HOW TO
FARM YOUR
BACKYARD
THE
MULCH-ORGANIC
WAY

HOW TO FARM YOUR BACKYARD THE MULCH-ORGANIC WAY

MAX ALTH

McGRAW-HILL BOOK COMPANY

NEW YORK   ST. LOUIS   SAN FRANCISCO   AUCKLAND   BOGOTÁ
DÜSSELDORF   JOHANNESBURG   LONDON   MADRID   MEXICO
MONTREAL   NEW DELHI   PANAMA   PARIS   SÃO PAULO
SINGAPORE   SYDNEY   TOKYO   TORONTO

Library of Congress Cataloging in Publication Data

Alth, Max.
    How to farm your backyard the mulch-organic way.

    Includes index.
    1. Vegetable gardening. 2. Organic gardening.
3. Fruit-culture. 4. Mulching. I. Title.
SB324.3.A47   635'.04'8   76-15158
ISBN 0-07-001128-1

1234567890   HDBP   786543210987

The editors for this book were Robert A. Rosenbaum and Lester Strong, the
designer was Richard A. Roth, and the production supervisor was Teresa F.
Leaden. It was set in Palatino by University Graphics, Inc.

Printed by Halliday Lithograph Corporation and bound by The Book Press.

Dedicated to
Char
Syme
Mish
Sal
Arabella and
Mendel

Original line drawings by Simon Alth.
Photographs not credited to others are by the author.

Contents

Preface

U NTIL I BEGAN researching this book I honestly believed I was the laziest backyard farmer around. I believed I was bringing in the crop with less work and at less cost than anyone else. In the 15 or so years I had been working my little backyard plot and applying my inventive little brain, I found by the continued hard application of no work that weeding was almost unnecessary. I found that in most but not all cases insecticides were also a waste of time and money. I found that chemical fertilizers weren't all they were cracked up to be. (I once put 50 pounds of fertilizer on my 25 square feet of ground to give my corn crop a kick in the pants, but the results weren't much better than the year before.)

But once I began reading the literature, as we scientists are wont to say, I found to my surprise that I was working much too hard. I found that there are farmers that do not plough, weed, or spray. They simply plant their seed and lie back until harvest time.

It isn't exactly that easy, but compared to the gardener who carefully tills his soil, weeds thoroughly, sprays as per directions, and cultivates, the mulch-organic method of farming (as I have named it) requires perhaps as little as one-fifth of the time, money, and labor expended when farming by conventional methods.

At the same time, foods grown without the aid of pesticides and herbicides are almost always perfectly safe for ingestion by man or beast. (Lead from nearby highways can collect on plants.) There are no poisons that need to be removed. Foods grown without chemical boosting have a greater proportion of trace elements, which make them tastier and more nutritious.

Mulch-organic farming is simple enough. Enrich the soil by in-place composting of last year's plant remains, and your new plants will grow fast, fat-, disease-, and bug-resistant. Cover the earth between growing plants with a layer of organic waste—leaves, grass clippings, etc.—and you will not only rid yourself of almost all unwanted weeds; you will also conserve soil moisture, and moderate soil temperature. Doing so speeds seed germination and plant growth and encourages worms and bacteria, both of which are vital to healthy soil and plants.

Although mulch-organic farming has been proved invaluable for truck farming, it is far from universally accepted. Most commercial growers assume that mulch-organic farming is uneconomical on a large scale. They believe they cannot profitably harvest a crop without "boosting" their soil with chemical fertilizers. A century and a half ago or thereabouts, commercial farmers believed the only cure for a worked-out farm was abandonment. In the United States, those that could, moved West to new lands. At that time farmers had no faith in chemical fertilizers. They had to be convinced of their value, and it required years. Today, commercial farmers need to be convinced of the value of mulch-organic farming.

Whether or not they will ever be convinced remains an interesting question. But the pressure to change is increasing. The cost of fertilizer continues to increase. The decreasing quality of many farm products in terms of taste and flavor is reducing their consumption.

Lack of flavor and smell in many of our supermarket fruits and vegetables is only partially due to maltreated soil. A good portion of the unnatural taste is due to green picking and chemical ripening. (For example, some tomatoes are "degreened" by exposure to ethylene gas.) The continued hardening of the soil due to unending loss of humus makes plowing and tilling more difficult, necessitating larger engines which burn more fuel that costs more each year. And the fields themselves are ever more voracious, demanding more and more fertilizer each year just to produce the same crop quantity.

Backyard farmers are more readily convinced, or perhaps they have not been so severely conditioned to established ways. Many have turned to organic farming. Unfortunately, many have had unsatisfactory results. Whatever the individual reasons for poor crops may have been, the major cause that probably underlies all the difficulties is the fact that impoverished soil cannot be revitalized overnight. It takes time, and during that time a certain amount of conventional fertilizer must be used if reasonably satisfactory crops are to be harvested.

This writer hopes this book will encourage you to farm your backyard and, if you are already farming, to switch to the mulch-organic system as it will save you time, money, and labor, and produce better results.

When sufficient numbers of backyard farmers grow their crop the mulch-organic way, commercial farmers will see the light. Then everyone, even those not fortunate enough to have a backyard farm, will benefit from tastier, healthier, and (let us hope) less expensive produce.

The author wishes to acknowledge his appreciation to Mr. John W. Albert, Coordinator of the Gardencrafters Program of the New York Botanical Garden for his encouragement and technical assistance, without whom this book would not be as accurate nor as useful as it is.

MAX ALTH

HOW TO
FARM YOUR
BACKYARD
THE
MULCH-ORGANIC
WAY

CHAPTER ONE

What It's All About

WHY FARM

U NTIL THIS CENTURY turned, a major percentage of Americans ate fruit and produce grown on their land and in their backyards by members of their family. Usually it was mother and her brood who planted and harvested the kitchen garden. Now, all this has changed. Only a few of us are fortunate enough to be within easy distance of a small farmer still doing business directly with the consumer. The rest of us make poorly do with supermarket fruits and vegetables, which in the main are pitiful and unsatisfactory.

The small farms are almost gone. The big farms are actually factories. It is fertilizer and pesticides and herbicides in one day and fruits and vegetables out several weeks later. The plants are selected for size, rapid growth, and traveling ability.

As a result, most of the fruits and vegetables offered at our supermarkets are force-fed hybrids generally grown on chemically fertilized soil. These fruits and vegetables are usually large, pretty, and high in starch, fiber, and water content; but low in trace minerals, and thereby low in taste and flavor. Fruits and vegetables grown in naturally fertile soil are sweeter and have a better aroma.

A good example of common, commercial growing practices is the dropping of the old, small, red strawberries of yesteryear and their replacement with the very large (as large as a golf ball), pale pink Mastadons now offered for sale today. The Mastadons are easier to harvest and probably travel better. (Those in my supermarket travel cross-country from California.) They are stodgy, tasteless, sweetish

Harvesting dwarf Starkrimson Delicious apples. Full-grown dwarf isn't much higher than the little girl. (Courtesy Stark Bros.)

lumps not worth eating. The small, dark red berries of yesteryear were piquant and very tasty. The difference is so great that I can honestly say that if you have never tasted anything other than Mastadons you have never tasted strawberries. The same can be said of sweet corn. If you have never eaten sweet corn within an hour or two of picking, you have never tasted anything but horse corn, which is what my mother used to call sweet corn more than a few hours old.

Another commercial practice that further reduces the taste and value of pressure-grown fruits and vegetables is that of too-early picking. Some fruits, like pears and peaches to a smaller extent, ripen off the tree. But pick them green enough and they never ripen; they simply rot. From the grower's and shipper's point of view, you can't pick anything too green because the harder the produce, the less it will be damaged by handling and shipment. The result is that much of the produce rots without ever getting ripe and the remainder is so tasteless there is no pleasure in eating it. One development is that fewer and fewer people eat fruit today, and many families buy fruit for display only; something to use as a table decoration when company is coming.

One answer to the question of why farm is that growing your own will provide you with fruits and vegetables as good as those your grandmother raves about. It is not her imagination. The fruits in her youth were better.

Another answer to the question of why farm is that your produce will be much better for you—safer and more nutritious—than their commercial counterparts. Taste is related to trace minerals, and more and more doctors and scientists are finding that much of our health is predicated on what we eat. The absence of certain trace minerals can have a tremendous adverse affect on our physical and mental well-being.

If this appears far fetched, think for a moment of pellagra, beriberi, and scurvy. Three mysterious diseases which afflicted mankind's body and mind not too long ago. Pellagra caused an erysipelatous eruption of exposed skin, melancholia, and a strong propensity to suicide. Eventually the skin became permanently enveloped in a thick, livid crust, and the victim died. It is prevented and easily cured by a good diet strong in protein, and in niacin, a vitamin.

Beriberi attacks the nerves, digestive system, and heart. It is caused by the lack of thiamine, another vitamin, in the system. (In some individuals it is caused by their inability to assimilate this vitamin.) Beriberi can be and is cured and prevented by proper diet. Scurvy, which rotted the flesh and generally debilitated the ancient mariners before it killed them is caused by the absence of vitamin C, which every schoolchild knows is found in great quantities in citrus fruits.

We pity the ancients who died for lack of this simple, basic knowledge, but scientists and doctors who ascribe many of our still unsolved diseases to trace mineral deficiencies are ignored. Specifically, there is strong opinion that many allergies are due to lack of trace minerals in the system.

Growing your own produce will enable you and your family to reduce this shortage to a great extent.

Still another reason for farming your own plot is that you needn't use any pesticides or herbicides on your plants. Although there is no proof that pesticides on the surface of produce are absorbed, it is true that traces of the poison can remain, and that by oversight and carelessness in washing we may ingest a quantity of poison.

Starkspur Earliblaze apples. Considered one of the best of the summer apples, this strain sets a very heavy crop of uniformly large fruit. (Courtesy Stark Bros.)

By the same law of chance, many farm animals must also consume some pesticide and herbicide. Cows, for example, sometimes stray into the fields after harvest to glean what they may. Pesticide and herbicide may remain on the stalks and on the ground, and some of this is bound to be picked up by the animals. The herbicide used with corn, Atrazine for example, is so powerful that if a farmer sprays a field with it and walks through the field weeks later and then across a lawn, the footprints across the lawn will be detailed in dead grass. Thus, another reason for growing your own is that you can reduce your family's intake of poisons.

Still another reason is financial. The cost of seed is negligible. If you follow the precepts outlined, you will need very little chemical fertilizer and eventually none; very little insecticide and eventually none.

Although there are published per-acre crop figures for all crops, it is difficult to be specific, as much depends on local soil, water, and climate. However, some of my results may be enlightening. I have a 40-foot row of raspberries. Last season my family picked better than 30 quarts. I do not fertilize or water these bushes. I merely cut the old cane back and tie the new cane to the retaining fence. Once in a

Author's daughter gathering berries. Forty-foot row of blackberry and raspberry bushes provided more than 30 quarts of fruit over a single season.

while I move some bushes around. Exclusive of picking time, I estimate my total labor at 6 hours for the year.

I had three tomato plants (in addition to other vegetables). They occupied a 10 by 4-foot space along with some cucumbers which don't mind tomatoes and some string beans I trained to hold the tomatoes in place on the trellis. Total cash investment for seed, plants, and a little dry manure was under $1.00. As I rarely watered, and weeded even less, total labor time required amounted to well under 5 hours. The harvest from this one 10 by 4-foot area ran to some 40 pounds of tomatoes, several pounds of cucumbers, and perhaps a half a pound of string beans. Beans don't like sharing a trellis with tomatoes.

My plot is in a valley, to put it gently. To be blunt, it is actually in a hole. There are tall trees immediately to the West and a hill immediately to the East and North. I can't imagine that my plot receives much more than 50 percent of the day's available sunlight. Certainly, it isn't an ideal little backyard farm by anyone's measure.

I have, among other plantings on my little plot, some string beans climbing poles. I estimate I will eventually harvest about 5 pounds of strings from each pole. I let my beans grow a foot long; so perhaps others will not get as much. Those with better locations and better soil may get more. My soil is as yet not very rich. I haven't used chemical fertilizer in three years, but I added a handful of dry manure to each hill of beans when I planted them. Cost for the bean plants, plus the manure, less the pole, is under 30 cents. In my supermarket, fresh string beans are going for better than 60 cents the pound.

Yet another reason for backyard farming is that it will, to some small degree, return you to the land. The time you spend on your farm will be at a pace totally different from the pace you follow at your job, be it manual, mental, or, like most of the jobs we hold, a combination of both. Farm time follows the seasons. Farm time is slow and regular and most of all, dependable. In a world that often appears to be crumbling before our eyes; in a world that continually changes in ways we often find painful, only nature is stable. Each spring the birds return, the seeds put out their green arms and go about their business of growing and reproducing. During the hours we spend on our farm we can believe this is the way it was, is, and will always be. It is comforting.

In a very literal sense, people were made to get their hands dirty. You can work very hard sitting still at a desk or behind the wheel of a truck, but the feeling of satisfaction isn't there. Perhaps it is because most of our jobs are limited in scope. Few of us have the satisfaction of seeing a job all the way through, as for example an architect does. Most of our work is confined to a small portion of a whole. We lay brick or we sell rental space in the finished structure but few of us take any job from concept through completion.

When you farm, you take it all the way yourself from seed to harvest. There is also, I believe, a primitive association with the soil itself that you cannot get any other way. Serving an ace in tennis, for example, or hitting a ball solidly for four bases have their moments of intense satisfaction. Getting a promotion or succeeding at some business venture also has its emotional rewards, but all these differ from the pleasure of bringing home food that you have grown yourself. I don't know why, but it is different and deeply satisfying.

If you are a real dirt farmer at heart, you will enjoy working the farm as much as the earth's rewards, which can be bountiful. You will take pleasure in making things grow, watching the seasons go by, and just being outdoors and a part of the land.

Picking cucumbers. To prevent damage to the vine, the stem is separated from the fruit by pushing.

NO ONE IS BORN WITH A GREEN THUMB

Farming isn't like baking a cake or building a television receiver. It is difficult to fail completely when you plant something, whereas you can go for zilch baking a cake or trying your hand at making a TV set without trying very hard.

Seeds are living things. Once you have placed them in the ground they will do their level best to produce. If they receive water and the sun shines on their home the seeds will sprout and grow.

The difference between a full, rich growth and a puny yellow thing is what agriculture is all about. This is knowledge man has taken 13,000 years to accumulate and understand. During the 13 millennia since the last glacier retreated, humanity has been planting, harvesting, and pondering. With each passing season farmers believe they are closer to understanding what it is all about, and if you farm you will also fall into this pattern: "Next year I'll put the rows of corn closer together; next year I'll try the new seed. . . ." The information has been garnered very slowly and painfully, but as we know more about plant growth today than ever before, the practice of agriculture is simpler and easier than it has ever been.

People are born with perfect pitch and the ability to pick up a speeding ball on the fly, but no one is born with a green thumb. The green thumb, the ability to make things grow, comes with a knowledge of how things grow; and as you shall see as you read on, this isn't at all difficult to learn and appreciate. In fact, you will learn as you farm.

ORGANIC VS. INORGANIC FARMING

Organically grown foods, both plant and animal, are presently being loudly touted as the panacea for all our remaining bodily ills. The relationship that may exist between the absence of essential trace minerals in our foods and our modern propensity toward allergies of complex kinds has already been mentioned. This is but one connection. Many others are also made between everything from mental illness to weak knees. Put simply, their arguments are: The absence of trace minerals plus the presence of generous traces of actual poisons and substances foreign to the body are the cause of many of the illnesses we presently cannot cure.

The pity of it all is that the Organics (can I call them Organists?) must shout loudly to make themselves heard, and in doing so they lose a considerable amount of credibility, which is most unfortunate *because much of what they claim is true.* The full scope of their arguments is beyond the space available here. But let me state I am in full accord with their views, which are not limited to merely growing food but include strong condemnation of such practices as the use of fumigants to control the growth of pests in stored grain; the removal of the tips of grain which contain natural vitamin E merely to facilitate storage; the addition of preservatives to cheese and on ad infinitum. (Read Jim Hightower, *Eat Your Heart Out,* to learn more of the lengths to which the food corporations have gone and are going to rob us of nutrition.)

But we have wandered from the subject. To return: Organic farmers grow their crops without the aid of chemical fertilizers, chemical bug killers and chemical weed killers. Inorganic farmers, that is to say, conventional farmers, use chemical fertilizers, chemical bug killers, and chemical weed killers.

WHAT IS THE DIFFERENCE?

Let us compare organic and inorganic fertilizers first. When Europeans first broke the sod (layer of grass) in this country they needed only to plant their seed to harvest a bountiful crop. The soil was black and rich. As they kept planting and harvesting, the soil became progressively poorer. The reason was that they took but did not return anything to the soil. Possibly they practiced crop rotation and possibly they let the earth lie fallow every seventh year. But more likely they simply moved on to new, low cost, and richer ground. In the Plymouth Colony they reportedly planted their corn Indian style, one fish to each corn seed. It works but it certainly isn't a practice you can follow any distance from the sea, and a dead fish doesn't do the corn seed much good the first year. In fact it probably robs the soil of considerable nitrogen while it is decomposing. And it is hard to believe hungry Pilgrims really did this: went to the trouble of catching fish to fertilize their corn.

Whether or not early American farmers used fish as a fertilizer is unimportant now. The fact remains that in the short span of some 150 years the American farmer had by and large exhausted the soil. After 1910 homesteading was finished. There was no more free land to farm, no more fresh sod to bust and so start anew.

With the reduction in crops the American farmer turned increasingly to chemical fertilizers. They worked. Add fertilizers and you bettered your crop.

At the same time the use of animal manures, which are organic fertilizers, continued. However, with the introduction of the automobile the horse population declined, and as the horse went the manure followed. In addition, farms became larger and more specialized. There was less and less manure on the farm, and besides, it was easier to apply fertilizer than to shovel manure.

And, as the land became increasingly impoverished, more and more chemical fertilizer was and still is needed to produce economically feasible crops.

The fertilizers most used are nitrogen, phosphorus, and potash. When you purchase a bag of chemical fertilizers, this is what you get in any of a number of different chemical forms.

Now there is absolutely nothing wrong with these chemicals, and the organic purists who decry chemical fertilizers as poisons are completely wrong. Their calumny is misguided. It is not the chemical fertilizers that are at fault; it is the absence of other valuable minerals, albeit only needed in small quantities, that is the root of the problem. Put another way, meat and potatoes are fine foods, but a diet confined exclusively to meat and potatoes will kill you in time.

This is the true fault of chemical farming. The plants are not supplied a complete diet and are therefore low in taste and nutrition. We who depend on produce and grains for much of our food are therefore equally deprived.

The difference in nutrition between similar produce grown in fertile soil and infertile soil can be tremendous, far greater than the difference in taste alone might lead one to imagine. For example, comparative tests made of similar produce grown in naturally rich, well-composted soil and non-fertile soil can be as much as two to one in phosphorus, five to one in calcium, three to one in potassium, six to one in sodium, boron, and cobalt, and as much as 1,940 to one in iron content. This, you must admit is much more than a mere difference in taste.

Organic farmers eschew the use of all chemical fertilizers. They use manures and humus exclusively. Both are excellent sources of plant food. The only trouble is that both are expensive when purchased. As it is estimated that few of our farms have soils containing more than 1 percent of the quantity of humus necessary for soil to be self-sufficient (rich), the quantity of humus and manure that would be required is staggering. How then do the organic farmers do it? The key is in the phrase, "when purchased." The making of good humus is almost free for the asking. Anything that is organic can be converted with a little work and a lot of time into humus. If you were to buy enough humus to prepare an acre of soil the cost would run into thousands of dollars. But if you collect all the leaves and stems that remain every year after the crops are harvested you could, in a number of years, have all the humus you required, and each year following you could supply your farm's needs with that year's crop remainder.

Once the soil is replenished, no chemical fertilizer is required. Each year, of course, additional humus is needed which is supplied by the previous year's growth.

This is the financial beauty of the organic farming argument, the almost complete removal of the need for costly chemical fertilizers.

Conventional farmers employ a large quantity and variety of insecticides. They do this for two reasons. To reduce the losses caused by insect pests and to protect the appearance of their fruits and produce. To some extent this is understandable. A bad infestation can put them out of business. Our argument is that by changing their farming methods, the use of pesticides certainly could be greatly reduced, if not entirely eliminated.

Organic farmers use no insecticides. They depend on the natural resistance of *healthy* plants to bug attack; they depend on the natural balance of insects and animals in any pesticide-free area, and they accept a small percentage of bug-marked fruit.

It has been proven that plants grown in rich soil, soil black with humus, are less vulnerable to bug attacks. It has also been proven that indiscriminate spraying kills the troublesome insects' natural enemies as well as the bugs themselves, thereby making it easier for the unwanted insects to come back. As for bug-marked fruit, one can accept a blemish if one expects it. There is nothing basically repellent in a small hole or dark spot in a vegetable or fruit. It is just a matter of conditioning. In any event, people who limit their diet to organically grown foods have come to expect imperfections. A bushel of perfect apples, for example, would lead them to believe chemical sprays had been used.

The organic farmer uses no herbicides, which are chemicals that destroy weeds or certain classes of plants while not harming others. The reasons are of course obvious; why use any poison at all in the field when it isn't essential to plant growth.

Conventional farmers think in terms of costs, and for them herbicides make sense. Yet does it really make sense when they and their families may inadvertently ingest some of the herbicide, as well as the rest of us?

WHAT IS BEST FOR THE BACKYARD FARMER?

In this writer's opinion, the best course is to start with whatever chemical fertilizers may be necessary for a good crop, to use as little pesticide as possible and no herbicide at all.

At the same time, whatever organic material can be scrounged should be collected for the compost heap and mulching so that some humus will be available for soil improvement in the coming season. And so that eventually no chemical fertilizer and no insecticide will be necessary: You will be farming organically, depending upon nature to do most of your work.

This writer takes the position that mulch-organic farming is the way to go, but at the same time it should be appreciated that one cannot successfully organically farm a plot of worn-out land without building it up.

CHAPTER TWO

How Nature Replenishes the Soil

ECOLOGICAL BALANCE

WHEN A PLANT GROWS, it receives energy from the sun and nourishment from the soil. When the plant dies its leaves, stem, and roots return to the soil. The cycle is complete; nothing has been lost. (Actually, something has been gained.)

When people first began farming some 13,000 or so years ago when the last glacier began retreating, they must have sensed the balance and that they were to some extent disturbing it. The few records that remain of humanity's farming activities through the millennia indicate a constant preoccupation with fertility. There were sacrifices of various sorts to fertility in general and to specific fertility gods and goddesses.

In lands where an annual flooding replenished the soil, civilizations flourished, and the entire economy was geared to the event. Surveying supposedly began in Egypt because the floods wiped out the land markers every year, and only by measuring from fixed points could land ownership be accurately reestablished.

Land not favored by annual flooding was often abandoned when crops grew thin. The entire human population of the globe at the time people first turned to farming is estimated at no more than five million. Thus the abandonment of a farm and beginning again elsewhere did not present a particular problem. If we estimate from the American experience, good crops could be secured from one piece of land for perhaps 75 continuous years of farming. The practice of deliberate abandonment, coupled with the shifting of population due to wars and plagues and the slow rise of total population, made farming by abandonment practical for many thousands of years.

It wasn't until fairly recent times that improvements in sanitation and increased medical knowledge enabled our population to grow to where increased farm yield was not only desirable but necessary.

As the need for increased farm production grew, the efforts of scientists and laymen to spur production grew apace. In the light of what we know today, some of their efforts and conclusions appear ridiculous, but at the time these were bright-burning candles in a world of dark ignorance.

In 1635, Jan Baptista van Helmont, a Flemish chemist, planted a small willow tree in exactly 200 pounds of oven-dried soil. For five years he carefully protected the small tree from everything except rainwater. Then he removed the tree from the soil, washed it, and weighed it. As he knew the tree's original weight, he knew for a certainty the tree had gained exactly 165 pounds. Then he carefully returned the soil to the oven, dried the dirt, and reweighed it. The soil had lost 2 ounces. Helmont concluded that the 2 lost ounces were due to experimental error and credited the 165 pounds of plant growth to water alone.

(We now know that the 2 ounces lost were soil minerals and that they combined with carbon, oxygen, and hydrogen—taken mainly from the air—and the rainwater to produce the plant's growth. But this is not germane to our story.)

In England, John Woodward, another experimenter seeking to increase man's knowledge of the relationship between plants and soil, tried growing plants in pure rainwater, water taken exclusively from clear-flowing streams, and muddy water. He found his plants grew best in muddy water, and he then credited soil as the container of the "principle" of growth.

Other experimenters decided that the principle of plant life was passed on from dead plants to living plants, and unless the soil contained some measure of once-living plants in the form of humus or manure no new plants would grow.

And so it went on until some time in 1840 when Baron Justus von Liebig, the foremost organic chemist in Germany at the time, published his findings. Liebig had the advantage of the tremendous improvement and refinement that had been made in analytical chemistry in the previous decade. He was able to actually measure the mineral changes that occurred in plants and the soil from whence they grew. His view was straightforward and to the mark, "The crops in a field diminish or increase in exact proportion to the diminution or increase of the mineral substances conveyed to it by manure."

Liebig reaffirmed the balance theory. Nature held all plant-soil relationships in balance. Plants grew and in doing so removed certain chemicals from the soil. Replace those chemicals, and a bountiful harvest followed. Fail to replenish the missing chemicals, and the crops were certain to be poor and stunted.

There were some known holes in his theory. For example, if plants removed nitrogen (one of the chemicals he specified as necessary to plant growth), how come clover does not remove nitrogen? Another was, how do plants in the wild continue to grow for centuries without the application of chemicals?

The known discrepancies notwithstanding, Liebig's prestige and skillful debate swept all the old alchemists theories into limbo. After Liebig published, there was no more public talk about the "principle" of plant life.

But much more telling than his rhetoric and his scientific reputation were the results. When the farmers followed Liebig's advice and spread manure over their land, they prospered. Plant growth improved, and in some areas doubled. When the supply of manure and guano (bird droppings) dwindled, scientists developed chemical fertilizers. The Haber process, for one, made it practical to remove and "fix" nitrogen from the air. We are still using these almost pure chemicals today.

THE FALLACY OF CHEMICAL FERTILIZERS

Almost all commercial farmers and home gardeners use chemical fertilization exclusively. The number of "organic" commercial and amateur farmers is minimal. Chemical fertilizers have a number of advantages over organic fertilizers. Chemical fertilizers are neat, clean, fast, and until recently fairly economical. (The price of chemical fertilizers has gone up with the increase in energy costs and greed.) Chemical fertilizers produce immediate, visible results. Organic fertilizers such as manure are now hard to come by, and humus, which is decayed organic matter, is slow-acting, messy, and not commercially available; you have got to make your own, and this requires very little effort but lots of time. You can, of course, buy topsoil which contains humus. But this is a very expensive way of fertilizing a field and would more than negate whatever savings resulted from growing your own vegetables.

Unforeseen by Liebig and his followers, chemical fertilizers (and we exclude the manures in this classification) have many long term drawbacks. For one, chemical fertilizers can wreak havoc with the organisms inhabiting the soil. (It depends on the chemical, quantity, and soil condition.) In time, continued applications of fertilizers will destroy them. For another, chemical fertilizers encourage the farmer to clear his land after each crop.

The current farming practice among many if not all commercial farmers and many noncommercial farmers is to plow the land, apply fertilizer, and follow with seed. In the fall the crop is harvested. Most often, if not always, the land is thereupon cleared of all plant remains. In some instances farmers may put in a winter cover crop and plow it under in the spring. In many instances they do not. A cover crop costs time and money, and it is easier and cheaper to depend on fertilizer. No matter the reason, some farm experts estimate that present-day American farms comprise less than 1 percent humus. Ideally the quantity would be about 30 percent. The change is so drastic that we have been accused of mining the land, removing the nutrients from the soil without ever replacing any of them the way a miner removes metal from the earth.

In Colonial times farmers simply planted their crops and harvested bountifully time and time again. No one ever even thought about fertilizer or humus. It was just there. When the sod was busted on the Great Plains (top layer of buffalo grass was turned over), the farmers found three and more feet of rich, black topsoil underneath. Today, when the soils on all our farmlands are averaged out, very little topsoil and humus remain. This is the direct result of poor farming practices, most of which stem from the almost complete dependence on chemical fertilizers.

Another unforeseen result of chemical fertilization is the need for increasing quantities of chemicals to produce the same crop year after year.

Still another is that the physical work of turning over the earth and cultivating becomes increasingly difficult as the earth loses humus and tightens up (hardens). Horses become more quickly tired; tractor size must be increased.

Tight soils restrict plant growth, absorb little water, and change more quickly with temperature than loose, humus filled soils. Plants grow slowly in tight, hard soil. Rain does not sink into the earth when it is tight. The rain runs off, causing dangerous and damaging erosion. And in running off, it leaves the earth dry, necessitating artificial irrigation: more work and more costs.

Soils bereft of humus do not and cannot refertilize themselves. Such soils are composed of pieces of stone of varying size and little else. They form a support system for plants and little else. Fertilizer must be added, or nothing will grow. These soils are exactly as Liebig pictured all soil or chose to depict all soils. In such barren soils the balance between the minerals added by the farmer and those removed by the growing plant is exact, or almost. In its extreme form it is called hydroponic gardening. The plants may be grown on a wire mesh suspended directly over a tank or pool of plant nutrients dissolved in water.

This method was used to a great extent in World War II to provide fresh vegetables for our troops in the South Pacific. (I think it was the South Pacific; thank God I served in the ETO and never had to eat hydroponic vegetables.) The method works beautifully. The returns per square foot of tank are phenomenal, but no one ever mentions how the vegetables tasted. No one ever writes about their trace mineral content. At least I have never encountered such data.

In any event, there is no doubt that plants do require food in the form of water-soluble minerals, which in concentrated form we call fertilizer. There is no doubt that the good Baron's work was and still is most useful. Yet one wonders if Liebig ever looked up from his chemist's scales. One wonders if Liebig ever accompanied the workers who carted the manure from the stables to the fields Liebig was testing. If so, did he ever ponder the forests he must have seen? Did he wonder how the wild apple and the wild berry bush thrived in the absence of manure of chemical fertilizers?

Fact is that most farmers in the world, even today, do not rely on manures or chemical fertilizers for crop growth and many do very well without them. Giant forests covered most of North America before the lumbermen put the axe to them. The forests were never fertilized. Can you imagine Indians building piles of dead fish at the roots of the giant California redwood trees, some over four thousand years old. Grass grew in abundance and fed the millions of wild buffalo on our vast prairies without the help of chemicals or human assistance.

But how? According to Liebig and his followers, the bin should have been emptied millennia before. The Midwest should have been barren well before Clark and Lewis crossed the country. The forests should have died from lack of food eons ago.

The answer lies in the very nature of plant life, and when we study their life's cycle for a few moments, we will see how they manage to feed themselves.

Plants are the only living creatures on earth capable of "digesting" minerals. A shovelful of soil is nothing but dirt until it is "eaten" by plants, at which point the minerals become organic and edible, and life as we know it becomes possible for all higher-order creatures such as mice and men. Without plants our life would be impossible.

Plants in turn are highly dependent on water. We all know that they cannot grow without water, but one portion of the plant world's dependence on water is a little more subtle than even many farmers realize.

Water is a powerful solvent. It will dissolve almost anything. When water seeps downward through the earth, the water dissolves a quantity of the disintegrated rock it encounters. It is this mineral soup that is absorbed by the plant's roots and drawn up to the plant's leaf by capillary action. At the surface of the leaf, the sun acts to convert the dissolved minerals to sugar and starch and other things needed by the plant for growth and reproduction. A portion of the liquid is evaporated, reducing the volume of liquid in the leaf and thus causing more mineral soup to flow upward from the plant's roots. The remainder of the now organic liquid is routed around the various parts of the plants, causing more leaves, roots and stem to grow.

The process of converting a water and mineral solution to an organic mixture is called photosynthesis. When we figure out just how it is done, we may be able to survive without plants. Right now scientists barely understand the process. We can expect to be farming for a long, long time.

PLANT LIFE AND DEATH AND SOIL FERTILIZATION

So long as a plant is alive, exposed to sunlight, and above freezing temperature, it continues to draw water containing dissolved minerals from the soil and continues to form carbohydrates in its chlorophyll-containing tissues, which are the green parts of the plant. In actual weight the quantity of minerals leached from the soil is very small. If we recall van Helmont's willow, the 165 pounds of tree consisted of no more than 2 ounces of minerals. The remainder of the tree was composed of water, carbon, oxygen, and hydrogen.

When the plant dies, it falls to the ground. All the minerals present in the plant at the time return to the soil. The water, carbon, oxygen, and hydrogen do also, but plants cannot absorb these elements; so there is no gain in plant food thus far. And if the plant's cycle were complete at this point, it would be impossible to farm without fertilizer; that is to say, we could not continue to grow crops without adding the specific minerals plants require.

Fortunately the plant's cycle is not completed when it falls to the ground. In a sense it is only half complete. The second half consists of decomposition. The plant is attacked by bacteria which inhabit the earth and live by ingesting dead plants and other organic substances.

Bacteria are tiny creatures about 1/25,000th of an inch long. Millions of them can comfortably fit themselves on the head of a pin. They are mobile, whipping themselves along with tiny legs, and they know where they are going because they can sense where the richer nutrient lies and head in that direction. Many scientists consider them plants. Other scientists consider them a special group of creatures which are neither plants nor animals. Given suitable food and the right temperature, they split every hour or so and thus multiply. However, given the proper encouragement in the form of a higher temperature and suitable nutrient, they copulate in a weird fashion, one taking the role of male and the other the role of female.

Exciting as that may be, their most important contribution to our well-being, and it is very important, is the carbon dioxide they generate during their digestive process. The carbon dioxide combines with water to form carbonic acid which is a very powerful dissolver of rocks, much stronger than water. Rocks are composed of minerals; and soil is, of course, composed of tiny particles of rocks. If the thought of microscopic creatures materially contributing to our material well-being appears preposterous, remember every tree that falls to the earth, every leaf, every blade of grass eventually rots; and that all rotting is the digestive work of bacteria. They may be small but their numbers run to the googolplex (which is number 1 followed by 100 zeros raised to the power of 1 followed by 100 zeros; ten raised to the power of 3 is a thousand).

Thus, when a plant returns to the soil, it not only brings with it all the nutrients it absorbed while alive, but it feeds countless bacteria whose digestive processes act to dissolve and provide even more food for plants to come. The cycle of plant life and death is not one of simple balance. It provides a gain. When the plant is finally, completely digested by the local bacteria, there is more plant food present in the soil than ever before. The point to bear in mind here is that normal plant growth does not deplete the soil; it enriches it, *but only if the plant is not removed.*

ADDITIONAL NATURAL SOURCES OF FERTILIZER

Of all the many elements drawn by plants from the soil, nitrogen is the element absorbed in the largest quantity. It is therefore almost always found in commercial chemical fertilizers and almost always in the largest quantity. Nitrogen is present in all living things. It is responsible, among other effects, for plant and animal growth.

Seventy eight percent of the air, as measured by volume, is nitrogen. The total weight of nitrogen in the air above every acre of ground (at sea level) amounts to approximately 30,000 tons. None of this is of any direct value to ourselves or plants. Neither flora nor fauna can assimilate nitrogen in its gaseous form. It must first be "fixed," which is to say, combined with another substance and converted to a water-soluble solid.

Fortunately, we have many little friends who do this for us. There are soil bacteria belonging to the genus *Rhizobia* that live symbiotically on the roots of leguminous plants (peas, vetch, rye, etc.), and in concert with types of fungi form lumps or nodules of solid nitrogen. Farmers often plant these legumes between growing seasons and plow them under to fertilize the soil. They are often called green manure. The quantity of nitrogen that is fixed by the Rhizobia varies from 50 to 150 pounds of nitrogen per acre. The nodules on individual plants can amount to 4 percent of the plants dry weight (alfalfa).

There are bacteria that fix nitrogen without the presence of plant roots. They belong to the nonsymbiotic or free-living genus called *Azotobacter*. It is estimated that these bacteria can fix as much as 50 pounds of nitrogen per acre per year. And there are algae, a very simple form of plant life that also fixes nitrogen.

Still another natural and free source of nitrogen are electrical storms. As the lightning flashes through the air, it fixes nitrogen which then falls to the earth in a gentle, unnoticed rain. Over the year an average of 9 pounds of nitrogenous compounds fall down on each acre of land in the temperate zones.

Between the nitrogen bequeathed the earth by deceased animals, fixed by bacteria and algae, and falling from the sky, a virgin acre of fertile soil will hold between 3,000 and 7,000 pounds of nitrogen. No wonder soil can be mined by farming so many years without replenishment.

So far we have only discussed the fixation of nitrogen by microflora. Microflora do many other important tasks to promote plant growth. For example soil microflora (bacteria, fungi, etc.) continuously recycle as much as 20 tons of carbon dioxide per acre per year. They do this by returning the carbon that has been photosynthetically combined with nitrogen and other elements to form plant tissue to the atmosphere in the form of gas. Plants cannot use carbon in any but its gaseous form.

Microflora also transform other compounds into forms useful to plants. For example, insoluble phosphate becomes soluble and available to plants by the action of sulfuric acid produced by bacterial oxidation. Sulfur will not counteract the undesired salinity of sodium until the sulfur has been changed to sulfate by soil bacteria.

This is but a small sampling of what the microflora—microbes, algae, actinomycetes, and fungi—do to promote plant growth. Unfortunately, everything they do is not advantageous to plant life, but in the main, plants and ourselves who depend on plants could not exist without the microflora.

If all this useful activity on the part of creatures too small to see with the naked eye appears to be exaggerated, bear in mind that the microflora comprise .03 percent of the top foot of fertile soil. An acre can contain upwards of 1,000 pounds of these microscopic links between the plant and the animal kingdoms.

CHAPTER THREE

Wondrous Humus

S OIL IS DISINTEGRATED rock, particles of stone ranging in size from tiny crystalline pieces too small to see without magnification to stones the size of hen's eggs. Pure soil is all mineral. There are no organic substances mixed in with the pieces of stone. Pure soil is devoid of life and the remains of life. If the particles of rock are very small and fine, the soil is called clay and while it can absorb and hold a tremendous quantity of water for a long time, it also hardens into a rock-like substance when the water is gone. And whether it is dry or moist, clay does not absorb water quickly. Falling rain runs off clay almost as rapidly and completely as it runs off concrete.

On the other hand, if the rock particles are large, the soil is termed sand. Sand holds very little water. Whatever water falls upon sand percolates right through in a matter of minutes. If the rock particles are larger, water run-through is even faster.

Seeds find it very difficult to germinate in clay, and once germinated the tiny plant finds it very difficult to grow. Clay is sticky and tenacious. Clay lies solidly in place. It has no cracks and air passages for young tendrils to follow to sunlight and water. Seeds germinate much more easily and quickly in sand. Sand, however, doesn't hold water very long, and unless the sand is constantly moistened by nature or the farmer, the plant soon dries out. Sand alone doesn't support plants very well. A strong wind will knock many plants down.

A combination of sand and clay combines the advantages of both, but only if there is several more times the sand by volume than the clay. If a little sand is mixed with a lot of clay, the mixture behaves exactly, almost, as clay alone. If just a little clay is mixed with a lot of sand, the clay provides some degree of particle adhesion without completely blocking the voids and passages between the grains of sand. However, if the mixing is not thorough and complete, the result will be small areas that act like sand alone and small areas that act like clay alone.

When the sand-clay mixture is correct, the rate of water percolation or run-through is greatly decreased. Root passage and plant growth are eased, and some air can filter down. However, the clay-sand mixtures do not offer any more plant nutrients than either size of crushed stone alone.

The food available to plants growing in pure soil is only that which the water can dissolve from the rock. There will be more in clay, because the finer particles of stone present a greater surface to the water than sand, but at best it will be very thin gruel indeed. Few plants can survive on it, let alone feed the farmer sufficiently to return the energy he expended.

Poor, worn-out soil is just this mixture. Sometimes a little more clay, sometimes a little more sand. Poor soil has very little color and almost no organic content. There is nothing alive in worn-out soil except the farmer's crop (if there is any), and a few weeds. On the national average our commercial farms may well be 99 percent pure, unadulterated rock. Only chemicals keep them going.

Rich, fertile soil is almost one third organic matter. It is black and alive with plants and creatures of all kinds. There are the microflora we discussed a few pages back. There are mites, bees, wasps, ants, beetles, spiders, and other insects. There are protozoa, slugs, nematodes, snails, moles, mice, shrews, other creatures and worms, lots of worms. A fertile acre will house and feed more than half a ton of worms.

All these creatures, large and small, are born, play, reproduce, feed on, and die in the wondrous composite substance we call humus. Just as plants and their ability to convert minerals to carbohydrates makes all higher orders of life possible, humus makes plant life possible and practical. Without humus (or artificial feeding by means of chemical fertilizers) and the creatures that inhabit the top one foot of soil, plants would not grow as luxuriantly as they naturally do, if they would grow at all.

THE FORMATION OF HUMUS

When a plant dies and falls to the ground it is immediately attacked by a multitude of creatures, each in its own way. Snails chew holes in the green leaves, ants tear off pieces and carry them away. Fungi extend their silken threads into open pores. In time the entire plant will pass through the digestive systems of these creatures. The animals will swallow, digest, and excrete portions of the plant in the ordinary manner. The fauna will consume the plant in a process we call rot.

The span of time that passes between the death of the plant and its complete dissolution depends on the nature of the plant. Soft, green plants filled with sugars and starches are more attractive and satisfying to hungry animals and are therefore attacked more energetically. Moist leaves support bacterial growth much better than dry leaves or twigs. Animals and bacteria work from the surface inward. Therefore you will always see the skeletons of branches and logs on the forest floor long after the leaves are gone. Fungi work from the inside out. You see their activity as white or colored growths (mushrooms, toadstools, mold, mildew) on the outside of logs and tree branches.

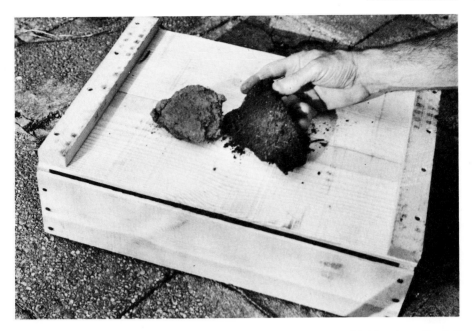

Humus is dark, soft, and loaded with plant food. Worn-out soil is highly mineralized. It contains little if any organic material. And generally it is very light in color.

The forest creatures work most actively when it is warm. When the temperature drops, they hibernate, each in its own fashion. The bacteria simply quit splitting and feeding and wait for a warmer day. Even subzero temperatures will not harm them.

All the topsoil creatures require moisture. The animals will die if there is a severe drought, but the microflora will survive to continue their eating and multiplying when water becomes available.

Most of the creatures require air. But some of the bacteria are anaerobic; they live without oxygen.

When the temperature is high, the leaves soft and moist and loosely packed so that there is plenty of air, complete breakdown, as some farmers call it, can take place in a month or so. When conditions are unfavorable or a log or heavy branch is present, complete breakdown can require several years.

In the process the plants turn black and coarsely granular. What was once a mighty oak is now a handful (quite a few) of light, crumbly material that appears to be soil. It is black because the carbon, which is black, is the last substance to be broken down.

The soft, black crumbly residue, the remains of plants after their chemical change, is called humus. It contains everything present in the original plants, almost all the nitrogen collected at the roots of leguminous plants, almost all the nitrogen collected by the free-living bacteria and algae, plus all the minerals present in the creatures large and small that died in the humus either in the natural course of their lives or as prey to larger creatures. Bacteria, for example, are eaten by the zillion by the slightly larger protozoa which belong to the animal kingdom. Some protozoa are large enough to be seen by the naked eye. In fertile soil there may be over 200 pounds of them to the acre. Although soil protozoa feed on bacteria, it has been found that decay and nitrogen fixation proceeds as fast and even faster with the protozoa present.

Bacteria also gather phosphoric acid, and when they die or are eaten by the protozoa, their little bodies contribute valuable quantities of phosphoric acid to the soil.

HUMUS DEPTH

In the preceding, we spoke of plants falling to the earth. These plants, naturally, remain on the surface of the soil. Thus the depth of humus on virgin soil would appear to be the total of the fallen plants. Actually, it is not so. A goodly portion of the plant is underground. When the plant completes its cycle and falls, its roots also cease to grow. These also are decomposed by soil bacteria and small creatures. As a result, while there may be several solid inches of humus atop the soil in an undisturbed forest or glade, there is also a considerable quantity of humus beneath the surface of the soil. In many areas you can dig and find no clean line of demarcation between the humus and the soil itself (topsoil and subsoil).

The point here, perhaps laboriously made, is that in the natural course of plant growth, nature provides more than just a top layer of fertility. The natural growth and decay of plants loosens and enriches the soil to a depth almost equal to the normal depth of the plant's roots.

HELP FROM OUR LARGER FRIENDS

The microflora decompose the plant remains. The larger creatures live on the plants before and after decomposition, depending on their nature. In the course of their lives they dig and burrow and muck about. In a very real sense they till the soil. Their tunnels and burrows admit air and water into the soil. And they generally carry the soil from their retreats up to the surface of the earth.

Of all the tiny burrowing animals, the earthworm is most important to the farmer. As stated, a fertile acre may contain several million wrigglers weighing as much as a half ton altogether. When conditions are right, they become the dominant animal life in the soil, and their total weight can exceed that of all the other in-earth creatures.

Earthworms do best in soils rich in organic matter, well drained and well supplied with calcium.

An earthworm is one long stomach. It feeds by tunneling through the earth, mouth first. Most of their time is spent in the top 6 inches of soil, but the more adventurous souls do dig down as much as 6 feet. As the worm tunnels and feeds, it ingests a mixture of soil and organic matter. It excretes the digested soil and organic material combined with calcium carbonate and a secreted mucus in the form of a granular cast. Some worms drop their castings on the surface of the soil, but some are not as neat and litter their tunnels as they move on. Over a year's span a healthy acre's worth of worms can move as much as 20 tons of soil.

The multitude of tunnels the worms dig in the process of feeding are extremely beneficial to plant growth. The tunnels aerate the soil without disturbing it, as plowing does, and the tunnels serve as water reservoirs. Plants often send their

Push aside the surface mulch, and you will see moist soil with happy, busy, little worms working for you. The worms in a fertile acre of soil will move as much as 20 tons of dirt a year—all without interfering very much with plant growth.

roots along old worm tunnels, and worms gobble their way back down these tunnels after the plant has died.

Sometime back in the 1800s, the great natural philosopher, Charles Darwin, wrote an entire book on the fertilizing activities of earthworms. Ever since then, or so it appears, more and more people have been extolling the virtues of the wriggly little creatures, crediting them primarily for the fertility of our soils. Although the value of worms to soil fertility cannot be slighted, worms are not the primary source of fertility. The primary source is humus. Worms thrive and multiply when and where there is suitable food, namely humus. Worms will not live in pure clay or sand or in a mixture of both. Without the ameliorating presence of humus, which not only feeds them but loosens the soil and enables them to worm their way along underground, worms perish.

There is no point in purchasing worms and encouraging them to loosen barren soil. No matter how loudly you urge them on, they will fail. On the other hand, if you add humus to barren or "pure" soil, worms will appear of their own accord and thrive.

By the same token there is no profit in purchasing worm castings, which are also marketed commercially, for the purpose of fertilization. The plant nutrition present in worm castings is always less than the nutrition present in the soil and humus that the worm ingested. Just as a cow plus grass does not result in manure that has more plant nutrition than the grass alone, so a worm plus humus does not result in castings that are nutritionally advantageous over the humus. In both cases, something has gone to power the beast.

In the case of the worm, the nutrition he or she or it consumes in the process of digging tunnels and producing castings is more than offset by the results. There is no practical way a farmer can dig so many tunnels and move so much soil during the growing season without seriously disturbing the plants.

In the case of the cow and other farm animals, the question of end product versus nutritional consumption is moot. Cows and sheep consume a tremendous quantity of feed in relation to the weight of food they produce. If we assume that the meat from one full-grown cow will feed two individuals for one year, then I would estimate that the food consumed by that cow from birth to maturity, which takes about a year or so, would feed six to ten individuals for a year. When you convert grain to beef, and beef to steak, you lose a tremendous amount of food.

THE VALUE OF HUMUS

Humus is about 50 percent air. It is light in weight; extremely porus; and rich in carbon, nitrogen, oxygen, and all the minerals drawn from the soil by the plants and the little topsoil creatures we discussed. Humus improves the soil and aids plant growth in many invaluable ways.

Soil amendment. A soil amendment is any substance added to the soil to improve its tilth and fertility. When humus is mixed into the soil, either naturally as discussed, or by the farmer as would be necessary if the humus was brought from one location to another, the humus loosens the soil and makes it friable. "Friable" is a farm word meaning loose, easily broken into small pieces. Tilth is supposedly the result of persistent tilling of the soil, turning it over and over again through the years. "Supposedly" is used advisedly. As will be explained in a chapter to come, tilling the soil, turning it over, does not improve its tilth; does not make soil more friable as so many farmers believe. In fact too much tilling, or even a little at the wrong time, can do just the opposite.

Humus is a wonderful soil amendment. Whereas the addition of a small percentage of sand to clay is almost a complete waste of effort because the change effected is negligible, the addition of a small quantity of humus to the same stubborn clay produces a marked improvement. Work a few bags of sand into a field of clay, and nothing happens. Work a few bags of humus into the same ground, and you have the beginning of fertility. The clay is loosened.

Fertilizer. Humus is a wonderful fertilizer. Not that it contains more nutrients per pound or per cubic inch than chemical fertilizers, but it contains a far greater number of different nutrients, and, in addition, it releases them slowly. Whereas chemical fertilizers must be applied with care to prevent them from making direct contact with plant roots and seeds, there is no such problem with humus. Whereas chemical fertilizers never contain anything more than the bag states, except by accident, humus naturally contains all the elements required by plants for normal growth (though not necessarily in proportions suitable for all plants).

This is because humus is the dead plant in toto, plus all the soil organisms that live more or less symbiotically with plants in the soil.

Now, how can a plant, perchance grown in poor soil, provide by means of its humus all the elements necessary for rich soil and well-fed plants?

The answer to this puzzle lies in the nature of plants. They have the ability to extract from the earth elements that may be present in such small quantities as to defy measurement by most laboratory techniques and instruments. And modern chem labs routinely measure in fractional parts per million (ppm).

The extractive power that plants have is a mixed blessing. While it enables them to survive in barren soils, it also enables them to collect minute traces of poisons that may be present in some soils. Thus poisoned soil can produce a poisonous plant, still another reason for eschewing insecticides and herbicides.

Returning to humus, our original subject, humus is in short a balanced fertilizer providing all the nutrients that plants need at a rate they can use without harm. (Please note that while humus alone is an excellent soil for many vegetables, it is not for all vegetables because of its acidic nature. But more on this later on.)

At this point it may be well to differentiate between humus and other natural, organic fertilizers. Some organic fertilizers, such as fresh manure, for example, can and will damage seeds and plant roots if the manure makes direct contact. The mere fact that a fertilizer is organic in its origin does not automatically render it safe for all fertilizing applications.

Bed and board. Humus is home and food to countless small creatures that spend their lives improving the earth's tilth and fertility. Without humus, these creatures cannot exist. Without these creatures, many essential plant nutrients remain in chemical forms that cannot be assimilated by plants. Without these creatures soil is tight and barren. Such soil must be supplied with food, i.e., fertilized. And as soil bereft of humus houses no worms, beetles, ants, and other busybodies, the farmer must himself keep constantly on the hoe, cultivating the land to keep it from solidifying into one giant cake of mud.

Sponge. Humus is a marvelous sponge. It can hold several times over its own weight in water. Many farmers call it drought insurance. Rain falling on humus does not run off but is absorbed and held until it is needed. As the presence of humus encourages worms and their ilk, the absorptive powers of the earth are tremendously increased by worm tunnels and animal burrows.

Protective blanket. A layer of humus atop the earth protects it from heavy rains. Whereas bare soils will be washed down the slightest incline in a heavy rain, humus-covered soils will be unaffected. In dry weather bare soils lose water rapidly to the sun. The ground is baked and the water evaporates quickly. When there is a blanket of protective humus, the soil remains relatively cool. Moisture is retained.

When the wind blows strong, it carries with it all dry exposed soil. Bare soil suffers from wind erosion. In certain areas and at certain times wind erosion can be very serious. (Witness the Dust Bowl of the 1930s.) Humus protects the soil from wind erosion.

A layer of humus atop and mixed in with the earth protects the plants and the tiny denizens from the cold. Humus is an insulator when reasonably dry. Not only does the blanket of humus on top keep the surface of the soil warm in cool weather, but also humus mixed with the earth reduces its thermal conductivity. Whereas pure moist clay or clay and sand exposed to prolonged subzero weather might freeze solid to a depth of a foot, fertile soil with a high humus content probably wouldn't freeze solid for more than an inch, even without a protective humus covering.

When there is a blanket of humus atop the earth and humus mixed in with the soil, winter frost does not penetrate as deeply. The earth warms up much more rapidly in the spring and the growing season is extended at that end of the calendar. At the end of summer the same thermal protection extends the season a few more days and possibly weeks.

Counterarguments. The value of humus is not accepted by everyone. Arguments have been put forth challenging some of the claims for humus. One such counterargument is directed against the advantage of humus atop the earth during winter: Humus is an insulator; ergo it slows the warming of the cold earth in the spring. Humus shields the earth from the warming rays of the sun.

This is not true in temperate zones. Up north, in Alaska for example, where there is permafrost, an insulating layer atop the ground would encourage freezing because the frost would work its way up. In a temperate climate the earth beneath the surface is always warmer than the earth at the top during the winter. Therefore the earth's heat would work upward during the winter and reduce the soils tendency to freeze.

When your soil is covered by a layer of humus, you will find that the earth underneath will be free of frost weeks earlier. And further, at the end of the growing season the earth will remain warm a little longer so that you benefit then too. More important, the protected earth is not subjected to alternate frosts and thaws which beat the heck out of the aforementioned denizens and the roots of perennial plants.

Another criticism is that humus shelters unwanted insect pests and encourages them to return for their spring depradations. True, without the protection of humus, with nothing but the bare ground to lie upon, few insects survive a cold winter. Humus may be therefore credited with the return of insect pests.

However, while humus provides housing for the "bad guys" it also houses and feeds their enemies. Thus when the battle in the spring is joined, the ratio of desirable to undesirable insects remains unchanged. As healthy, strong plants are better able to resist insect attack, and as humus encourages plant growth, the sum total is beneficial.

Still another criticism is that rich, humus-filled soil encourages field mice, shrews, and moles. This is also true. However, a serious infestation of small animals is rare. They are afraid of people, and unless you have a really large backyard farm, so large that your presence can go unnoticed for long stretches of time, you may never see a mouse or mole during your entire career as a backyard farmer. And even if you have a normal complement of these small creatures, the value of their burrowing and soil tilling more than offsets whatever small portion of your crop they may steal.

A remaining criticism is that humus-topped soil is messy and far from neat. Many people *do* find humus-topped garden soil far less attractive than neatly raked, barren soil. This is unfortunate, but unavoidable.

CHAPTER FOUR

Selecting and Improving Your Site

I F YOUR FARMING is limited to a window box, much of your planning is already accomplished. But if you are fortunate enough to have a choice of farming plots, then you will do well to take the time necessary to select the plot best suited to vegetable gardening and the crops you plan to harvest.

BEST LOCATION

If you live in the northern half of the country and your farm must be located near a building, the best spot to farm would be the south side of that building. This area will receive the most sunlight and the building will provide north-wind protection. Should the south side be unavailable, select the north side in preference to either the west or east side. If the building is tall and the farm close by, the building will shade your crop a portion of each day. We are assuming, of course, that the building is roughly rectangular and that its sides are directly in line with the major points of the compass. We are also assuming that you are planning hot weather crops like corn and tomatoes, and that you are seeking maximum sunlight.

If you have a choice of a hilltop or a hillside location, the top would be better if it wasn't the highest hill in the area and completely exposed to heavy winds. In such cases the southern side of the hill might be better and might average a higher

Even a single flower-
pot can produce a
worthwhile crop.
Tomato plant shown
was developed
especially for indoor
farmers. It's Burpee's
Pixie Hybrid. *(Courtesy
W. Atlee Burpee Co.)*

temperature over the summer than the hilltop with its possibly higher noon temperature.

The side of a hill is usually warmer than the valley below where the cold air gathers at night and remains until the sun is high. In very windy areas, however, a small valley location might be preferable because of the protection afforded by the hills forming the valley.

WINDBREAKS

Anytime there is a natural windbreak it pays to take advantage of it. The windbreak can be in the form of a stout hedge, stone wall, row of trees, or a fence. The windbreak doesn't have to be on top of the plot to be effective. It can be a dozen yards windward and still protect your plants.

Don't assume that all crop-destroying winds come from the North. They don't. Check the troublesome direction with your local weather station. Out on the plains, for example, the prevailing wind changes direction with the season. Another thing to determine in areas of changing wind directions is whether it is late spring or early fall winds that cause the most trouble. Once you have the data, you can plant on the correct side of the windbreak, or erect a windbreak of your own.

You can make a windbreak from stones gathered in the field and piled into a wall. You can plant trees or bushes in a tight row. When you do, think about fruit trees and berry bushes. While these plantings will suffer the most from wind

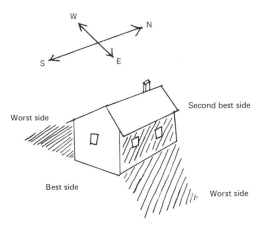

If you are forced to plant within the shade of a building, first choice is the south side if you are living up in the Northern half of the country. Second choice would be the north side of the building. Least desirable would be the east or west sides of the building.

damage and you will possibly lose considerable crop each year, whatever remains will still be much more than you would get from a string of poplars or yews.

Don't plant any of those "living fences" you may see advertised now and again. They will provide the fencing all right, but they will also provide you with all the exercise you want keeping them from overgrowing your farm.

Small farm to side of garage produces about 50 pounds of assorted vegetables a season.

And don't erect a "tight" fence. Plants require air movement, and if you erect a solid wooden or brick fence, you may do your plants as much harm as good.

Enclosed areas. By the same token, don't, if you have a choice, crowd your plantings up against a building or wall. Don't plant within a tight enclosure such as results from a circumferential fence or a stone wall. The cold night air will collect and remain within the enclosure for a goodly portion of the day. Crops planted in such areas tend to ripen weeks later than crops planted in open fields do.

LEVELING THE LAND

Although I have seen Scotch farmers harvest wheat on the sides of hills almost impossible to stand on, the side of a hill is no place to farm if you can help it.

The best farm land is perfectly flat and level. All the water that falls remains in place until it is either evaporated by the sun or absorbed by the soil.

When land is not perfectly level, rain water tends to run off. Water that does not seep into the soil is water that you have lost and that will not nourish your plants. Water that runs off carries soil and soluble plant nutrients with it. The quantity of soil and nutrients that may be lost in this manner depends on the pitch of your land, the quantity of water flowing at any given time, and the nature of your soil.

If your soil is soft, porous, and rich in humus, it is highly absorbent. It will hold roughly half its volume or more in water. Not until it is fully saturated will surface water accumulate. If your soil is tight and hard and lacking in humus, it is almost impervious. It will quickly saturate. Therefore, given the same pitch and rate of rainfall, there will be little runoff from the porous soil, while at the same time there will be almost complete runoff from the hard soil.

All this is of course obvious. The point that may be overlooked at least until after the first hard rain is that the soil most in need of water, the hard soil, will be the one most harmed. Given a little pitch and a summer storm, your entire application of fertilizer and whatever little topsoil you may have developed can be washed away if the underlying soil is hard and impervious.

How much is too much pitch? If you can see evidence of any scouring action after a moderate rain, you have too much pitch and should take some measures to correct the condition. If this direction is too vague, you can take a length of string and a string level and determine your land's pitch. Drive a stake into the high point of your plot and a second stake into the low point of your plot. Run a taut line

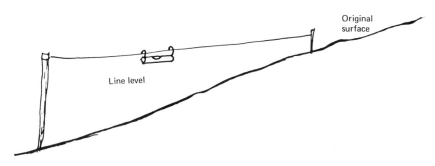

Use some stakes, a string, and a line level to establish your land's pitch.

between the two stakes, each end of the line just a foot above the earth. Now hang a string or line level in the center, and see which way the bubble goes. That indicates the high side. Next raise the low end of the string until the bubble is in the center of the level. The string is now level, and by measuring the distance between the string and the earth you know how much higher one end is than the other. If the difference works out to be more than ½ inch to the foot, I'd terrace if my soil was hard and poor.

TERRACING

A terrace is simply a retaining wall installed across the natural flow of water down the side of your plot. The amount of material and labor involved depends on the size of your plot and its pitch. The steeper the pitch or grade as it is commonly called, the more work involved.

Materials. Your choice of material for building a retaining wall will depend on how high you need to make your wall, how much space you can spare for it (in terms of width, not length, of course), and available material.

If you have the space, the simplest, least difficult solution is to omit the wall and merely slope the end of your terrace down to the lower level. As the surface of the slope should not be more than 45°, and preferably at an even smaller angle, you lose at least one foot of growing surface (it becomes hillside) for every foot of terrace height.

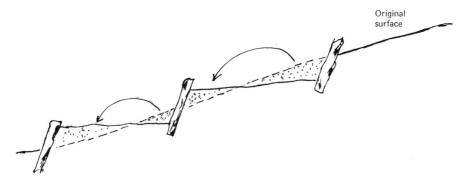

Original surface

Transfer the dimensions to a sheet of paper and then plan the number of terraces that are best suited. By moving soil from upper terrace to fill in lower terrace, work is reduced to a minimum.

An alternative that uses up less growing space is a wall of fieldstone (whatever you can pick up), old railroad ties, logs, timbers, rubble (which is quarry waste), or any type of concrete block. If your wall is going to be more than three feet or so high and almost vertical, you will have to go to some form of masonry, even poured concrete, which can be quite expensive in terms of material, forms, and labor.

CONSTRUCTING A RETAINING WALL

Start by drawing a profile of the land. Drive a stake into the earth at the highest point and a second stake into the earth at its lowest point. Then run a string from

Using 4-inch concrete block to make a retaining wall.

the first stake to the second. Following, either a line level or a mason's level is used to make the string level. You cannot use your eye to do this as you will be deceived.

With the string level you measure the distance between the two stakes, and then from the ends of the string to the earth to determine the pitch. These dimensions are transferred to paper by means of a simple sketch. Now you can see the pitch and decide how many terraces and retaining walls you want or need.

The more walls you build, the lower each wall needs to be, and the easier it is to construct.

Building a wall-less terrace. Mark the center of the width of the slope that will terminate your terrace with a couple of stakes and a length of string. Dig a trench along the lower side of the string. Make the trench just half as deep as the desired height of the slope. Take the dirt from the trench, and pile it into a wall on the other and higher side of the string. Remove the string and stakes. Use your shovel and pack the soil down, forming a slope facing the trench you have just dug. You now have a sloped surface half of which is trench and the other half of which is the side of a mound of piled dirt.

If you have some spare sod in your garden, cut it loose and spread it over the slope. If not, seed the slope with grass, tamp the seeds down, and cover with burlap to foster quick growth.

You can build an earth retaining wall of this type to any height so long as you make its downhill side slope sufficiently. Obviously, as you increase its height,

Using fieldstones to make a retaining wall.

more and more of your farmland becomes retaining wall slope and useless for farming.

Concrete block retaining walls. If all you need is a couple of inches, purchase 2-inch solid blocks and set them on their sides in a shallow trench. Then pack the earth firmly around them. If you need more height than a few inches, you will need 4-inch solid block which is 4 inches thick, and like the thinner block, 8 × 16 inches in size. Set these on end, a half inch or so apart inside a trench about 5 inches deep, and tamp firmly in place.

Fieldstone or rubble retaining walls. Start by laying out the string and digging your trench a few inches deep. Place the removed soil loosely on the high side of the trench; then place the largest of your stones in a line on the loose soil. Dig some more trench, and place the dirt atop the stones. Following, lay down a second layer of stones, preferably flat stones that overlap the in-place stones. Then more dirt and more stones. The stones help hold the dirt in place, and the dirt bars the flow of water.

Leveling the terrace. After you have completed your retaining wall or walls, the old surface of your land still runs downhill, albeit it is broken up by the retaining walls. You now have to level each terrace, which is just a matter of shovel work. However, do not stop when you have moved enough soil to make the surface level. Instead, keep on hauling dirt until the surfaces of your terraces run or pitch into the hillside by a few degrees. In other words, when you are finished, rainwater should run in a direction opposite to that in which it ran before. This is necessary because the soil you just moved will pack down with time, and when it does you want it level or pitched gently toward the hill.

TREES AND SHADE

Of the two, trees are the worst. Shade, such as is thrown by a house or wall means the absence of light. A tree not only throws shade; it draws hundreds of gallons of precious water from the soil. A tree's roots extend as far out as its drip line, which is the farthest reach of its branches. It is more or less along this line that the water drips down; hence the name, drip line.

Although trees do not throw the solid shade of walls and buildings, the presence of the tree's roots will effectively stunt and possibly destroy any plants you attempt to grow within the tree's reach. So if you must choose between planting beneath a tree and next to a wall, choose the wall.

And although a tree's roots are not supposed to extend beyond its limbs, don't bet on it. Give your plants as much tree clearance as possible. The hundreds of gallons of water that a large tree evaporates each day from the soil will drain an area of water much larger than the mere stretch of its branches. Should you be forced to plant your crops near a tree's drip line, you will note in the midsummer dry season that the plantings nearest the tree suffer most from the drought.

DRAINAGE

Plants require their roots to be moist. If the soil underneath dries out, the plants will die from drought. If the plants roots are continuously submerged in water they will also die, from drowning (lack of air at the roots). To prevent the first contingency we pray for rain to end a drought, and if the rain fails we irrigate. To prevent the second calamity, drowning, we plant only where subsurface drainage is satisfactory, or we provide drainage in one manner or another.

Obviously, hilltops and hillsides are well drained. The exceptions would be thin layers of soil atop a pocket of some sort in the underlying rock. Level ground, valley bottoms, and depressions may and may not be satisfactorily drained.

In some instances poor drainage is obvious. The earth is always soaked, no matter what its condition elsewhere. In other instances a simple test can give you the data you need.

Drainage test. Dig a straight-sided hole, 1 foot deep in the earth. If water

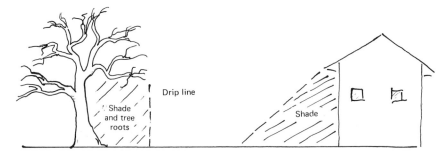

Plant growth is almost impossible under a tree. Not only does the tree rob the plant of sunlight; its roots also rob the plant of groundwater.

appears, drainage is nonexistent. If there is no water, fill the hole to its brim with water, and measure the time it takes for the water to be absorbed. If the water disappears in an hour or less, drainage is satisfactory. If it takes more than an hour, drainage may not be satisfactory. Just how unsatisfactory depends on how long altogether it takes the water to drain off, and the general condition of the nearby soil. If there have been several days of rain, slow drainage may be temporary. If there hasn't been any rain for weeks and the water hangs in there overnight, very little will grow well there. You can try it, but don't be surprised if your crop is a failure.

IMPROVING DRAINAGE

There are two general approaches to improving drainage, and neither of them is easy. The first is raising the level of the land. The second is draining the land.

Raising the level. Divide your plot into a number of smaller areas, leaving walk spaces between them. Build a retaining wall 8 or 10 inches high around each subplot. Build the wall from logs, old rails, concrete block, fieldstone or even turf-topped soil. Fill the enclosed areas with soil hauled from elsewhere or from your walk spaces. If the existing soil isn't high in sand content, consider mixing in sand in order to raise the level of the soil. Add one cubic foot of sand for every three square feet of plot area. If you can, purchase the sand by the truckload. If you can, have the truck dump the sand in place, and if you can, rent a Roto-tiller; it isn't too expensive or difficult. Once the sand and soil are mixed, it never has to be done again.

Draining the soil. The following suggestions presupposes that your soil is fairly open, meaning a goodly quantity of sand is present. (If you encounter nothing but clay as you dig down, there is a good chance all your work will be for naught.) Whereas you can drain a sandy field with a trench or pipe every 8 or 10 feet; you need much more piping and trenching to do the same with solid clay. Water just won't travel through clay, because clay is almost impervious.

If your subsoil is clay and it needs to be drained, it is advisable to call in an expert for advice before you waste your time and money trying to drain it.

If your field is fairly loose, you can drain it with either open trenches or covered drain pipe; however, you must have somewhere to drain it. There must be an area nearby that is lower than yours. There is an alternative, which is discussed some paragraphs on, but it isn't always practical.

To drain your field by trenching, dig a number of trenches leading to a lower area. Make each trench at least 1 foot deep, preferably two, but no more. Pitch their bottoms toward the disposal point. Check their effectiveness by digging a number of test holes, as discussed.

To drain your field with pipe, dig the same trenches, fill them with an inch or so layer of crushed stone. Lay down a continuous run of bituminous fiber drain pipe (it has a row of holes along its sides). Pitch the pipe toward the drain area. Cover the pipe with crushed stone. Follow with a layer of tar paper and soil.

The advantage of pipe is that you eliminate the open trenches in which you can trip and fall, and the open water puddles in which bugs can grow.

As the pipe requires much more work and expense, my suggestion is that you check the results of your trenching before you go further and install the pipe.

When there is no lower area. When there is no place to lead your water, you can try making one. The trenches are pitched to one central point where you lay to and

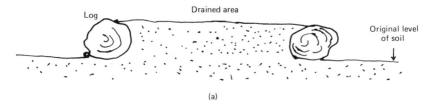

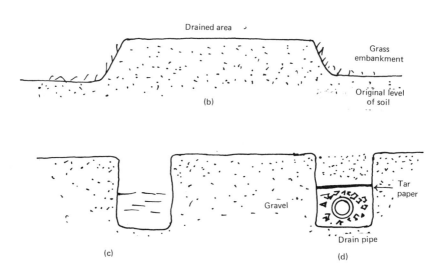

You can rid your soil of excess water by either raising the soil above the water or by draining the water. (*A*) Raise your soil by piling it up into a flat-topped mound, and hold it in place with logs or railroad ties. (*B*) Slope the sides of the mound, and hold the earth in place with grass. (*C*) Drain by simply digging a number of open ditches alongside your plot. (*D*) Drain the ditches with drain tile or perforated bituminous pipe laid in coarse gravel topped by tar paper and covered by soil.

dig a large deep hole. Your trenches drain into the hole and form a pond. Hopefully the water will evaporate and seep out of the pond faster than the trenches bring water to it. To speed evaporation, plant a few willow trees nearby. As they evaporate a couple of hundred gallons of water every summer day, they will help.

It would be nice if I could say this will do it every time, but I can't. It may and may not work.

CHOOSING THE BEST PLOT

If you are happily land-rich and have a choice of backyard farms you can by examination usually determine which is best.

Dig a straight-sided hole about 1 foot deep in each plot. Wait until the ground is fairly dry. Examine the sides of the holes. The exposed earth is called its profile.

You may find the earth soft and black and friable all the way down to the bottom of the hole. If so, you are in luck; you have virgin soil, rich and fertile.

You may find that the soft, black, or dark layer of earth isn't very thick, and that it is clearly separated from a lighter-colored layer of earth below. The top layer is called topsoil.

You may find that there is no topsoil, that as far as you have dug there is nothing but disintegrated rock. There is no humus at all. This is not good, but still not necessarily all bad.

While the layer of topsoil is valuable, it takes years to produce it; the nature of the underlying soil is more important in the long run. If the underlying soil is clay or mostly clay, you have a farm that will not take kindly to deep-rooting plants and which will take a very long time to improve.

On the other hand, if the underlying soil is mostly sand, it will quickly respond to plant growth and will soon improve.

The difference is so great that given the choice between bare sandy soil and a shallow layer of topsoil on clay, the clay shouldn't be given a second thought.

DIFFERENCE BETWEEN SAND AND CLAY

The difference is one of particle size. Sand particles are many times larger than clay. Silt is an intermediate size. For those who by some strange mischance have not encountered either, let me describe them.

Sand is like sugar, granular. Sand cannot be molded into any shape when it is perfectly dry; it falls apart. Sand will not hold water, it percolates right through.

Clay is like putty. It can be molded into complex shapes which it will hold. It can hold large quantities of water for a long time. When it dries, it becomes rock-hard. In the desert, clay is used as a building material. When fired, clay turns into ceramic ware.

Both clay and sand are easily recognized in their pure form. The problem arises when the two are mixed. In such cases and they are the norm, not the exception, we need to know their ratio. The reason can be a matter of comparison: evaluating one farm site against another. And it can also be that knowing the mix will better prepare us for the amount of work that a soil may need to bring it to maximum productivity. Ideally, a mix of 10 to 20 percent clay and the remainder sand is best—we are ignoring humus for the moment.

An accurate determination of the sand/clay ratio in a soil sample is difficult, especially if humus is mixed in. It is something best done in a laboratory. However, you can get a fair appreciation of the ratio by working a quantity between your fingers. The higher the clay content, the more easily you can shape the soil; the more readily you can smear the sample between your fingers. The higher the sand content, the more friable the soil, the more quickly it crumbles when you work it; the less smear you get when you rub it between your fingers.

FARM SIZE

While there is a natural limit to the size farm you can or may want to work, be advised that the larger farm is proportionally easier to work. Let me explain why.

The more plants you put in, the more plants you can lose to insects, disease, and predators, such as hungry rabbits and little children, and still harvest a satisfactory crop. The more plants you put in, the less you have to weed because you can lose some plant efficiency to the weeds and still harvest a good crop. If you put in very few plants, you must make every one come through, and that requires considerable attention.

The larger the plot of ground you devote to your farm the farther apart you can place your plants. The more space between plants, the easier they are to cultivate and harvest. The more space between plants, the larger and stronger each plant will become, thereby making them better able to resist insects and weeds, assuming that you mulch. (Farmers who do not mulch sometimes set their plants close together to keep out weeds.)

The more space you have, the more space you can devote to walks and paths, and this too will reduce the amount of work involved.

WALKS AND PLANT BEDS

Be advised that you cannot reach more than 2 feet or so without getting a crick in your back or neck. This means that you should not make any plant bed wider than 4 feet at the most. If you do you will find your self straining to reach the center of the bed. If you make the bed a little narrower, it will be still easier to reach its center.

At the same time, the walks you provide between beds should be at least 12 inches wide. If you don't leave this much space at a minimum, you will hardly have room to place your feet. If you have the space, make your walks half a dozen inches wider than your lawn mower. If you do this, you can keep the weeds down on your footpath by simply running the mower down the walk now and again.

CHOOSE CAREFULLY

One final word on selecting the ground for your farm. If you follow the mulch-organic principles expounded further along in this book and advised by this writer, your piece of land will grow more fertile with each passing season. As it does, the work you will need to do will lessen while your returns will increase. The land that you mulch-organically farm is therefore an investment. If you plant one season here and one season there, you will not benefit from the work you do beyond the immediate harvest. So when you start backyard farming choose a site you can continue using through the years to come.

CHAPTER FIVE

Conventional vs. Mulch-Organic Farming

I F YOU HAVE never grown a crop of fruit or vegetables the title to this chapter probably means little or nothing to you; so as a way of introduction to mulch-organic farming let me describe both techniques. First, however, let me forestall criticism by agreeing now that there really isn't any one conventional method of farming. A large variety of methods or techniques can be classified as conventional. Each farm, each locality, each soil, and each crop requires a somewhat different treatment, not to mention the differing farming opinions held by farmers and agronomists.

The same is true of mulch-organic farming, and while there are probably millions of conventional farmers for every mulch-organic farmer, there are also variations in this relatively new technique. Perhaps even more variations because it is, in a way, so very new.

CONVENTIONAL FARMING

In the spring the soil is tilled. It is either turned over by a moldboard plow or a disk plow pulled by horse or tractor, or it is turned over with a shovel by hand. The purpose of tilling is to loosen the earth, make it more friable, expose more surface to the air, and destroy or at least discourage weeds that have begun to grow and insects that have survived the winter in the earth.

At this time fertilizers and other amendments such as lime may be spread over

Conventional farming is neat and very pretty if you work hard at keeping the weeds out. The results, however, are not very good unless you fertilize heavily. The farm in the photo is obviously worn out, judging by its light color and sandy texture. *(Courtesy Ferry-Morse Seed Co.)*

the soil. The type and quantity depending on the condition of the soil, the crop to be planted, and the farmer's disposition. But almost always, finance permitting, a little more fertilizer than the year before will be used.

After, or sometimes before the spreading of the fertilizers and amendments, the soil's surface will be made relatively smooth with a power-drawn harrow or a man-operated rake.

The next step is planting. Again, this may be done by man or machine, depending on the size of the plot and the crop.

As soon as the seeds sprout and grow large enough to be recognized, the summer-long, double task of weeding and cultivating begins. For those of you who have never operated a garden hoe, let me say it is the art of breaking the crust that forms on "tight" soils after a rain. It is an art because the crust must be broken, and the soil underneath loosened a bit, all without damaging the plants or their roots.

The crust is broken so that a following rain will seep into the ground rather than run off. Also, breaking the crust and the clods that form underneath permits more air to enter the soil, encourages plant growth, and supposedly reduces water loss by evaporation. I say "supposedly" because the more surface exposed to the air, the higher the rate of evaporation. Some farmers break the clods into fine pieces which they use to "mulch" the soil and so protect it from sunlight and evaporation.

Weeding is another art, which is also done with a hoe or smaller hand tool. It is an art similar to cultivating. The trick is to remove the weeds without damaging the plants or their roots. To say it isn't easy is an exaggeration: It is nigh impossible in most instances. Plant and weed roots intertwine. If you cut the weed at its stem, its roots remain to continue their spurt toward the sun. If you pull the weed out by the stem, and this can only be done in friable soil or shortly after a rain, you stand a good chance of pulling your desired plants out too, or at least damaging them.

Most farmers combine cultivating and weeding in one fell swoop. They just hack away at the earth between their rows of plantings with a garden hoe. If you ever hear a farm boy complain that he spent all morning chopping, that was what he was doing.

Although it is a compromise, the simple solution of hacking is a necessity. If the soil's crust isn't broken you will lose water, which is the most vital single element in a plant's makeup. You need 700 to 1,000 pounds of water to make one dry pound of edible plant. If you don't fight off the weeds they will overrun your garden and stunt or destroy most farm plants. There are some exceptions. Corn and tomatoes come to mind, but there aren't many. Weeds are native, tough, and determined. They are the natural inhabitants of the area; your farm plants (and we are speaking of your produce garden plants) aren't.

Weeding can also be accomplished chemically by the use of herbicides. Generally the weed killer is sprayed between the plants and onto the soil that is not to support growth. In theory, it works wonderfully well. In practice, much is left to be desired. Herbicides cannot be used with all plants because some weeds are too closely related to the crop. Some crops cannot tolerate herbicides, even when they are sprayed on the earth nearby, and all herbicides are poisons. No matter how careful we may be, the wind is bound to carry some herbicide onto the plants we eat. Most of the herbicide is washed off, but a trace is bound to remain. Some herbicide is bound to enter the protected plants through their roots. The herbicide seeps into the earth. It cannot be prevented from moving sideways in some small quantity from the weed area to the plant area. And our farm animals cannot help but ingest a quantity, living on the farm as many do, and eating corn and other grains protected from weeds with herbicides.

Herbicides are therefore very expensive. There is their initial price; they are not given away for free, and there is the added price we pay in our health; small, perhaps, but it is all cumulative. (Lose a day to herbicides, a couple of days to pesticides, a few weeks to smoking, tainted fish, smog, etc., and there is hardly any time left for procreation.)

Which brings up pesticides. During the growing season and for fruit trees and the like, insect pests are controlled, but never eliminated by the application of various insecticides. Whatever can be said about herbicides can be said with greater emphasis about pesticides: More is used and in generally greater strength.

In the fall the crops are harvested. Afterward the earth is carefully cleared of plant remains. They are removed and dumped somewhere, even burned. The reasoning is that plant debris harbor insects and fungi harmful to the next year's crop. If the earth is swept bare, they have no shelter to protect them from the winter's cold, and most of them will perish.

Some farmers plow their fields in the fall. This increases surface area, allowing more air to make contact with the soil. The roughened surface holds water better, and discourages weeds in two ways. Weeds and plants prefer a relatively level, smooth surface for growing. They do not grow well when the soil is all hills and valleys. Also, those weed seeds that have taken hold in the fall are disturbed and to some extent destroyed.

Some farmers plant a "cover crop" or "green fertilizer" in the fall. Generally this is a vetch or clover crop that is plowed back into the soil in the spring. Its purpose is to add humus and nitrogen, which our little bacteria friends have affixed to the plant's roots. When farmers do this, they are no longer farming by purely conventional methods; they are leaning well into the organic realm of farming.

A well-planned and well-operated mulch-organic garden looks like an abandoned lot. However, the return in produce per square foot of ground and per hour of labor is several times higher than usual. This is a corner of the author's garden, where he is trying to convince tomatoes, string beans, lettuce and cucumbers to live in harmony.

While the foregoing doesn't pretend to be an exact or complete review of modern American farming practices, it does present an honest, if simplified picture. Farming by conventional methods is long hard work. It used to be hard, dawn-to-dusk toil. That is why so many fled the farms when they could, opting, surprisingly to us, for city slums and factory sweat; it was far easier. That is why our population shifted. Whereas some 90 percent or more of our people lived on lovely, romantic farms before 1900 or so, less than 5 to 7 percent earn their living by farming today, though many would return now that farms have machinery (the delay is caused by lack of money).

The major reason why most of us who have the space do not grow fruits and vegetables are possibly the tribal or even family memories of the work associated with farming.

If that is your reason for not farming your backyard, be advised that it no longer exists. It may be disconcerting, to put it very gently, but it is a fact that the millions of man-hours spent behind the plow and on the end of a hoe weren't necessary (for many crops, not all). Some 90 percent of the labor normally associated with truck farming can be eliminated and has been eliminated by mulch-organic methods. One such farmer of whom you may have heard or read her book is Ruth Stout, and her book is *How to Have a Green Thumb without an Aching Back* (Exposition Press, New York, 1955). Another, who has restored an impoverished, worn-out farm to full production on a commercial scale without the use of fertilizer is Edward H. Faulkner. His books on the subject in general and his particular approach to mulch-organic farming include *Plowman's Folly*, 1938; *A Second Look*, 1946; and *Soil Development*, 1952 (University of Oklahoma Press, Norman).

MULCH-ORGANIC FARMING

You may start this method almost anytime in the year. For literary convenience we will assume that it is fall and that the crop has just been harvested.

The plants are cut off near the ground and permitted to lie where they fall. The entire growing area is covered with a layer of mulch which can be any organic material from peanut shells to hay. Preferably the layer is several inches thick.

In the spring, when it is time to plant, the mulch is pushed aside to bare sufficient earth space for planting. If you are planting a row of radishes, a space 2 inches wide by the length of your row is cleared. A long scratch is made in the earth, and the radish seeds are laid within the tiny ditch and covered with the thin layer of earth they require. If you are setting out green pepper plants, a suitable hole is dug, and the pepper is planted in the usual style.

During the summer you sit in the shade on your porch and watch carefully. If a couple of weeds do somehow manage to push through, you threaten them with your hoe. It isn't necessary to get up. There won't be enough weeds to matter.

In the fall you harvest and enjoy your crop. Again the plants are cut down to the

Leaf lettuce planted rather closely together and mulched with grass clippings. When grown this way weeding is negligible. If the outer leaves alone are removed, the plant will grow new ones.

roots, which are left in the ground. Now you add whatever mulch you have accumulated: leaves, grass clippings, vegetable leaves, compost, and so on. There is nothing more to do until spring.

You haven't turned the earth over.
You haven't cultivated.
You haven't weeded.
You haven't used herbicides.
You haven't used pesticides.
You haven't added fertilizer.

The picture painted of mulch-organic farming is not false. It is not a television commercial pushing the miracle kitchen cleaner that does the job by itself. This is really how mulch-organic farming can work and does.

However, it presupposes two conditions: The soil is fertile and friable to begin with. The soil is neither highly alkaline nor highly acidic.

If your soil isn't fertile and friable, it can be made that way. Some fertilizer and soil amendments may be necessary at first, but with each succeeding season you will need less and less until you will need no more.

How many seasons? An exact figure is of course impossible. But we can give you some general guidelines. If you add nothing whatsoever to your soil and it isn't all clay to start with, you can probably bring it to the condition described in 3 to 5 years. If you add a little fertilizer and lots of organic material and possibly lime, you can do it in 2 years or so. Again we are assuming that your soil is not hopelessly solid clay, which can be improved, but which requires much more time.

Meanwhile, and this is a very important "meanwhile," you will be harvesting crops. Not as much as when your soil is in top condition and not without some work beyond what we pictured, but increasingly better crops each season with decreasing amounts of fertilizer and pesticides.

BASIS OF OPERATION

Nature may surprise and trick you but it doesn't cheat. A dirigible flies because despite its huge size, engines, and passengers, it is lighter than the air it displaces. A teak log sinks because though it is wood it is heavier than the water it displaces. Plants thrive when organically farmed because conditions so produced are favorable to plant growth.

Tilling the soil. For countless centuries people tilled the soil. They began with a straight stick, moving on to a hooked stick attached to any animal they could force to do the work. Today we have ganged plows pulled by giant tractors. And while it is true that the mulch-organic system cannot be used for crops such as oats and wheat, it is becoming increasingly evident that tilling the soil does not improve it. The ancient word "tilth," denoting friable soil well suited to growing plants, is a misnomer. Tilling, working the soil does not improve its tilth. On the contrary it can reduce its tilth.

All through the farming literature we are informed that it is most important that plowing, tilling, be done when the soil's condition is just right. The soil should not be wet, but it should also not be too dry. If you can work a sample into a ball that holds its shape, it is too wet. If you can't work the soil into a ball, it is too dry. The exact condition is elusive. The reason for the difficulty in ascertaining the exact condition best for tilling is, in this writer's opinion, due to the fallacy of the effort.

W. A. Raney and A. W. Zingg, writing on the Principles of Tillage in *Soil,* the 1957 Yearbook of Agriculture, published by the U.S. Department of Agriculture, state:

> Excessive tillage breaks down the structure of the soil and leaves it susceptible to crusting. The small pore sizes associated with surface crusts impede water intake, increase runoff and reduce the amount of moisture stored for crop use.

Other agricultural writers advise farmers to be careful not to "smear" the clods as they break them up, to avoid compaction, and to avoid "blocky" soil for formation.

It is this writer's opinion that soil should be tilled only when there is some direct mechanical benefit to be derived. For example, should your land be covered by a clay runoff produced by some ancient or even recent stream discharge, and should the soil underneath prove to be sandy, mixing the two would rid you of the layer of clay and possibly benefit the underlying layer. Should your land be like so many other backyard plots, it may comprise a collection of various types of soils, dumped there by the contractor who hauled whatever soil he could find that was free or almost so. In such instances a thorough rework of the soils may act to produce one soil with fair texture.

Unless a soil is completely clay or nothing but sand, rainfall and plant growth both act to improve it. As the rain percolates down through the earth, it carries with it the finer particles of soil, which are of course the clay. The downward movement of the water is not straight, but constantly changing, moving first in one direction and then in another, much like the progress of a drop of rain down a pane of glass. The passage of a single drop of water alters the texture of the soil to the extent that the drop has transported a quantity of clay and has dissolved a minute amount of soil. Following the downward passage of that single drop there now exists a microscopic path through the earth that did not exist before. Subsequent drops of water will preferentially follow that path as it offers less resistance to their passage than the rest of the earth. In time, repeated rainfalls will form innumerable tiny passages through the earth. In time, rainfall alone can and will form air passage that did not exist before in the soil, assuming that the soil is not pure clay, or pure sand. In the latter case, of course, there are already too many passageways into the earth.

When soils are worked or tilled, they are subjected to a sliding, smearing action that forces the clay that may be present into the tiny pores formed by passing rainwater. Thus tilling helps to destroy the very soil texture that the tiller is seeking. The smearing action takes place most readily when the soil is wet because water is a lubricant. Little smearing action and pore closure occur when the soil is very dry, but when soils are really dry, they are next to impossible to work, especially soils high in clay.

Plant growth acts to improve soil in two ways. When the plant completes its cycle and dies, its root structure is turned into humus, providing food for plants to come and food and passageways for worms and their ilk. The second way is a mystery, at least to this writer. Pull a weed from a bone-dry, rock-hard field, and you will find that the soil immediately surrounding the weed's roots is slightly moist and friable. Somehow the weed has been able to conserve moisture in and near its root system, and somehow the weed has been able to sheath its roots in topsoil. The remainder of the field may be infertile, but the earth near the weed's roots is obviously not. My guess is that the weeds, or any plant's roots, absorb water containing dissolved minerals. This solution is drawn up into the body of the plant and its leaves by capillary action. Clays and silts are dissolved first by water action because they have more surface. Thus in the process of growth a plant enlarges the area surrounding its roots, leaving the desirable granules of sand. All plants accomplish the same results, but it is more noticeable around weeds growing in abandoned fields.

There is yet another reason why the earth should not be turned over and otherwise tilled in the process of introducing desired plant life. The thinking behind this reason falls into the romantic or philosophical category: Why change nature? The entire earth catalog of plants live, die, and reproduce on untrammeled earth; why change it? You wouldn't add or remove salt (if you could in meaningful quantities) from the sea because you didn't catch as many fish as you desired. Yet farmers almost continuously trouble to turn the top foot or so of soil topsy-turvy. Plants growing unaided by farmers thrive on soil that is undisturbed. The soil near and at the top is different from the soil a foot or more down. It is not a homogenous mixture as it is when the soil is tilled.

We know that continuous watering causes a plant's roots to lie near the surface of the soil, which isn't good, as they crowd and fail to get the nutrients they require. Isn't it possible that plants require their nutrients to be stratified? Isn't it possible that they need to reach down into the earth, not only for water but for food? Isn't it possible that the unvaried diet presented by an unchanging nutrient profile hinders their growth?

Cultivation. Cultivation, loosening the soil around a plant while it is growing, probably did not start until fairly recently in historical perspective. So long as the soil retained a goodly portion of humus, so long as there was "color," there was little need for cultivation. Not until after the soil became worn out and tight did the need arise. Whether it is harmful or not depends on the nature of the soil, the type of plant, and the care with which the farmer handles farming tools.

Carrots, for example, are deep rooted. On the other hand, beans and corn have a large percentage of their roots close to the surface of the soil. It is difficult to cultivate plants of these types without damaging their roots. And yet, if there is a crust on top of the soil, that crust must at the very least be broken as soon as possible. It is mostly clay and forms an airtight and watertight seal.

At this point an astute reader may point out that cultivation is not merely breaking the earth crust around the stems of plants; it also includes such practices as piling the earth into a hill around the roots of corn. Very true, but in our discussion we are limiting ourselves to cultivation practices that are eliminated by mulch-organic farming, a part of which is simply mulching. Mulching, of course, is covering the bare earth between desired plants with anything that will protect it. Organic wastes such as leaves and grass clippings and hay and the like are best because they decompose to add to the humus present. But in a pinch, almost anything can be and has been used. The list is long. Newspaper, plastic sheet, rocks, and boards can be and have been used to advantage.

The mulch breaks the force of the falling rain. Mud isn't kicked up and puddled. The mulch acts as a blanket, tempering the sun, reducing soil evaporation and keeping it warm on frost-filled nights.

Weeding. Mulching eliminates weeding. No plant can grow beneath a light-proof cover. When you mulch you stop weeding; not entirely, it is true. You can't mulch right up to the plant's stem; it needs some circulating air. But for all practical purposes, mulching eliminates weeding.

One point about mulch worth mentioning is that you don't have to mulch "solid" for it to be effective. If you have a limited supply, you mulch close to your plants, because that is where weed competition can cost you the most in harvest. If you have a little more, you can spread it around. Even a thin layer of mulch will discourage growth, raise soil temperature, and help conserve moisture.

Herbicides. These chemicals are mainly used by commercial growers who want to eliminate the labor of weeding. When you farm by mulch-organic methods, you eliminate weeds by mulching, thereby eliminating any need for herbicides.

Pesticides. It is a proven and accepted fact that stronger plants are not usually attacked by insect pests, and when they are, they are not harmed a fraction as much as pale, weak, spindly plants. No one seems to know the reason why. Perhaps the weaker plants have a different composition and flavor. Perhaps the better developed plants exude substances that discourage predators; perhaps the stronger plants merely replace the missing tissues faster than the bugs can eat. We know their greater resistance to be a fact, and little more.

At first your plants will probably be as susceptible to insect and fungi attacks as any others. During this period you may want to use some pesticides; when you do, there are kinds that are not harmful to man and beast. Pesticides are discussed in following chapters.

Fertilizers. As previously stated, probably more than once: as the soil loses its color and tightens up, as the soil loses its plant nutrients, these have to be replaced if productivity is to be maintained. As first you will probably need and therefore want to use fertilizers. With time, as the soil improves, this requirement will decrease, and in a year or two you will not need any at all, nor any in the years to come.

LABOR AND TIME

So far in this chapter we haven't mentioned labor and time, which are to a great extent synonymous, and of great importance to all those who farm for profit and not merely for exercise and entertainment. Profit, of course, need not include the sale of farm produce. If you can grow your own produce for less than you can purchase them, and if you can save more dollars by your effort than you can normally earn at another occupation you are profitably engaged. In the full sense of the word there is no profit in growing cabbage, for example, selling at 5 cents the head if it requires an hour of work per cabbage. It is, no doubt, fun and relaxing, but hardly profitable.

Mulch-organic farming is profitable farming in every sense of the word. No matter how poor your farm soil may be at the start, you will produce a crop, and with time, when the soil is reasonably fertile you will harvest bountifully. When all the hours of turning the soil over, raking, weeding, cultivating, spraying, and after-harvest cleanup are eliminated, there is really very little left to do. In fact, backyard farming may become so simple it may bore you. Mulch-organic farming makes it practical for every household with the space to have a kitchen garden and more.

Steps in setting out plants the mulch-organic way. (*A*) The mulch that has been protecting the earth all winter long is pushed aside.

(*B*) A hole is dug to receive the plant. If the soil isn't as rich as you would like it to be, a handful of manure or humus is added.

(C) The plant is placed in the hole, and the earth around it is firmly pressed down.

(D) The plant is generously watered for a few days. The mulch is pushed back into place, leaving a little clear space around the plant's stem. As this is a pepper plant, a stake will be required. Other than this, there is little to do but wait for harvest time.

CHAPTER SIX

Examine Your Soil

WHEN THE EARTH is loose and friable, when the earth is filled with nutrients, plants grow rapidly and strong. When the earth is tight and hard, where there is little nutrition or it is unsuited, plants do poorly, even though there may be an abundance of sun and rain.

Neither friable soil nor nutrition alone can produce good crops; both conditions, loose soil and proper nutrients, are necessary. Therefore, to assure ourselves of a bountiful harvest before sowing our seeds, we must examine our soil both chemically and physically beforehand. If our soil is deficient in either major characteristic, we can correct the deficiency or select crops better suited to the soil as it is.

The physical makeup of a soil depends to a great extent (but not entirely) on the size or sizes of the mineral particles that comprise the soil and the percentage of humus that may be present. The physical makeup of a soil determines how fast or rapidly water percolates down through, how much difficulty plant roots may encounter while making their way, how much support the earth provides plants buffeted by the wind, which plants will fare best, and so on.

The physical makeup of the soil also determines whether or not soil amendments are required, in what quantity, how much labor will be needed, and whether or not the soil should be turned over and otherwise tilled.

The chemical composition of a soil is literally its chemical response to plant life: whether it is acidic or alkaline, how much plant food is present, and in what quantities.

This chapter discusses the physical aspect of the land. Following chapters cover the chemical nature of soil.

PHYSICAL COMPOSITION

Agronomists, soil scientists, commercial farmers, and the rest of us green-thumb people describe and define the physical composition of our soil in a number of ways. When we say clay or sand or pebbles, we are talking about soil particles of more or less specific size.

Particle (soil) name	Diameter in millimeters
Clay	Less than .002
Silt	.002 to .05
Fine sand	.10 to .25
Medium sand	.25 to .50
Coarse sand	.5 to 1.0
Pebbles	Larger than 2.0

When the particles or separates cluster and form clumps, the clumps are considered soil structure and are defined as either granular, meaning that the soil breaks easily into coarse granules, or are classified as blocky, meaning that the soil does not break into small crumbs but remains in large, blocklike clods.

When we speak of texture, we mean the proportion of the various particles in the soil. When a soil's texture is classified as sandy, it means that there is so much sand present that the soil has the texture of sand. When a soil is called clayey, it has the texture of clay though it may also contain a high percentage of sand, silt, and even humus. The deciding factor is that the soil behaves more like clay than like any of its other ingredients.

Soil classification may appear to be academic and somewhat useless. It is not. For unless you examine your soil and determine its class or type, all the information that follows concerning soil treatment, both physical and chemical, is useless.

SOIL CLASSIFICATION

Soils are classified according to their physical composition and humus content. The figures are approximate.

Gravel	All or mostly pebbles and stones
Gravel and sand	A mixture of stones and sand
Sand	More than 75% sand
Sandy loam	50 to 75% sand, 40% silt, and the remainder clay
Loam	50% sand, 40% silt, and the remainder clay
Clay loam	Up to 25% clay, 30 to 50% silt, and the rest sand
Clay	More than 25% clay
Muck	Up to 25% humus, the remainder clay and silt
Peat-loam	Up to 35% humus, a lot of sand, and a little silt and clay
Peat	More than 35% humus; the remainder sand, silt and clay

Gravel. Gravel cannot be used for farming. The rainwater runs right through. If you have uncovered a gravel bank on your property, don't complain. Purchase a truck, and go into the contracting business. Gravel is valuable.

Sand and gravel. The same holds true for a mixture of sand and gravel that is so coarse that water doesn't hesitate on its way through. However, if there is lots of sand and few stones, you may be able to treat it the same as sand.

Sand. Sand alone will not hold water, though it will not pass water as fast as gravel.

To check whether you have sand alone, or sand plus silt, clay and/or humus, moisten a sample, and try to mold it into a stable shape. The best you can do with wet sand is to make a sand castle. On the other hand, clay can be molded and carved into intricate shapes that it will hold.

Another test consists of placing a sample in a funnel and adding some water on top. If it is pure sand, the water will run through almost as fast as you pour. If anything else is mixed in (excluding pebbles and rocks), the passage of water will be slowed.

Pure sand can be mixed with clay, silt, or humus to reduce its permeability and make it useful for growing plants. However, the mixing job is a big one in both labor and material, and so it is advisable to run a few tests to find just how much amendment you must add to your sand to make into plant soil.

How to find the minimum quantity of amendment needed with sand and alternatives to the use of amendments is discussed in Chapter 10, "Amendments."

Sandy loam. This is a soil that is mostly sand but contains sufficient silt and clay and possibly humus to enable it to retain water fairly well. It will feel sandy in your hand when you rub it between your fingers, but you should be able to mold it into a simple shape, and it should retain water a fairly long time when given the funnel test. Sandy loam is excellent for root crops, and good for all other plants.

Loam. This is the soil called for on seed packets. It is ideal or near ideal for all crops; best for leaf crops such as lettuce, cabbage, etc. If you have loam, your gardening problems are all but licked. However, the word itself as used by agronomists denotes a mixture of sand, silt, and a little clay. Loam is simply a texture; it does not imply the presence of humus, though this may be present.

Clay loam. When a farmer speaks of a "heavy" loam, he means loam with a higher-than-usual percentage of clay. It still feels soft in the hand, and it still crumbles easily when dry. However, when it is moist and rubbed between the fingers, you can feel the slippery trace of clay as well as the sand granules. Clay loam is a good soil suitable for many plants just as it is, and for almost all plants with the addition of a little humus.

Clay. If your soil dries rock hard and cracks, if you can smear a wet sample between your fingers and feel few or no particles, if you can mold it like putty, you have pure clay. If some humus, sand, and/or silt is present, if it isn't completely puttylike you have a clayey soil, which can be made to grow plants with the addition of amendments. The quantity depending on the percentage of clay present.

Tips on working with clay and clayey soils may be found in Chapter 10, "Amendments."

Muck, peat-loam, and peat. Technically the difference between peat and muck is that muck is much further along the road to complete decomposition than peat. In other words, peat turns into muck, given the time and proper conditions.

From our point of view, the three different types of soils are similar in that they can grow crops if they are not too wet (a usual problem) and are not too acidic. Excessive moisture can be drained off. Acidity can easily be cured by the application of lime. However, before troubling to do either of these, you would be well advised to remove a sample and dry it. Doing so will enable you to better judge its clay content.

Examine your soil's profile. Dig a straight-sided hole in the earth about 2 feet deep. Note whether there are any horizons (layers) and what their colors and textures are. This profile of the author's soil shows very little change from bottom to top: just a gradual darkening indicating an increasing quantity of humus. There is nothing to be gained by turning this soil over, except exercise.

EXAMINE YOUR SOIL'S PROFILE

Now that we know more or less what soil structure and composition are all about, it is time to examine your soil's profile. This is best done when the ground is fairly dry, as excessive moisture will, to a great extent, disguise the nature of the soil.

Exposing a profile. Dig a hole in the earth 2 feet deep and 1 foot wide. Use your shovel to make one side of the hole fairly smooth, flat, and reasonably vertical. Dig as many exploratory holes as you believe there are soil variations in your land. If your land is fairly level, and it is clear that it is not fill, chances are that there is little difference in soil composition and profile from one area to another. In such cases

You can judge your soil's humus content and fertility by its color. You can judge its texture by its appearance and its feel between your fingers. This soil sample has very little humus. It consists mainly of a mixture of sand and clay.

one exploratory hole in the earth, dug wherever convenient, should do. If you are going to farm fill, which is a broad term meaning soil that has been moved from one place to another, there is no telling what you may find when you dig. Builders and contractors haul whatever dirt is close by and cheap. Then they level it all and cover it with a kiss of topsoil to nurture the grass cover. If you suspect that your farm is fill, dig a number of exploratory holes. You may find a bonanza in loam, and you may find pure clay, but at least you will know what you have to work with and will be able to take whatever corrective steps may be necessary.

Profiles and what to do about them. Wait until the earth is reasonably dry; otherwise the soil will look much darker and more fertile than it really is. Look at the earth's color. Note whether or not there is a difference between the side of the hole near its bottom and its top. Note whether there are any layers or horizons, as they are commonly called. Test the texture of the soil with your fingers. Note whether there is any difference in textures between the top and bottom sides of your test hole, whether there is any textural difference between the horizons. Try to classify the horizons according to the previously given list of soil types. Try to estimate how much clay or sand may be present in the horizons if there are any.

Possible profiles. Many profiles are possible, but only a few are probable. Ignoring any thin layer of black topsoil that may be present on top and considering only the soil exposed by our 2-foot cut into the earth, you may encounter a single, consistent texture accompanied by a single, consistent color; a single texture with a graduated change in color; a single texture with varying bands of color; a graduated change in texture with either a single color or a graduated change in color; or two or three horizons with differences in both texture and color.

Color, of course, is partially caused by the inorganic soil matter (the red clays of our southeastern coastal areas, for example) and partially due to humus. The more humus, the darker the soil, and the more fertile it is.

Assuming that your soil has a uniform texture and a uniform color, if it is pure sand or nearly so, there is no point in turning it over. Nothing will be changed. But you do need to add an amendment to make it usable. Amendments are discussed in Chapter 10.

If your soil is all sandy loam, you are in luck. Sandy loam is excellent for a limited number of crop plants and good to very good for most of the rest.

If your soil is all loam, you are even luckier.

If your soil is clay loam, you are still in fairly good shape unless the soil is on the heavy side, in which case you may want to work in some amendments.

If your soil is all clay, you are definitely going to need amendments and probably in good quantity.

Assume that your soil has a uniform texture but shows color change across its profile. Assume additionally that the color is darkest at the surface and lightens more or less gradually as it goes down. This would be natural, indicating undisturbed earth with a maximum percentage of humus on the surface, decreasing in quantity with depth. In such cases it would be inadvisable to turn the soil over if you have sand, sandy loam, loam, or clay loam. If you have clay and a thick, heavy section of humus on top, there would be an advantage to turning the soil over and mixing the humus in. If you have a lot, you would possibly need little additional amendments; but if there is little humus, the soil would definitely require additional material to make it suitable for farming.

(Please bear in mind that in all these directions we are providing specific guidance for what are rarely specific conditions: When it gets right down to the dirt, readers will have to draw their own conclusions.)

Assuming that your soil has textural horizons (differing layers of soil), if one horizon is sandy and the other is clay or clay loam, you will improve both layers if you mix them together.

If you have several inches of rich humus-laden topsoil overlaying clayey subsoil, it is advisable to work the topsoil into the clay for a distance of a foot or so. Plants do not grow in the top few inches of soil alone; at least most crop plants do not. If there is excellent soil atop impermeable undersoil the seeds will take off fine, but the tough undersoil will stunt their growth. Better a fair soil to a depth of a foot or so than just a few inches of exceptional soil.

If there is a layer of humus-laden soil atop sandy loam, there is no need to turn the soil over. The sandy loam will retain moisture and plant food. Even if there is a sharp line of demarcation, indicating that the topsoil was dumped in place, there still isn't any reason to mix the two. The rain will wash some of the plant nutrients down into the sandy loam, and the plant roots will follow, eventually enriching the entire soil profile and eliminating the boundary between topsoil and subsoil.

If there is a layer of humus atop sandy soil and it contains a goodly quantity of in-place plant growth and is not merely dumped topsoil, do not mix the topsoil into the subsoil. In doing so, you will disturb the old growth. The roots of these plants, even though they may be dead and partially decomposed, form a kind of organic net which binds the grains of sand together. If you turn the soil over, you will break these vegetable strands and reduce the soil's ability to retain water, thereby reducing its ability to support plant growth.

Assuming you encounter muck or peat loam, dry a few samples of the soil before estimating their clay content. This will help you secure a more accurate estimate. If there are horizons with notable differences in clay content, they will benefit by being mixed. If there is no difference in clay content across 'he face of your cut, there is nothing to be gained by mixing except exercise, even if there is considerable color difference.

Summary. At this point we have a fair evaluation of our soil's physical nature, whether or not amendments are needed, and whether or not mixing the soil as it is will help. Before proceeding with any mixing and turning it is necessary to evaluate our soil's chemical condition, its pH, nutrient content, fertilizer, and amendment requirements. All this is discussed in following chapters.

CHAPTER SEVEN

pH Testing and Correction

P LANTS LIVE BY ingesting inorganic chemicals dissolved in water. The chemical composition of the soil is therefore as important as its physical composition. Without the presence of the proper chemicals in their proper ratios and combinations, plants will starve to death, despite friable soil and plenty of sunshine and water.

By determining the chemical composition of our soil in advance of planting we can assure ourselves of a good crop. If certain chemicals are lacking, we can add them. If others are present in dangerous overabundance, we counteract their presence by adding still other chemicals. If the soil's chemistry is not too far from optimum, we can make do by planting crops suited to the existing chemical condition of the soil.

The chemical composition from a farmer's point of view can be ascertained by testing and by examining the previous season's crop. Generally both methods are used. The reason is that a really thorough and comprehensive chemical test is very expensive and unnecessary. A few basic chemical tests coupled to a careful examination of the plants during their growth and afterward can usually provide an experienced agronomist with all the necessary information.

One of the basic chemical tests involves the pH of soil. This test, easily made with low-cost equipment, determines whether a soil is sweet or sour.

Sweet and sour soils. Soils are a mass of complicated chemical compounds involving hundreds of different elements and compounds and perhaps as many almost constantly changing relationships. Just as fertile soil is alive with creatures large and small, marrying, begatting, and divorcing, so is the soil "alive" with chemicals joining, separating, and rejoining. The common denominator of all or of at least much of the action both animal and chemical is the acid-alkaline condition of the soil.

Years ago when soil was considered little more than decomposed rock, farmers judged a soil by tasting it and noting what grew well. If the soil tasted sour and sorrel thrived, the soil was called sour. If the soil tasted soapy or slightly sweet, and if clover and alfalfa grew well on it, the soil was classified as sweet.

Sometime during the past 50 years or so, simple litmus paper was brought in for testing. Placed in moist acidic soil, blue litmus paper turns red. Placed in moist alkaline soil, red litmus paper turns blue. In neutral soil, both types of paper turn purple. In a sense, "acidic" is the opposite of "alkaline," while the term "neutral" means that the substance is in between, neither acidic nor alkaline.

Tasting is an ancient method, and litmus paper is not much more accurate for measuring the pH of a soil. pH is an abbreviation for the phrase, power of the hydrogen ion; and when used in conjunction with a number, it is a simple chemical notation for expressing the relative acidity or alkalinity of a substance.

For example, vinegar has a pH of 3, which indicates that it is a mild acid. Ammonia, which is a moderately strong alkali, has a pH of 11. The reaction of pure water is pH 7, which is exactly neutral.

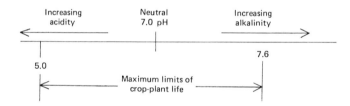

Graphic representation of pH, showing the acidic-alkaline limits in which the plants we grow for food and animal use can live.

Although the pH scale ranges from 0 through 14, and the pH of soils varies from 3.3 to 9.8, few if any plants can exist in soils more acidic than pH 4, or more alkaline than pH 8. All our farm crops do best within the range of pH 5.0 to 7.6. Some plants thrive in a pH band no more than half a unit or so wide. For example, potatoes, sweet potatoes, and watermelon do their best in soil that ranges from 5.0 to 5.6 pH.

At first glance it would appear as though the pH of a soil is very critical since the numerical difference between plant preferences appears to be small. It is not. The numbers used are actually exponents to the log base 10, which, if you have forgotten your high school math, means that the difference between pH 6 and pH 5 is not 1 but 10. Thus, a soil with a pH of 5 is 10 times more acidic than a soil with a pH of 6, and a soil with a pH of 4 is 100 times more acidic than a soil with a pH of 6.

The importance of pH. In addition to the facts that few if any plants at all will grow in soil more acidic than pH 4 or more alkali than pH 8 and that some of our food plants prefer a narrow range within the boundaries described, the pH of the soil is important in a number of other ways.

The pH of a soil controls to a measurable extent the availability of several important and desirable plant nutrients. For example, phosphorus, which is one of the elements most vital to plant life, becomes almost insoluble as the acidity of the soil increases. When phosphorus cannot be dissolved, it cannot be absorbed by the plant. Thus you can spread bags of phosphorus over your land and still fail to feed your plants if the soil is too acidic.

On the other hand, when the soil is too alkaline, phosphorus combines with iron and aluminum to form another, different but still insoluble, compound that is once again useless or almost useless to plants. As aluminum is the third most abundant element in the earth's crust and iron the fourth, there is little or no chance that your soil will not contain some aluminum and some iron.

Aluminum and manganese are relatively insoluble in moderately acidic soils. When the soil's acidity increases sufficiently, these metals dissolve and form toxic (poisonous) compounds which are absorbed by plants, weakening them.

pH also has a strong effect on our friendly, neighborhood microorganisms. They do their best when the soil is slightly acidic or neutral.

Soil texture (structure) is also closely tied to pH. When clay or clayey soil is either strongly acidic or strongly alkaline, it becomes very tenacious and sticky when wet and rock-hard when dry. When the same clay is neutral or only slightly alkaline, and especially when a high percentage of calcium is present, the same clay is far less sticky and troublesome. In fact, correcting a clayey soil's pH can be almost as effective as adding physical amendments in making blocky soil granular.

Soil pH also affects plant diseases. Some plants are less susceptible when the pH is shifted in one direction or another. Potatoes, for example, are less susceptible to scab when the soil is more acidic than that in which the potatoes grow best. Potatoes will grow in soil with a pH of up to 6.5, but you will have far less scab if you keep the soil more acidic and hold pH in the 5.0 to 5.5 range. Cabbage is attacked by "clubfoot" fungus when the pH is lower than 7.0

The effect of pH on plants, soil, soil creatures, plant nutrients, and poisons is a highly complex, fascinating field of study. Fortunately, backyard farmers need know little more than has been discussed so far to produce excellent crops. So long as you have a general understanding and appreciation of pH, all you need to know is how to measure it and how to make changes if necessary. The rest can be left to mother nature.

MEASURING SOIL pH

There are several approaches: You can purchase simple "indicators," which are just a little better than the old method of tasting the soil. You can purchase an inexpensive kit for about $5.00 from most if not all of the mail-order gardening supply houses. These kits will enable you to secure a numerical pH figure. You work by matching the color resulting from your test against five different colors, each indicating a specific pH ranging from 4 through 8. With a little practice you can easily estimate fractional differences. With care these kits will provide all the pH accuracy you need. In addition, these kits enable you to measure the nitrogen, potash, and phosphorus in your soil. Unfortunately the inexpensive kits do not provide numbers for the aforementioned chemicals. You are given four colors marked deficient, low, doubtful, and adequate. The more expensive kits do produce numerical results, but in this writer's opinion they are unnecessary.

Still another approach is to send a sample of your soil to one of the agricultural colleges or government stations listed on an accompanying page. Some charge;

some do not. If any are free, they will be those in your state. In any event, write for instructions first.

STATE AGRICULTURAL EXPERIMENT STATIONS

ALABAMA	FLORIDA	MAINE	NEW MEXICO	SOUTH DAKOTA
Auburn	Gainesville	Orono	Las Cruces	Brookings
ALASKA	GEORGIA	MARYLAND	NEW YORK	TENNESSEE
College	Athens	College Park	Geneva	Knoxville
ARIZONA	Experiment	MASSACHUSETTS	Ithaca	TEXAS
Tucson	Tifton	Amherst	NORTH CAROLINA	College Station
ARKANSAS	HAWAII	MICHIGAN	Raleigh	UTAH
Fayetteville	Honolulu	East Lansing	NORTH DAKOTA	Logan
CALIFORNIA	IDAHO	MINNESOTA	Fargo	VERMONT
Berkeley	Moscow	St. Paul	OHIO	Burlington
Davis	ILLINOIS	MISSISSIPPI	Columbus	VIRGINIA
Los Angeles	Urbana	State College	Wooster	Blacksburg
Riverside	INDIANA	MISSOURI	OKLAHOMA	WASHINGTON
Parlier	LaFayette	Columbia	Stillwater	Pullman
COLORADO	IOWA	MONTANA	OREGON	WEST VIRGINIA
Fort Collins	Ames	Bozeman	Corvallis	Morgantown
CONNECTICUT	KANSAS	NEBRASKA	PENNSYLVANIA	WISCONSIN
New Haven	Manhattan	Lincoln	University Park	Madison
Storrs	KENTUCKY	NEVADA	RHODE ISLAND	WYOMING
DELAWARE	Lexington	Reno	Kingston	Laramie
Newark	LOUISIANA	NEW HAMPSHIRE	SOUTH CAROLINA	
	Baton Rouge	Durham	Clemson	
		NEW JERSEY		
		New Brunswick		

For additional information on your farming problems and an occasional free bulletin write to any of these agricultural extension services; they work with the U.S. Department of Agriculture.

Auburn University
Auburn, Alabama 36830

College of Agriculture
University of Arizona
Tucson, Arizona 85721

University of Arkansas
Box 391
Little Rock, Arkansas 72203

Agricultural Extension Service
2200 University Avenue
Berkeley, California 94720

Colorado State University
Fort Collins, Colorado 80521

College of Agriculture
University of Connecticut
Storrs, Connecticut 06268

College of Agricultural Sciences
University of Delaware
Newark, Delaware 19711

University of Florida
217 Rolfs Hall
Gainesville, Florida 32601

College of Agriculture
University of Georgia
Athens, Georgia 30602

University of Hawaii
2500 Dole Street
Honolulu, Hawaii 96822

College of Agriculture
University of Idaho
Moscow, Idaho 83843

College of Agriculture
University of Illinois
Urbana, Illinois 61801

Agricultural Administration
Building
Purdue University
Lafayette, Indiana 47907

Iowa State University
Ames, Iowa 50010

Kansas State University
Manhattan, Kansas 66502

College of Agriculture
University of Kentucky
Lexington, Kentucky 40506

Louisiana State University
Knapp Hall, University Station
Baton Rouge, Louisiana 70803

Department of Public Information
University of Maine
Orono, Maine 04473

University of Maryland
Agricultural Division
College Park, Maryland 20742

Stockbridge Hall
University of Massachusetts
Amherst, Massachusetts 01002

Department of Information Service
109 Agricultural Hall
East Lansing, Michigan 48823

Institute of Agriculture
University of Minnesota
St. Paul, Minnesota 55101

Mississippi State University
State College, Mississippi 39762

1-98 Agricultural Building
University of Missouri
Columbia, Missouri 65201

Office of Information
Montana State University
Bozeman, Montana 59715

Dept. of Information
College of Agriculture
University of Nebraska
Lincoln, Nebraska 68503

Agricultural Communications
Service
University of Nevada
Reno, Nevada 89507

Schofield Hall
University of New Hampshire
Durham, New Hampshire 03824

College of Agriculture
Rutgers, State University
New Brunswick, New Jersey 08903

New Mexico State University
Drawer 3AI
Las Cruces, New Mexico 88001

State College of Agriculture
Cornell University
Ithaca, New York 14850

North Carolina State University
State College Station
Raleigh, North Carolina 27607

North Dakota State University
State University Station
Fargo, North Dakota 58102

Ohio State University
2120 Fyffe Road
Columbus, Ohio 43210

Oklahoma State University
Stillwater, Oklahoma 74074

Oregon State University
206 Waldo Hall
Corvallis, Oregon 97331

Pennsylvania State University
Armsby Building
University Park, Pennsylvania 16802

University of Rhode Island
16 Woodwall Hall
Kingston, Rhode Island 02881

Clemson University
Clemson, South Carolina 29631

South Dakota State University
University Station
Brookings, South Dakota 57006

University of Tennessee
Box 1071
Knoxville, Tennessee 37901

Texas A & M University
Services Building
College Station, Texas 77843

Utah State University
Logan, Utah 84321

University of Vermont
Burlington, Vermont 05401

Virginia Polytechnic Institute
Blacksburg, Virginia 24061

Washington State University
115 Wilson Hall
Pullman, Washington 99163

West Virginia University
Evansdale Campus
Appalachian Center
Morgantown, West Virginia 26506

University of Wisconsin
Madison, Wisconsin 53706

University of Wyoming
Box 3354
Laramie, Wyoming 82070

Federal Extension Service
U.S. Department of Agriculture
Washington, D.C. 20250

The kit's advantage is that you can make as many tests as you wish, when you wish. You do not have to wait. The disadvantage is that you cannot possibly work as accurately as a laboratory can, and you do not have the equipment to test for the presence of as many elements as they do. However, inaccuracy is not a serious handicap; as we stated before, the pH range in which plants thrive is far broader than the figures themselves might lead you to believe.

Another reason why it is not necessary to have your soil's pH very close to the figures recommended for the various plants is that the plants themselves are very tolerant of variations. Plants that thrive in the range of pH 6.0 to 7.0 will do almost as well when the soil is 5.5 or 7.5, and even better when there is plenty of humus present. No one seems to know why this is so, but humus helps make plants thrive in soil with a pH one or even two points away from what tests have proved to be optimum in highly mineralized soils (soils that lack humus).

This writer suggests that you secure a kit *and* send off a soil sample to one of the labs. The lab will back up your test procedures and give you data on elements you cannot measure.

When to test pH. The best time to test, meaning that your reading will be most accurate, is after the earth has warmed to 60° F or more and about a week or so after a rain.

Bacteria are inactive when the soil is cold; air temperature has little affect on them. If you measure the pH of cold soil, you will get a false reading.

The reason why it is necessary that the soil be moist for several days before you make your test is that drought will inactivate or destroy the bacteria present. When bacteria die, they release organic acids which will make your pH lower (more acidic) than it really is. On the other hand, if the soil is slopping wet, your test solution will be diluted, and you will be measuring ground water that will soon percolate down into the earth.

Also bear in mind that the season affects pH to some degree. Your pH tests will show a minimum of acidity in the fall and a higher reading (more acid) in the winter; so shave your readings accordingly.

Make your pH tests before you do anything at all to alter your soil's chemistry. Then wait at least several weeks for whatever chemicals you have added to dissolve and react with the soil before taking a follow-up test. Once you have

Using a spoon to scrape a soil sample for testing.

brought the pH of your soil close to optimum, you can limit your pH tests to once a year. That will be sufficient to keeps tabs on things.

Taking samples. Dig a hole about a foot deep. Make one side as vertical as you can. Use a clean knife or spoon, and scoop a shallow groove out of the side of the earth. Start the groove about 7 inches from the surface, and quit before you reach the topsoil, if there is any. If not, stop about 1 inch below the surface. Transfer the soil thus collected into a clean, dry plate or saucer. Mix the soil with the same clean utensil. Do not touch the soil sample with your fingers or permit any cigarette ashes to fall onto and be mixed in with the sample. Either action, fingers or ash, can alter the pH reading.

Take as many samples and make as many tests as you believe there are variations in your soil. Do not dig half a dozen holes and mix the soils from each. That will give you an average, and though the average may be excellent for your purpose, the various areas contributing to the average may be way off.

Making the test. If your kit is like mine, you take a small sample of the soil, place it in a test tube, add the specified reagent, and after mixing and waiting, you compare the resultant color with that of the chart. After you have fiddled with the tiny test tube a few times and learned to differentiate between the color of the solution and the color of the dirt, you can move on to using a clean plate. Just put a pinch of the soil on the plate, mix in the reagent, and compare the resultant color. It is a lot easier.

HOW AND WHEN TO ALTER pH

An accompanying chart lists the more popular vegetables and their pH prefer-ences. For pH data on other vegetables and fruits refer to the rear section of this book.

At this point you know the pH of your soil, and having at least made a tentative selection of your plantings, you know whether or not you are in the pH ball park, and if not, how far out you may be and in which direction.

To alter your soil's pH in one direction or the other requires the addition of any of a number of chemicals. The chemicals necessary to go acidic or alkaline are definite. The quantity to be added is not. It all depends on the nature of your soil, as well as how much you wish to alter it. But bear one general guideline in mind: It is always better to add a little less than necessary rather than more.

When to alter pH. If this is the first year you are farming a particular plot and the soil is loaded with humus, leave it alone unless your tests indicate that the pH is more than two units from optimum.

If the soil is clayey, and it is more than one-half unit acidic than optimum, alter its pH with limestone because this will make the soil more flocculent (granular) as well as more alkaline (less acidic).

If your soil has very little humus and its pH is one or more units away from the desired pH, the soil should be corrected. If the same soil is less than one-half unit away from optimum pH, leave it alone. For one reason, it is difficult to add just sufficient chemical to produce an exact pH condition. For another, a simple color chart test cannot be trusted to get closer than one-half unit to either side of the truth (actual pH).

If you have worked the plot before and your crop was good to excellent, don't fiddle with the pH, no matter what the reading indicates, and no matter what condition your soil may be in. If you feel you must alter the soil's pH, add half or less than the quantity suggested. Then wait and take some more tests. (Your equipment may be defective or you are using it improperly.) Plant growth is a much more dependable indicator than a simple chemical test.

Time, quantity, and amendment. You add lime, which is alkaline and has a high pH, to soil that is acidic and has a low pH. You preferentially add sulfur, which is acidic and has a low pH, to soil that is alkaline and has a high pH.

Use sulfur, if you can secure it, and not aluminum sulfate because it takes 6 pounds of aluminum sulfate to equal the effect of just 1 pound of sulfur. More important, soluble aluminum is toxic to plants; so you don't want any more aluminum in your soil than may already be there.

Preferably lime or sulfur is added to the soil in the fall, and chemical fertilizers, if used, are added in the spring. If this is not possible or practical, the pH amend-ments should be added at least one week after the application of fertilizer, and at least another week should be allowed to pass before sowing seeds or setting out plants.

Should you wish to change the pH of your soil after you have planted, do so very guardedly, adding just a sprinkle a little at a time whether you are adding lime or sulfur.

Which lime? Technically, the term "lime" is restricted to pure calcium oxide. However, as ground limestone is the "lime" most frequently used on farms, and as ground limestone is almost all calcium carbonate, ground limestone or calcium carbonate is the yardstick by which the effective neutralizing ability of all other

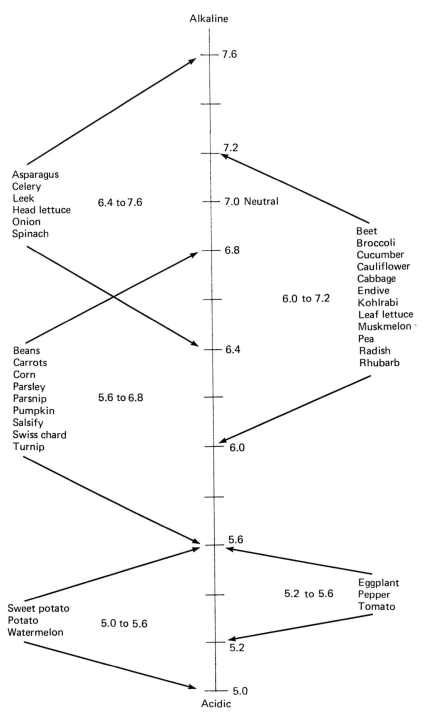

Alkaline

7.6

7.2

7.0 Neutral

6.8

6.0 to 7.2

6.4

6.4 to 7.6

Asparagus
Celery
Leek
Head lettuce
Onion
Spinach

Beet
Broccoli
Cucumber
Cauliflower
Cabbage
Endive
Kohlrabi
Leaf lettuce
Muskmelon
Pea
Radish
Rhubarb

Beans
Carrots
Corn
Parsley
Parsnip
Pumpkin
Salsify
Swiss chard
Turnip

5.6 to 6.8

6.0

5.6

Eggplant
Pepper
Tomato

5.2 to 5.6

Sweet potato
Potato
Watermelon

5.0 to 5.6

5.2

5.0

Acidic

pH preferences of various plants. *(Connecticut Experiment Station data.)*

"limes" is measured. By common consensus, ground limestone is rated as 100 percent effective and other liming materials are rated proportionally.

For our purpose ground dolomitic limestone is best because it contains both calcium carbonate and magnesium carbonate. Magnesium is a highly essential element of plant growth too often in short supply in many truck gardens, especially in the acid soils common to eastern and southern United States. Magnesium deficiency is aggravated by adding low-cost superphosphate and other chemical fertilizers containing sulfates (aluminum sulfate for one) to the soil. The sulfates combine with whatever magnesium is present to form magnesium sulfate (Epsom salts, no less), which is highly soluble. Thus, by adding ordinary fertilizers and amendments containing sulfates the magnesium present in soil is reduced by leaching. Every time it rains some of the magnesium is washed deep into the subsoil.

Ground dolomitic limestone has the additional advantage of variable or self-changing solubility. It does not readily dissolve in neutral or alkaline soil; thus, its tendency to make alkaline soil even more alkaline is nil. However, as the soil to which it is added becomes increasingly acidic, the dolomitic limestone becomes increasingly soluble and in a sense more effective. Dolomitic limestone is never as soluble (fast acting) as burned or hydrated lime, but it is fast enough to do the job. Because dolomitic limestone is slow acting, and because it works only as fast as it is needed, it is difficult to overlime with reasonable quantities of this material, whereas it is easy to do so with other limes.

Although ground dolomitic limestone contains less calcium carbonate than ordinary ground limestone (dolomitic limestone is 60 percent calcium carbonate and 30 percent magnesium carbonate), magnesium carbonate molecules are so light that the dolomitic limestone is 97.5 percent calcium carbonate by weight and therefore rated equal to ground limestone in neutralizing power.

Ordinary limestone is your second best choice. Since it doesn't contain magnesium, it is advisable to add this in the form of magnesium sulfate at a rate of 2 to 5 pounds per 1,000 square feet. In case you have forgotten your high school math, a plot of 1,000 square feet would measure 50 by 20 or any other two numbers that multiplied to give you 1,000.

Marl is a kind of a stone usually found under muck in a swamp. Generally it contains some silt and clay, which degrades its effectiveness as a liming agent. However, it is mostly calcium carbonate, and when it is clean, it is considered on a par with ordinary limestone on a pound-for-pound basis.

Seashells, either burned or ground, are also suitable for liming. Generally they are rated as 90 percent effective compared to ordinary limestone.

Burned lime, quicklime, and lump lime are all different names for ordinary ground limestone that has been literally burned. The result is almost pure calcium oxide, which is a far more effective neutralizing agent than ordinary ground limestone. Therefore 56 or so pounds of burned lime equals 100 pounds of ground limestone.

Unfortunately, burned lime is just about the gardener's last desperate choice for liming material. When burned lime is mixed with water, it becomes very hot and dangerous. When the reaction is complete, the result is a very sticky, slippery, smooth mass, excellent for plastering walls (which is its reason for manufacture) but difficult to apply to the soil. If lime isn't applied evenly, you end up with areas of acidic and areas of alkaline soils, neither of which are suited to farming.

Slaked lime is burned lime that has been mixed with water and dried. Sometimes called hydrated lime or lime hydrate, it is calcium hydroxide and is as effective on a weight basis as burned lime (it is packed dry). The trouble with burned lime and slaked lime is that both work very, very fast and are therefore difficult to evaluate. And once the burned or slaked bag of lime is opened or exposed to moisture, the lime quickly forms one solid lump.

Wood ashes are excellent for liming purposes. The ashes of a hardwood fire that haven't been leached contain about 4 percent potash, up to 2 percent phosphoric acid, and other minerals, as well as strong neutralizing agents. Pound for pound, fresh hardwood ashes are on a par with ground limestone.

Coal ashes should never be used with soil that is to be farmed; they contain soluble chemicals inimical to plant life.

Particle size. Although limestone is limestone, the particle size is extremely important in predicting the results. Ordinary limestone and even dolomitic limestone broken into pieces the size of small peas are often touted as being most desirable, as they last the longest and do their work over the greatest period of time. Very true, but lime does not migrate. Its only motion is downward into the earth by the action of water, which dissolves a quantity of the stone and carries it along. If you mix limestone the size of peas in with the earth, it will remain there for dozens of years. Its neutralizing effect will be almost nil, and in this writer's opinion, not worth adding.

You need finely ground lime, the finer the better. The finer, the more quickly it will do its job, and the sooner you will be able to measure and see the results. If you are adding lime to loosen your soil, you want as many fine particles of lime as possible. Each particle of lime gathers round it a layer of clay and becomes a granule. The more granules, the looser your soil.

Lime quantity. Before you even consider purchasing lime, bear in mind that there are many soil conditions which are best not limed though the pH may be a little low.

As previously stated, if your soil is rich in humus, it it generally advisable to let it be unless the pH is more than two units off. If your soil is low in humus you still should leave it alone unless it is more than one unit off in pH. If it is only one-half unit away from optimum, it is best not to add lime unless it is clayey.

All the Northeast and portions of the North Central and Eastern sectors of our country are underlain by ancient glacial till that is high in lime. There is a constant rise of groundwater from deep within the earth in these areas. The groundwater contains dissolved limestone and in time it tends to correct excessive surface-soil acidity. This is not true of every farm and garden plot in this part of the country, but it is true enough to warrant your leaving your soil's pH alone unless it is far off and unless it is incorrect for a year or more.

If you live more or less east of the Mississippi, you live in a perennially moist area, at least when the ground isn't frozen. If you live here and your soil is somewhat alkaline, the trouble will be solved when you add humus. The bacteria always present in humus will produce the required acid as they digest the organic debris.

The point of all this is that while it is important to know your soil's pH, it is also important to exercise restraint in the matter of lime and sulfur and give nature a chance to work its magic.

Secondly, if your soil does need an application of lime or sulfur, never try to alter its pH by more than one unit at a time in any direction, and preferably less.

Use hydrated lime if you want fast results, but as fast as it might be, wait a couple of months before taking your follow-up pH tests. And don't try to hit it on the nose. It is better to be off a half a unit than add too much sulfur or lime.

Use ground limestone or ground dolomitic limestone when there is no rush, and give the limestone 6 months or more to settle in before you conclude that you have secured a correct reading. Remember, even if you use finely ground limestone it isn't necessary to lime a field more than once every 3 to 4 years.

If you overlime, you can bring the pH down with sulfur. It isn't easy in that it takes a long time for one to react with the other and even longer for you to be certain you are reading the final results, but outside of the expense and labor, no permanent harm is done.

Before going on to provide more or less specific figures on the quantity of lime necessary to raise pH by a unit or so, there are still some more sides of the picture to be explained.

One is that the effect of lime you add depends on the size of the lime particles. This is because the finer the particles, the more of the lime's surface that is touched and dissolved by downward moving water. Thus the result of finely ground lime will be more immediate but not as long-lasting as the lime broken into larger particles.

Another is that a lot depends on the book you read. The quantities suggested by this writer are based on a U.S. Department of Agriculture publication. Suggestions for roughly double the quantity can be found in a bulletin published by the Virginia Experiment Station, which is under the indirect auspices of the U.S. Department of Agriculture. Other gardening books suggest even greater quantities of lime.

As stated, sulfur is the preferred amendment to use to lower soil's pH and make it more acidic. Like the lime, the sulfur works most rapidly and most effectively when it is in powdered form.

FINELY GROUND LIMESTONE NECESSARY TO RAISE THE pH OF A 7-INCH LAYER OF SOIL

Region and texture	Quantity in pounds per 100 square feet		
	pH 3.5 → 4.5	4.5 → 5.5	5.5 → 6.5
Warm-temperate			
Sand	1.5	1.5	2
Sandy loam	1.5	2.5	3.5
Loam	1.5	4	5.5
Clay loam	1.5	6.5	9.5
Clay	1.5	8	11
Muck	13.75	18.15	20.9
Cool-temperate:			
Sand	2	2.5	3
Sandy loam	2	4	7
Loam	2	6.5	9
Clay loam	2	8	11
Clay	2	10.5	12.5
Muck	15.75	20.9	23.6

If you are using hydrated lime, use three-quarters of the quantities given.
If you are using burned lime, use one-half of the quantities given.
If the soil is unusually low in humus, reduce the quantities by 25%.
If the soil is unusually high in humus, increase the quantities by 25%.
Don't attempt to change the pH of your soil by more than one unit in any direction at one time.

APPROXIMATE POUNDS OF SULFUR NEEDED TO LOWER THE pH OF 100
SQUARE FEET OF SOIL TO A DEPTH OF 8 INCHES

Starting	Final pH					
pH	4.0	4.5	5.0	5.5	6.0	6.5
	Pounds of sulfur (S = sand, L = loam)					
	S L	S L	S L	S L	S L	S L
4.5	.4 1.2					
5.0	.8 2.4	.4 1.2				
5.5	1.2 3.5	.8 2.4	.4 1.2			
6.0	1.5 4.6	1.2 3.5	.8 2.4	.4 1.2		
6.5	1.9 5.8	1.5 4.6	1.2 3.5	.8 2.4	.4 1.2	
7.0	2.3 6.9	1.9 5.8	1.5 4.6	1.2 3.5	.8 2.4	.4 1.2
7.5	2.7 8.0	2.3 6.9	1.9 5.8	1.5 4.6	1.2 3.5	.8 2.4

Note: If you are treating soil with a texture between that of sand and loam, use an intermediate figure. If you are treating clayey soil, use about twice the amount suggested for loam.

SALINE AND ALKALI SOILS

Soil is weathered rock. Soils formed in moist areas are constantly leached by rain. The salts released as the rock disintegrates under the influence of the weather are washed deep into the earth. Soils formed in arid areas, areas with less than 20 inches of rain per year, tend to accumulate salts. There is, of course, some rain, and when it falls, it does carry some of the salt into the interior of the earth, but as the earth dries, much of the salt tends to return to the surface.

Other highly saline and alkali soils are ancient lake bottoms. These lakes were land-bound and their waters did not flow out to the sea but evaporated. The countless tons of salts that flowed into these lakes during their million-year lifetimes remain there.

You can recognize some saline or alkali soils by their color. Lake-bottom alkali soils are generally a dead-gray color (muck is black). Very often you can find snail shells and other crustacean remains in such soil, which is usually called black alkali. These soils are usually high in sodium carbonate and usually have a pH of 8.5 or higher. Technically they should be termed "alkaline" soils. Alkali soils are white in color and are usually called white alkali, though they are not strongly alkaline in nature. Saline soils, also white in appearance, contain 0.2 percent or more of neutral or nonalkaline salts, such as chlorides and sulfates.

Saline, alkali, and alkaline soils are to be found in particularly flat or low areas in desert and near-desert regions and in naturally low spots in moist parts of the country. If the area does support plant growth, the tip-off is that far less will be growing on the "difficult" soils than on neighboring land.

Saline, alkali, and alkaline soils can be brought into crop production by leaching and the addition of various chemicals such as limestone, sulfur, gypsum, and alum.

The first step is to determine the texture of the soil—sandy, clayey, or what have you. The second is to determine the soil's salts content and what should be added and in what quantity to remove or neutralize them. This is best done by a laboratory, though you can use your kit to measure pH. Until you have the lab's report and suggestions, it is inadvisable to go farther.

When you know what to mix into the soil and have done so, the next step is leaching the soil. Since there is small possibility that you can drain your leaching water off somewhere, your only practical alternative is to raise the soil above the level of the existing earth. This can be done by building a retaining wall around each plant bed and piling the soil into the space to a height of about 1½ feet. The top of each bed is flattened and indented to form a circumferential wall of dirt a few inches high. The end result is a giant baking-tin shape made of soil, its top more than 1½ feet above the surrounding earth.

Next, the "baking tin" is carefully filled with water. When that water has seeped out of sight, but before the bottom of the tin has even begun to dry, more water is added. This is repeated as many times as necessary until a quantity of water totaling 1½ feet in height or more has seeped down through the earth. (Use the sidewall as a guide.)

When this has been done, the edge of the "tin" will be seen to be filled with dried salt. The edge is removed and discarded. The soil is now ready for its crop. However, a second soil test is advisable, just to measure the effectiveness of the chemical and leaching treatment.

CHAPTER EIGHT

Nutrients

T HE BASIS OF all plant life and thereby all animal life is a process called photosynthesis. Green plant leaves contain a complex molecule called chlorophyll. Driven by the power of sunlight, the chlorophyll molecules somehow cause gaseous carbon dioxide, taken from the atmosphere, to combine with oxygen taken from water to form a glucose with which the plant synthesizes starches, sugars, cellulose, amino acids, organic acids, hormones, enzymes, and everything a plant needs to grow and reproduce.

Plants, however, cannot sustain their life on the elements found in water and our atmosphere alone. They need other, additional elements. So far as we know to date, plants require 16 elements for their sustenance and well-being. These are carbon, hydrogen, oxygen, nitrogen, manganese, zinc, iron, copper, molybdenum, boron, phosphorus, sulfur, potassium, calcium, magnesium, and chlorine. In addition, plants will also absorb other elements within reach of their roots. Just why plants will collect sodium, iodine, cobalt, aluminum, and silicon, along with other elements which may be toxic to both the plant and whoever ingests the plant, is not known. Plants do not appear to require these elements for growth and reproduction.

Plants secure the carbon they need for the manufacture of glucose from carbon dioxide drawn from the atmosphere directly by their leaves. Under average conditions, still air contains no more than .03 percent carbon dioxide. Typically, corn plants require 40 tons of carbon dioxide to produce 100 bushels of corn.

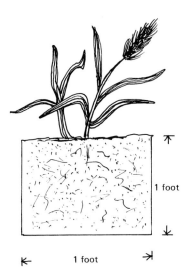

1 foot

1 foot

The root system of a single rye plant consists of more than 13,000,000 individual roots with an aggregate length of more than 385 miles and a surface area of close to 6,870 square feet. One cubic foot of loam contains soil particles with a total surface area of more than 560,000 square feet.

During a hot summer day, it is estimated that corn plants in full sunlight could utilize 20 times more carbon dioxide than is present in the surrounding atmosphere. Agronomists believe that the shortage of carbon dioxide is a limiting factor in plant growth.

Curiously enough, the quantity of carbon dioxide in the air above farmland is to a great extent dependent on the quantity of humus in the soil. As previously stated, one major by-product of microorganic activity is the gas, carbon dioxide. Therefore, soils rich in humus do more than merely feed the plant through its roots. They help furnish it with the essential ingredient of all organic life, carbon in a form that the plant can utilize.

Hydrogen is another major component of the all-purpose glucose, as is oxygen. Both are taken from water mainly absorbed through the plant's root system. However, oxygen in gaseous form is also required at the plant's roots for respiration. This is still another reason why plants in loose, granular soil fare better than plants in hard, tight soil. Granular soil is porous; air filters down to the roots through granular soil. Little or no air can reach through tight soil.

ROOT SYSTEM

Plants ingest the nongaseous portion of their mineral diet by means of absorption and transpiration. Their roots are in contact with groundwater which contains a portion of the minerals that the water dissolved during its passage through the earth. The roots are connected to the leaves by a multitude of microscopic tubes called capillaries. As it is the nature of all liquids to ascend whatever capillaries they contact, the groundwater containing minerals in solution rises to the surface of the leaf, where the water alone is evaporated by the sun. The minerals, actually nutrients from the plant's point of view, are left behind and are converted to glucose by photosynthesis. As the groundwater evaporates from the surface of the leaf, more groundwater enters the roots and ascends the capillaries. Thus the sun not only converts minerals to glucose and a host of other plant necessities; it also draws water from the soil into the plant's leaves. The process is called transpiration.

If you have casually examined the roots of a plant purchased from a nursery or the roots of a weed pulled from the ground, you may logically question the process of transpiration. There just doesn't appear to be nearly enough roots. But that is only because almost all the roots are left behind when a plant is literally pulled up by its roots.

Plant root systems are actually tremendous feats of engineering, so vast that they are difficult to comprehend. For example, the root system of a single rye plant grown in no more than a single cubic foot of loam has approximately 13,800,000 individual roots with an aggregate length of more than 385 miles and a surface area of close to 6,870 square feet. If this seems impossible, be advised that 1 cubic foot of loam contains soil particles with a total surface area in excess of 560,000 square feet. The roots of a single rye plant therefore make contact with less than 1 percent of the total soil surface available. Clay, having smaller particles, has several times more surface area. That is why clay can hold so much more water than loam, and why water passes so slowly through clay. Water adheres to the surface of each particle.

This is why a plant can draw its sustenance from the soil, and this is why a potted plant can exist for countless years, feeding on just a handful of soil.

So much for the function of water and air in a plant's diet and how a plant manages to extract its food from the soil and the atmosphere. Let us now consider the elements that plants remove from the soil.

NUTRIENT QUANTITY

The mineral elements ingested by plants in comparatively large quantities are called major elements or nutrients. Those required in very small quantities are called micronutrients or trace elements.

The difference between the major nutrients and the micronutrients appears to be limited to quantity only. Eliminate any one nutrient, major or minor, or limit its supply, and the plant suffers. It may fail to grow, change color, die, produce undersized, unripe fruit, or no fruit at all.

At the same time, if there is an oversupply of any one or more nutrients, major or minor, the plant may also be adversely affected.

Still another necessity is the proper ratio between available nutrients. If there is too much of one in relation to another, plant vigor and growth may be hindered.

This portion of farming is very interesting and complex. It is helpful to know or at least have reference to information that will enable you to recognize the cause or causes of plant malformation and failure. However, it isn't necessary to have these data at your fingertips. Your plants will make their way without your knowledge of even a smidgen of chemistry. All you need remember is that if your crop looks poorly, this is the chapter wherein you may find the simple cure.

MAJOR NUTRIENTS AND THEIR EFFECTS

Nitrogen. Nitrogen forms a part of all protein, and is therefore vital to the formation of plant cells. If any one plant nutrient can be singled out as all-important, it is nitrogen. It is utilized in a larger quantity than any other soil element.

When the supply of nitrogen in a soil is limited, plant growth is stunted. When the shortage is severe, the young leaves of the plant will become light green or yellow while the leaf's veins turn somewhat red.

In some plants nitrogen deficiency produces an appearance somewhat similar to that caused by sustained drought; all the leaves grow pale and change color somewhat, and some of the lower and older leaves may fall off. When nitrogen is the only nutrient in short supply, the plant may mature early and fruit much sooner than usual, but its fruit will be smaller than usual.

When the supply of nitrogen in the soil is overabundant, plant cells become larger than normal, but their walls are thinner. This makes for a more succulent and tender leaf, which to a limited degree may be welcome in leaf crops such as cabbage and lettuce, but also makes plants more susceptible to disease, drought, and lodging, which is a farm term for wind damage.

Excessive nitrogen produces lush dark green leaves at the expense of the root system. Therefore the plant becomes more susceptible to drought. Excessive nitrogen delays flowering and fruiting. Thus frost may kill the crop before it has ripened. On the other hand, if the growing season is long, an excess of nitrogen can increase the harvest.

Phosphorus. Phosphorus is another vital plant nutrient. It is not required in as large a quantity as nitrogen, but it also operates in the formation of plant tissues. Organic phosphorus compounds help transfer biochemical energy from one life process in a plant cell to another. In a sense, it is a control element. It regulates, if we may use the term, photosynthesis, plant respiration, the synthesis of new protoplasm, and other biochemical steps in plant life and growth.

It was once believed that phosphorus was of importance to plants only when they reached the fruiting or their maturity stage and that it wasn't needed for the early weeks of a plant's growth. With time, it was learned that the converse is true. Phosphorus added to the soil according to old gardening manuals for "firming up the fruit," is a waste of time. Phosphorus is so important to young growth and the formation of new leaves that a phosphorus deficiency often shows up as poor lower foliage on a plant having normal upper, young leaf growth. The plant transfers the phosphorus from where it has been used, the old leaves, to where it is needed at the moment, the new leaves.

Despite its importance, very little phosphorus is removed from the soil by plants. For example, an acre of corn will take up no more than 25 pounds of phosphorus. At the same time a fat, 100-bushel corn crop from the same acre will remove more than 150 pounds of nitrogen. Unfortunately you cannot add a mere 25 pounds of phosphorus to the acre that yielded the 100 bushels of corn and return that acre to its pre-crop state. The reason is that phosphorus is much too active to lie about waiting to be drawn into a corn plant root, or any root for that matter.

To provide approximately 25 pounds of "free" phosphorus it is necessary to add some 200 to 300 pounds of superphosphate (a form of phosphorus) to the soil. Phosphorus combines so readily and quickly with iron and aluminum to form almost insoluble compounds (insoluble in the acids and alkali solutions found in garden soils) that many experts estimate that no more than 1 percent of the phosphorus present in soil is ever available to the plants.

Some of the compounds that pure phosphorus forms in the soil, fluorapatite and hydroxyapatite, for example, are broken down into soluble forms useful to plants by weathering and bacterial action. These compounds and others break down more readily when the soil's pH is correct, and as you can guess, the correct pH for maximum phosphorus "availability" is within the range suited to plant growth. When an acidic soil is rendered less acidic, more phosphorus becomes available. For example, by adding lime and changing a soil's pH from 5.5 to 6.4, the solubility and therefore the availability of phosphorus is increased some 10 times. Shifting a soil's pH from 5.5 to 6.4 is shifting it toward neutral, which is pH 7. On the other side of neutral, adding sulfur to change a soil's pH from 8.3 to 6.9, again a move toward neutral, will increase the availability of the phosphorus present some five times or more. As you can see, there is more than one reason why plants thrive in that narrow range near neutral.

However, even when phosphorus is not locked into almost permanent partnership with other elements in the soil, its solubility is very low. So low that for all practical purposes the element is immobile. Whereas a goodly quantity of lime, for example, is washed down into the earth by rainwater; the crystals pure phosphorus forms are not. Phosphorus does not move to the plant's roots; the roots must move to the phosphorus. Thus phosphorus when added to the soil as a fertilizer must be broken up into a powder and thoroughly mixed with the soil to a depth equal to that of normal root growth.

Humus increases phosphorus availability in a number of ways. The organic acids produced as a by-product of organic decay, tartaric, isocitric, and others, combine with iron and aluminum to form metallic-organic ions which do not readily combine with phosphorus. Thus, when humus is present in the soil, less phosphorus is lost to insoluble compounds. The size of the crystals that pure phosphorus forms depends on soil moisture. High moisture content, which is normal to soil high in humus favors the growth of small crystals which dissolve more readily than the large crystals of phosphorus formed in dry soils.

As stated previously, humus encourages the growth of microorganisms which, in the course of their brief lives, collect considerable phosphorus. As microorganisms do travel about, they tend to disperse their legacy of phosphorus throughout the soil.

A shortage of available phosphorus makes itself visible by turning the veins of the leaves and leaf stems purple or deep red. At the same time, the leaves themselves may be mottled with yellow spots and/or show blotches of brown. And, as stated previously, when the plant doesn't have sufficient phosphorus, it will transfer this element from the older leaves to the new leaves in the process of forming and growth. Thus the lower, older parts of a phosphorus-deficient plant will have droopy or missing lower leaves, while the young, upper leaves appear to be growing properly.

Lack of phosphorus also slows plant growth. The stalks will be smaller and thinner than normal. Fruit and vegetables will ripen much later than usual. Grain and fruit harvests will be considerably reduced.

Although it is possible to have so much phosphorus in a soil that the soil itself can be used as a low-grade source of the element, it is difficult if not impossible to overload a soil with phosphorus. It combines too readily with other soil elements. And, more important, the plants themselves appear to use restraint in the matter of this nutrient. They appear to take what they need and no more.

Potassium. Potassium or potash is the third major nutrient required by plants. Its exact role in plant growth is not as yet understood. It is believed to favorably affect enzymatic processes, particularly those involved in transforming the various sugars found in plant tissues. An enzyme is a proteinlike substance that catalyzes or speeds up biochemical reactions.

Potassium helps form and transport the sugars and starches and other carbohydrates formed in the leaf of the plant during photosynthesis to other portions of the plant. Potassium helps stiffen plant tissue by counteracting the tendency of nitrogen to produce large, water-filled plant cells.

Potassium increases the oil content of seeds, increases the sugars and starches stored in root and cereal crops such as potatoes and corn. These same crops will withstand storage better if the soil's potassium content was suitable when they were grown.

The quantity of potassium drawn from the earth varies widely from crop to crop. For example, a good crop of oats will draw some 5 pounds of potassium per acre. The same acre planted to celery may lose as much as 200 pounds of potassium in one season.

Potassium deficiency affects crops in a number of readily visible ways. Cucumbers that curl at one end and never fill out indicate a shortage of potassium, as do small-size beans and peas.

A shortage of potassium makes plants more susceptible to drought, and stunts and slows their growth. If the deficiency is great the plant's leaves will dry up, turn brown, and fall off. If potassium is not immediately added, the plant will die.

Potassium shortage is aggravated by an abundance of nitrogen and phosphorus. In such cases the plant's stems will be weak, giving way under the slightest breeze. The plant's leaves may be abnormally green at the start of growth, turning to brown as the season progresses. Some plants will exhibit small gray, red-brown, or yellow spots on their leaves. Leaf edges and tips may turn brown and fall off.

When nitrogen and phosphorus are also in short supply, the plants will be grayish in color, and will bear few flowers and less fruit, often far earlier in the season than normal.

When potassium is in short supply and nitrogen is abundant, plant leaves become highly sensitive to fungus diseases.

An excess of potassium in the soil will cause plants to reduce their intake of other nutrients, especially calcium and magnesium. Thus the overall effect of too much potassium is to retard plant growth.

Calcium. Like potassium, calcium is a metal. In its pure form, which is never found in nature, calcium is hard and silvery. In its common form, calcium is found in combination with carbonate and is called limestone, or dolomitic limestone when it is in combination with carbonate and magnesium carbonate. Calcium is also found in marl and in seashells. In other words, calcium is our old friend, lime.

Calcium (lime) is not merely an agent for correcting soil acidity and structure; it is an essential plant nutrient affecting the action of certain cell enzymes. Particularly, calcium joins with pectate to form a substance that holds plant cells together. It is especially important during early plant growth because it serves as a sort of protein building block.

Calcium deficiency will distort and sometimes destroy the cells forming the growing tips of both plant shoots and roots. Young leaves forming a terminal bud will curl, and the plant's younger leaves will wrinkle. Some leaves will not unfold as they normally should but will remain tightly closed. A band of light green may form along the edges of the leaves. The plant's roots will be far shorter than usual, but at the same time they will have many more branches than normal.

Plants cannot transfer calcium from one leaf or branch to another the way they can transfer phosphorus. A plant cannot even transfer calcium from one root to another. If the calcium is not present in the soil at the very tips of the roots, the roots and plant will suffer. While plants can direct their roots toward moisture, they cannot direct them toward nutrients. As a result, if there is adequate or even more than adequate calcium in the top layer of soil, but not below, the roots will pass through the calcium area without difficulty, but will hardly penetrate the no-calcium area. Calcium to be useful must be thoroughly dispersed throughout the growing depth.

All the symptoms of calcium deficiency will appear in plants despite the proper amount of calcium in the soil if there is an excess of either magnesium or manganese.

When it is necessary to add calcium to acid soils, as for example soils required for growing blueberries, without altering the soil's low pH, calcium sulfate can be used. It will supply the calcium without affecting the acidity.

Magnesium. Another metal, it is silvery white in color, extremely light and highly combustible in its pure form. Magnesium used in fireworks and flares produces a bright white light. It is used in appreciable amounts by plants in the formation of chlorophyll. An atom of magnesium can be found in the central portion of every chlorophyll molecule forming the cells of a plant's green leaves. Magnesium takes an active part in many, if not all, the plant's enzyme systems.

Without magnesium, plants cannot form healthy green leaves. As dolomitic limestone contains as much magnesium carbonate as it does calcium carbonate, if you lime with dolomite there is little chance that your soil will be deficient in this metal nutrient.

Magnesium deficiency shows up as a lack of green in the leaves. Without magnesium the plants cannot manufacture chlorophyll, and the leaves are light in color. They may exhibit brown spots, or the entire leaf may develop a uniform brownish tint.

A simple test for magnesium deficiency consists of dousing the suspected plant with a solution comprising one tablespoon of common Epsom salts in a quart of water. If the plant's leaves become a darker shade of green, or turn from yellow to green, the soil needs magnesium. For quick treatment, dust the soil near the plants with finely powdered dolomitic limestone. Do not permit any of the limestone to fall on the plants themselves.

Magnesium deficiencies develop when a field is cultivated for years without humus and without the proper application of dolomitic limestone. The application of calcium carbonate or calcium oxide alone over a period of years will also produce the same results.

Sulfur. This is the sixth of the mineral elements or nutrients used in comparatively large quantities by plants. Sulfur forms an important component of the amino acids, which are organic acids containing nitrogen compounds. Amino acids form proteins. Sulfur is therefore just as important to plant growth as nitrogen. And although sulfur is hardly ever mentioned as a necessary plant nutrient, it is drawn from the earth in greater quantity than phosphorus, for example. An acre field of cabbage will remove about 25 pounds of phosphorus from the soil. At the same time this member of the mustard family will extract 50 pounds of sulphur. Radishes, turnips, kale, broccoli, cauliflower, and onions, in addition to cabbage, require a good supply of sulfur. It is sulfur, by the way, that helps onions produce the aroma that causes our eyes to water.

The reason sulfur is neglected is that it is present in most soils in sufficient quantities to supply plant needs. Some of the necessary sulfur is washed down from the sky in somewhat the same fashion that nitrogen and phosphorus are. In rural areas an estimated 5 pounds per acre accumulates in this way. In industrial areas, that sulfur which doesn't mix with atmospheric moisture to form sulfur dioxide and sting our eyes (smog), and the Lord alone knows what harm it may do to our lungs, accumulates on our fields in quantities of as much as 50 pounds per acre. Humus and microorganisms are another source of sulfur, as are many of the commercial fertilizers in use today. Superphosphate, sulfate of ammonia, sulfate of potash, and calcium sulfate are the more common commercial fertilizers applied for the presence of other elements, but they also supply most if not all the sulfur the soil may need.

Plants growing in soil short in sulfur have young leaves much lighter in color than they should be. Leaf veins will be even lighter in color. The plant will be stunted, its growth slow, its older leaves weak and flabby, and stalks will be thin and shorter than normal. Some of the leaves may develop spots, and the fruit will not ripen properly.

When there is insufficient sulfur, the plant moves some of this element from its older leaves to the growing tips of its new leaves. Amino acids, nitrogen compounds, and cystine accumulate in the tissues of the plant because protein synthesis stops. Plant growth is halted.

Too much sulfur in the soil can be toxic to plants, and too much sulfur in the air can also harm them. Sulfur dioxide concentrations of more than one part in a million can destroy the cells in leaves. This is why plants do not thrive in an industrial area. (We don't particularly thrive either, but our resistance is fortunately a little higher.)

TRACE NUTRIENTS AND THEIR EFFECTS

In addition to the six nutrients necessary to plant life in comparatively large quantities, seven additional elements are known to be equally important to plants. They are often called trace elements because the quantities required are on the order of a trace, a few parts per million of soil.

The elements are iron, manganese, zinc, copper, molybdenum, boron, and chlorine. If one or more are missing from the earth, the plant will suffer. If some of them are present in too large a quantity, the plant will also suffer.

Iron. An ordinary metal, the fourth most abundant element found in the crust of the earth, it is required for the formation of chlorophyll. Iron is not a part of the chlorophyll molecule, but is central to a substance called heme, which is a complex atom very similar to the cholorophyll that comprises a portion of our blood's hemoglobin. Heme regulates plant cell respiration by controlling various enzymes.

Iron deficiency results in chlorosis, which is a yellowing of the plant's leaves. Since green is the color that is most absorbent of sunlight, plants that suffer iron deficiency do not form the starches necessary for growth and are therefore smaller than normal.

A shortage of iron can be caused by an actual lack of the metal in the soil, but this is rare. More often it is caused by overirrigation, or excessive phosphate or lime, both of which act to lock up the atoms of iron. Lime is especially troublesome in this matter. If you lime an already alkaline or nearly alkaline soil, iron chlorosis often appears in a very few days. The cure is to bring the pH down with an application of sulfur.

On the other hand (and as farming is accomplished with both hands, there appears always to be an "other hand"), too much free iron in the soil is detrimental to a good crop. So don't add iron in one form or another just because your plant's leaves turn yellow; it may not be the trouble. (This is one of the reasons why you are well advised to send a sample of your soil to a lab, in addition to making your own tests.)

Manganese. This element was long a puzzle to scientists. Its lack seemed to be the cause of many obscure plant weaknesses and diseases. Finally it was found to be necessary, along with iron, to the manufacture of chlorophyll; and when the plant's chlorophyll production is off, the starches and sugars necessary to plant life and growth are also diminished.

Generally, when manganese alone is in short supply, the veins of the leaf remain properly green but the spaces between the veins turn yellow or brown and may sometimes disintegrate. The plant itself is also smaller and weaker than usual.

In some instances, a shortage of iron may also increase the plant's need for manganese. The exact relation between these two elements and plant growth is not completely understood.

Manganese may be absent from the soil, or it may be present but too tightly joined with other elements to be available to the plants. Overliming can do this. If the manganese is present but useless because the soil's pH is too high, the addition of sulfur will cure the trouble. If too little manganese is present in any form, lowering the pH will not put it there. If the pH of your soil is correct and you need manganese, add about ½ ounce of manganese sulfate to every 100 square feet of garden. If your soil's pH is high, add about twice this much manganese sulfate. Doing so will also drive the pH down as well as introduce the manganese you need.

An excessive amount of manganese will also cause a chlorosis of the foliage similar to that caused by a lack of the metal. However, only tobacco appears to be troubled this way.

Zinc. This metal plays a part in plant metabolism, the manufacture of protein and the regulation of plant growth. Although only a microscopic quantity of zinc is necessary, as little as one part in a million, plant cells do not divide when it is absent but continue to grow in size. Obviously this trace element plays some vital role in the cell nucleus.

Zinc deficiency results in peas and beans forming small, seedless pods. When just a little zinc is present, the pods will be slightly undersize but the plants themselves will be stunted. However, the total crop will also be far under par. Plant leaves will exhibit some chlorotic areas between the veins. The leaves themselves will be much thicker than usual, and the stems will be shorter than usual.

Unlike most of the other elements that are supplied or made available in the presence of humus, zinc is most often in short supply in organically rich soils.

To correct a deficiency of zinc, zinc sulfate in powder form or dissolved in water may be spread over the soil. One ounce of zinc sulfate dry or dissolved in water per 100 square feet of garden surface should do for several years. Beans, corn, and grapes are among the plants that seem never to get enough zinc from the soil. Potatoes, tomatoes, and onions are not quite as greedy, while asparagus, mustard, and carrots don't appear to care at all for this metal.

Copper. This red metal is important to the enzyme associated with plant respiration, and possibly many other chemical processes in a plant. Copper's importance to plant life wasn't recognized until 1927 when it was learned that its absence was the cause of reduced vigor in citrus trees.

One method that may be used to test for copper deficiency is to mix a little copper sulfate with water and spray your plants with the solution. If that is what they need, you will soon note a considerable improvement in color and growth. To add missing copper to your garden soil, spread ½ ounce of copper sulfate over every 100 square feet of garden surface.

Copper is sometimes missing in sandy soils and muck. Other soils seem to have all the copper necessary.

Molybdenum. Molybdenum is vital to many enzymatic processes in plant life, particularly those that convert nitrogen in nitrate form to an organic nitrogen, which is used to produce amino acids and proteins. Molybdenum also helps the free-living bacteria in the soil go about their business of extracting and fixing atmospheric nitrogen.

The quantity of molybdenum required is hardly measurable. Just one chunk of molybdenum in 100 million chunks of soil does the job. But without this metal many plants, including tomatoes, clover, and fruit trees, will not grow.

Molybdenum is released from bondage with other soil elements by liming, which is strange for a metal, but that is the way it is. If you lime regularly, molybdenum should not be a problem on your farm.

If your soil requires molybdenum, spread 1 ounce of sodium molybdate or molybdic acid over an acre of your farmland. That should do you for several years.

If you find that impractical, and this writer will be surprised if it isn't, add superphosphate fertilizer in the quantity recommended. This fertilizer is usually compounded with molybdic acid, and as soils low in molybdenum are usually short on phosphate, the problem of distributing the tiny amount of moldybdenum is easily solved.

Boron. It is believed that boron participates in 15 or more different life processes in a plant. Like calcium, boron is required in continuous supply. Like the absence of calcium, the absence of boron produces somewhat similar effects: The growing tips of roots and shoots die; terminal buds die. Side shoots are formed and reach out, but their buds also die. The plant has many branches but practically no leaves.

Without boron, sugars and starches accumulate, cells do not divide properly, flowering and fruiting are adversely affected, storage tissues become soft and porous, and pollen grains do not germinate.

The quantity of boron required in a soil is no more than one or two parts in a million; however, it is necessary that calcium also be present and in a ratio of not less than about 80 parts calcium to one part boron, nor more than 600 parts calcium to one part boron. If there is too much boron, say more than 10 parts per million, the boron becomes toxic and harmful to the crop. Beans and lemon trees are particularly sensitive to excessive quantities of boron.

It should also be noted that soil scientists differ on the quantities of boron necessary and toxic. Some belive that boron in even less than 10 parts in a million can be toxic.

Boron itself is sensitive to moisture. So long as the soil is moist, boron remains soluble. When the soil dries out, the boron becomes insoluble. The addition of humus to the soil will release boron that has assumed its insoluble form.

Boron can be added to the soil in a number of ways. You can purchase a borated fertilizer, which contains boron. You can add barnyard manure, which contains approximately 20 ppm (parts per million) of boron. Superphosphate contains 5 to

20 ppm of boron, and you can add ordinary borax, which is sodium tetraborate. The household grades contain 10 percent boron. Fertilizer grades contain 14 percent boron. As an excessive amount of boron is toxic, it is better to add less rather than more. Without lab guidance, try ½ ounce to every 100 square feet of garden surface, and see what happens.

Chlorine. It wasn't until 1954 that chlorine was proved to be a vital plant nutrient. On a weight basis, plants require several thousand times more chlorine than molybdenum; a good-size crop will extract about 5 pounds of chlorine from an acre of soil.

Plants grown without chlorine are severely diseased, displaying a variety of symptoms including wilt, chlorosis, bronze discolorations, and more.

Fortunately, we farmers need not worry about chlorine as it is brought from the sea on the wings of the wind. Near the sea, airborne deposits can amount to hundreds of pounds of chlorine per year per acre. Even areas distant from the sea receive some 10 pounds per acre per year. This is sufficient, as chlorine does not tie up with any of the other elements in the soil, but remains free to enter solution and be absorbed by the plants.

TOXIC AND OTHER NONESSENTIAL ELEMENTS

As previously stated, plants have a penchant for collecting whatever elements their water-fed roots may bring them. Traces of sodium, iodine, cobalt, selenium, aluminum, silicon, arsenic, and other elements are therefore often found in plant tissue, though none, so far, appear to have any value to the plant. In fact, some of the elements, as aluminum for example, are toxic to the plant; and some, like arsenic, are toxic to whoever consumes the plant, as well as to the plant itself.

Trace elements inimical to plant life and man are seldom a problem in "natural" soil. They become a problem when the soil is treated with a toxic chemical and then used for agriculture. One such danger and problem arises when an old orchard is converted to a truck garden. For years the standard treatment for many orchards was to spray the trees with water-soluble arsenic or compounds of arsenic. Generally this was done at the rate of 100 gallons of solution per tree, 15 times or so each year.

The arsenic so collected in the soil over the years can stunt and slow the growth of plants, produce holes and scorch (damage) the leaves of fruit trees, prevent legumes from forming seeds. Peas and beans are most susceptible to arsenic in the soil.

Arsenic in the soil can be rendered harmless by applying iron sulfate at the rate of 10 pounds per 100 square feet of garden surface. Alternatively, the topsoil can be plowed under to a depth of 2 feet.

Make certain you purchase the ferric iron form of iron sulfate and not the ferrous. Be further advised that too much iron sulfate can destroy your crop plants. This, of course, places you between those old horns: Eat your farm's produce, and take a chance on consuming a little arsenic. Or add sufficient iron sulfate to make certain there is no danger, and have no crop. The answer is having your soil tested by an agricultural lab. Advise them of your fears, and they will be able to advise you in return.

Should you convert a lawn that has been liberally treated with DDT over a period of years to a farm, you run the same risk and are advised to follow the same suggestion. DDT is not the only dangerous, persistent poison. Some of the herbicides, such as sodium arsenite, will prevent anything from growing for several years and pose a poison threat for an equal period of time.

Another danger, but one that can easily be circumvented, arises from dumping discarded African violets and their soil into the garden. These plants are often protected from insect pests by selenium. This metal can be poisonous in the concentrations normally used for pest control. Plants can take up considerable selenium without themselves necessarily showing any ill effects.

CHAPTER NINE

Fertilizers

THE DIFFERENCE BETWEEN plant nutrients and fertilizers is merely one of location. Plant nutrients are plant foods already in the soil. Fertilizers are plant nutrients which we add to the soil.

Although our goal is to eliminate the need to add fertilizers in one form or another to our soil, this goal is not always possible in a single growing season. Most often it is not. Crops without tilling and fertilization require a rich, humus-filled garden plot. Unless there has been a good crop the year previous, the mere presence of humus is not a certain sign (though it is a good one), that mother earth in your corner of the world is ready for seeding. You can, of course, seed away and hope for the best, but if you want to be certain of at least a fair crop, you should test your soil for nutrients and add whatever is indicated in one form or another.

Adding fertilizer does not eliminate the need to measure pH and correct the same if necessary. Nor does it eliminate the need to add soil amendments (discussed in a following chapter), if required.

TESTING FOR NUTRIENTS

As with pH, there are two approaches to measuring the quantity of plant nutrients present in your soil; and again as with pH, it is advisable to use both. The test kit has the advantage of immediacy and low cost. You can make your tests without delay, and once you have purchased the kit, there is no more cost.

Unfortunately, the inexpensive kits measure no more than pH, nitrogen, potash, and phosphorus, and only approximately. For our purpose this is good enough, but it is helpful to know of the presence or absence of the other nutrients required by plants. This information can only be secured with a more complex kit or with the aid of one of the government laboratories, a list of which appears on page 58. Therefore it is best to purchase a kit *and* send one or more samples off to be tested.

Making the tests. The same procedures used for measuring pH are repeated. Use great care to avoid touching your sample with your fingers; wait until there has been a rain and the soil has dried to a moist condition; do not take samples when the earth's temperature is 60°F or less. Do not dry your sample in an oven. If it is too wet, wait and take another sample. When testing for phosphorus, make certain that the tin rod is clean before you use it. If it is not, use fine sandpaper to clean it. It is also advisable to clean the rod this way two or three minutes after you have used it. If the solution gases, let the gas escape before you take a reading. Still another point: Don't let too much time elapse between taking a sample of your soil and testing it. Try to do both the same day.

As each kit contains its own instructions, there is no point in repeating them here. Besides, there is always the possibility that your kit may be different from most, at least in the recommended testing procedure. However, there is one point that bears explanation, and that is the method used to interpret the test findings. Like almost all accompanying instructions, it can be terribly confusing.

Deciphering the results. Your kit will include color bars for each of the "big three" nutrients. Some kits will have their bars accompanied by numbers—1, 2, 3, 4. Some kits rate their bars deficient, low, doubtful, adequate. No matter, their meanings are the same, though the percentages ascribed may differ. The kit that I have before me at this moment provides the following color bar ratings and percentages:

1. Adequate—minimum of 2 percent
2. Low—minimum of 8 percent
3. Doubtful—minimum of 12 percent
4. Deficient—minimum of 14 percent

You must admit that the above is confusing. What it means is this. If your tests indicate that you are deficient in nitrogen, for example, the makers of the kit advise that you add 3 to 5 pounds of fertilizer to every 100 square feet of garden surface, and the fertilizer should be 14 percent or more nitrogen. In other words, 6 to 11 ounces of pure nitrogen per 100 square feet is what should be applied.

If you can secure nitrogen alone and not in combination, and that is all your soil needs, fine. You simply add it or whatever your tests indicate. However, single fertilizers are not readily available in nonfarm areas, and few soils require one nutrient alone. This brings up multiple or "standard" chemical fertilizers. These are always a mixture of three fertilizers, the three you can test for. Keeping this thought in mind, test for potash and phosphorus. Let us assume that you need 8 percent potash and 12 percent phosphorus.

Your total needs are: Nitrogen 14 percent
Phosphorus 12 percent
Potash 8 percent

Your next step is to select a bag of chemical fertilizer that reads 14-12-8 and apply 3 to 5 pounds of the mix to your farmland. If you cannot find a bag that reads this

Using a soil test kit. With a little experience you can do your testing on a plate and not waste time with the tiny test tubes that are furnished with the kit.

way, there is little harm if the numbers are merely close. Plants are not finicky eaters.

Reading the bags. For the moment let us ignore the various chemical forms in which chemical fertilizers are manufactured and sold. They are important and will be discussed later. All standard chemical fertilizer bags are marked with numbers indicating the type and quantity of active chemicals that they contain. There are always three numbers, and they are always in the same sequence. The first number stands for the percentage of nitrogen present, the second for phosphorus, and the third for potash. Sometimes there will also be letters. N will stand for nitrogen, P for phosphorus, and K for potash.

If the numbers read 10-10-10, the bag contains 10 percent nitrogen, 10 percent phosphorus, and 10 percent potash. Thirty percent of the bag's contents are fertilizers; the remainder is some neutral substance such as sand. If another bag of equal weight reads 20-20-20, it contains twice as much fertilizer as the first and is therefore worth twice as much. This is something worth keeping in mind when shopping for fertilizer.

Fertilizer balance. This is a subject made much of by a considerable number of agricultural writers: The big three nutrients must be in a specific chemical balance to enable plants to achieve their maximum growth and health. The ratio is 100 pounds nitrogen to 20 pounds phosphorus to 37 pounds potash. If you were to add 200 pounds of nitrogen to 20 pounds of phosphorus and 37 pounds of potash, most of your nitrogen would be wasted, and the end result would not be as good as if you had remained with the ratio given. By the same measure, if you stinted on the others or added too much of either phosphorus or potash, the results would not be too good either. The key to success is to maintain that 10:2:3.7 ratio.

Be advised that the percentages suggested by the soil test kits usually direct you toward this goal. So, if you follow their recommendations, your soil will reach this balanced state.

Be further advised that this balanced state is far from critical and far from being universally accepted. According to the Connecticut Agricultural Experiment Station, just to cite one example, many vegetables favor a fertilizer balance other than that given here. In Connecticut asparagus prefers high and equal levels of nitrogen, phosphorus, and potash; as do cauliflower and potato. In the same state, radishes do better with a lower level of nutrition and less nitrogen.

This does not invalidate your soil tests. It merely proves that you do not need to slavishly follow the fertilizer recommendations given by kits and many agronomists. All you need do is bring the elements in short supply up to par, and not burden the soil with fertilizers already present in sufficient quantity.

Terminology. The chemical fertilizers we may add to our soil are usually combined with any number of different elements. As is the wont of chemists, each combination has its own special chemical name, which makes for a large variety of names. In addition, with the passage of years, manufacturers have changed the names they use. For these reasons, to apply potash to our land we may find ourselves applying sulfate of potash, potassium, or muriate of potash. To supply phosphorus we may add phosphoric acid, calcium metaphosphate or superphosphate. All that concerns us is the available percentage of the element we seek in the fertilizer. Its chemical name or chemical form usually (but not always) means very little.

TYPES OF FERTILIZERS

Fertilizers divide into two definite types or classes: manufactured or natural, or if you prefer, chemical and organic. Both types may contain the individual or group of plant nutrients we may wish to add to our soil. And when we consider the individual elements alone, as for example nitrogen, chemical fertilizers cost only a fraction as much as organic fertilizers. To put this in numbers: dried cow manure contains no more than 2 percent nitrogen by weight. Sulfate of ammonia, a manufactured chemical fertilizer is 20.5 percent nitrate. Ordinary sulfate of ammonia will contain a trace of the other plant nutrients, no more. Dried cow manure also contains 1.5 percent phosphorus and 2 percent potash, plus all the other trace elements that were present in the cow's diet. Thus a pound of dried cow manure is 5.5 percent fertilizer, or roughly only one-fourth as much fertilizer as is contained in an equal weight of sulfate of ammonia. However, organic fertilizers offer advantages which, in many applications, more than offset their higher "fertilizer" costs.

Organic vs. chemical fertilizers. First it might be good to repeat the fact that there is absolutely nothing wrong with chemical fertilizers. The chemicals found in chemical fertilizers are exactly the same as those found in organic fertilizers. Plants can take up straight chemical nutrients, as well as they can absorb more complex solutions resulting from organic fertilization.

The big difference, and again we are repeating ourselves, is that organic fertilizers contain a large variety of nutrients in fair percentages, whereas chemical fertilizers contain no more than two or three elements, at most. All other elements are present in trace quantities only, and not by intent but by accident. Actually, they are there as impurities.

Another important difference is that organic fertilizers release their nutrients slowly. Composted manures and other organic fertilizers cannot damage the plant in any quantity. (Fresh manures can do damage, though, if placed too closely and in too great an amount.) On the other hand, all chemical fertilizers will "burn" the plant on contact with its leaves or roots.

Burning is the term applied to the dehydration that results when fertilizing chemicals make direct contact with plant leaves or roots. The chemicals are hygroscopic and rapidly remove water from the plant tissues. The side of the plant that was touched by the chemicals may turn yellow or brown. And sometimes, depending on the plant species and the quantity of fertilizer on its roots, the entire plant may be completely destroyed. This is not a serious problem, as you can easily avoid fertilizer burn with a little care. On the other hand, the very rapidity with which plants absorb chemical fertilizers is sometimes advantageous. Organic fertilizers in general must be decomposed by the various earth organisms before they become available for use by the plant. If you want to feed hungry plants in a hurry, organic fertilization is not the way to do it, though there is a good "soup," highly appreciated by tomatoes, that can be made from manure.

Yet another reason for using organic fertilizers (and humus can be included in the group) is that the organic fertilizers also act as a soil amendment, loosening and aerating the soil. Very often the resultant crop will be far greater when manure is mixed with a heavy soil than when several more times the actual equivalent in chemical fertilizer is mixed with the same soil. The soil's organic content is as important to plant growth as the soil's nutrient content.

TYPES OF CHEMICAL FERTILIZERS

For clarity we will define a chemical fertilizer as one that is, except for accidental impurities, composed of a single plant nutrient. This is a necessary qualification because some "chemical" fertilizers are simply dug from the earth and, after grinding, used that way. Therefore, these chemical fertilizers are often called natural.

Ammonium sulfate. Also called sulfate of ammonia, this is still the home gardener's most available source of nitrogen. It is slightly on the acid side (low pH), and therefore good for alkali soils and acid-loving plants such as blueberries. It contains approximately 20.5 percent nitrogen. It can be spread dry or dissolved in water, a method preferred by many gardeners.

Sodium nitrate. Also called nitrate of soda, this is a naturally occurring combination of sodium, oxygen, and nitrogen found in huge quantities in Chile. For years this was our main source of supply, and all the old garden books mention it. Sodium nitrate is about 16 percent nitrogen and somewhat basic (high pH). It is not recommended for basic soils and is no longer first choice as a source of nitrogen.

Urea. If you have had dogs visit your front lawn, you may have noticed that their urine first "burned" the grass and then made it grow like mad. This is due to the 45 percent nitrogen content of urea which is a part of urine. Urea is now manufactured without the aid of animals; so though it is classed as an organic, we have classed it as a chemical fertilizer. Urea is not used in its pure form but is always mixed or diluted with a neutral substance. Urea is acid forming.

Ureaform. A man-made combination of urea and formaldehyde, this is 38 percent nitrogen, but it breaks down so slowly that it rarely if ever burns, even when placed in direct contact with plants.

Calcium nitrate. This fertilizer is a combination of nitrogen and calcium. Generally the calcium content varies from 15 to 25 percent, while the nitrogen content remains at about 15 percent.

Calcium cyanamide. This fertilizer is often called simply cyanamide. It contains 21 percent nitrogen and is alkaline and toxic. Supposedly its toxic properties disappear if it is mixed into moist soil several weeks before planting.

Ammonia. Liquid ammonia is the most widely used commercial source of farming nitrogen. The liquid is usually about 30 percent ammonia, and ammonia is about 85 percent nitrogen; so liquid ammonia is about 25.5 percent nitrogen. Unfortunately it is not available to home gardeners.

Ammonium phosphate. This is a combination fertilizer produced in two grades. One is called monoammonium phosphate and contains both nitrogen and phosphorus (in the form of phosphoric acid) in quantities of 11 and 60 percent, respectively. Actually it is a better source of phosphorus than of nitrogen. The second type or grade, called diammonium phosphate, contains 23 percent nitrogen and 53 percent phosphorus. The two types are highly soluble and quite alkaline (high pH).

Slag. A by-product of the steel industry, slag may contain calcium and a little magnesium in addition to phosphoric acid in quantities of 2 to 16 percent. Slag is basic.

Rock phosphate. Literally a rock that is mined and ground into a powder, rock phosphate is a mixture of limestone and phosphate. The available phosphoric acid present varies from 30 to 50 percent, with the limestone varying a like percentage. (Some authorities believe the phosphoric acid ranges between 20 to 30 percent—must depend on how the rock bounces.) Like other rock fertilizers, the nutrients are released very slowly. Full release takes several years. Some gardeners claim that you cannot see any effect at all the first year after application.

Since rock phosphate contains a lot of limestone, it doesn't work very well with soils with a pH of 6.2 or more. So before adding this fertilizer, figure it to be half limestone, and compute the resultant change in your land's pH before you add it.

Rock phosphate contains traces of sulfur, iron, magnesium, and other elements necessary to plant life.

Superphosphate. When ordinary rock phosphate is treated with sulfuric acid it becomes superphosphate. The available phosphoric acid is reduced, and the calcium carbonate is converted to calcium sulfate. The result is a fertilizer with a pH of exactly 7—neither acidic or basic (alkaline). Its phosphoric acid content will vary from 14 to 49 percent, depending on grade, but its acid is more readily utilized by plants than that offered by plain rock phosphate. Superphosphate is probably the single, most frequently used source of garden phosphorus today.

Calcium metaphosphate. One of the newer fertilizers, calcium metaphosphate is another neutral (pH 7) chemical containing 53 percent available phosphoric acid.

INORGANIC FERTILIZERS, PERCENT CONTENT OF CONSTITUENTS

Type	Nitrogen	Phosphorus	Potash	Other
Ammonia	25.5			
Ammonium phosphate:				
Grade 1	11	60		
Grade 2	23	53		
Ammonium sulfate	20.5			
Corn cob ash			20–30	Some lime
Calcium metaphosphate		53		
Calcium nitrate	15			Calcium 15–25
Kainite			12–22	Some magnesium
Manure salts			25–40	
Muriate of potash			47–63	Little magnesium
Potassium-magnesium				
sulfate			25–40	55 magnesium
Rock phosphate			30–50	30–50 limestone
Rock potash			3–15	Trace elements
Slag		2–16		Some calcium and magnesium
Superphosphate			14–49	
Urea	45			
Ureaform	38			
Wood ash			4–10	Some lime

Rock potash. Powdered rock potash can run from 3 to 15 percent potash and contain a fair percentage of other plant nutrients. In its most common form, rock potash is called greensand and will contain iron potassium silicate in small quantities. Like all other rock fertilizers, this one also releases its plant food very slowly. You therefore require quite a bit to show results. However, it lasts for years and the particles of stone act as an amendment and help to some small degree to keep the soil loose.

Powdered granite. This ultrahard stone contains a small percentage of available potash. If you can purchase it at very low cost and your soil can use a little sand, it is worth adding, though your crops will probably not show any results unless your soil is critically short of potash.

Muriate of potash. Muria is the Latin word for brine, and as it was deposited millions of years ago in ancient seas, that is the name that was selected and is still in use today. Muriate of potash is potassium chloride, contains some 47 to 63 percent water-soluble potash and a little magnesium. It is best used on acid-loving plants. The chlorine quickly enters the air and disappears when this fertilizer is mixed with the soil. However, many horticulturists believe muriate of potash harmful to many soil organisms and opt for the more expensive sulfate of potash.

Sulfate of potash. Technically called potassium sulfate, sulfate of potash contains 47 to 53 percent water-soluble potash and is probably one of the most used sources of potash.

Kainite. This fertilizer contains 12 to 22 percent water-soluble potash plus varying amounts of magnesium.

Manure salts. This chemical contains little or no magnesium and from 25 to 40 percent soluble potash. Both kainite and manure salts are mined as crude salts.

Potassium-magnesium sulfate. Sometimes called double manure salts, this mined fertilizer contains 20 to 30 percent water-soluble potash plus as much as 55 percent magnesia, which is a form of magnesium. It is used on soils that are deficient in both potash and magnesium.

Wood ash. The ashes of all trees and bushes contain 4 to 10 percent potash. The ashes of a tree's branches contain more than its trunk. The ashes of grapevines, maple, oak, willow, and elm contain more potash than those of other plants.

ORGANIC FERTILIZERS

Any substance, once alive, that will disintegrate or break down in the soil and provide nutrition for plant growth is an organic fertilizer. However, unless the nutrients are in somewhat concentrated form, the substance is not considered a fertilizer. Therefore, humus, which is disintegrated plant material and which is rich in plant food, is not classed as a fertilizer. It has too much bulk in relation to its nutrients.

Fish and animal remains, manures, seaweed, burned plants and plant parts, treated plant seeds, all of which contain a concentration of one or more plant nutrients, are considered organic fertilizers.

Rock phosphate, which is mined and used in its natural state, and other "rock" minerals are not organic fertilizers, though they are often called natural fertilizers.

So far as plant response is measured, it doesn't make one chloryphyll molecule difference whence the nutrient originated. If it is dissolved and in contact with the root, the plant will ingest it. Nitrogen is still nitrogen whether it comes from old fish bones or drops to the earth after a lightning discharge. What the plant needs and seeks is a daily supply of dissolved minerals; their source is completely unimportant.

Differences. While generalizations always leave one open to criticism and correction, a generalization often helps clarify a detailed subject. So, the major difference between organic and chemical fertilizers is that the organics almost always contain a fair quantity of secondary nutrients. The chemical fertilizers rarely contain more than one major element; whatever else is there is there as an impurity and is little more than a trace.

Thus, one major difference between organic and chemical fertilizers is that you run far less chance of starving your plants for micronutrients with the organic than the chemical fertilizers.

Another is the aforementioned tendency of chemicals to burn plants when they contact their leaves or roots. This can be avoided when applying chemical fertilizers, it is true, but it is something that limits and hinders their application in many instances.

Only the fresh manures need be watched in this respect. And even so, it takes a considerable quantity of fresh manure, very closely applied, to seriously damage a growing plant. Composted manures and other organic fertilizers never burn plants.

Still another important difference between the organics and the chemicals is that the organic fertilizers always add some quantity of humus to the soil. The humus loosens the soil and provides a home and food for our friendly microorganisms. It is believed by many that some chemical fertilizers can harm soil creatures, and only lime and sulfur have any effect on soil structure.

Another difference is cost. On a pound-for-nutrient-pound basis, the common chemical fertilizers provide much more nutrition than do most of the commonly

**ORGANIC FERTILIZERS, PERCENT CONTENT OF
CONSTITUENTS**

Substance	Nitrogen	Phosphorus	Potash
Ash, wood			4–10
Blood meal	15	1.5	.7
Bone meal	2–5	20–25	.4
Cocoa shell powder			2–3
Cottonseed	5–6	1.5	1.75
Fish scrap	5–8	10–15	.37
Ground bone, burned		35	
Hog manure, fresh	.6	.45	.5
Hoof meal and horn dust	10	1–2	
Horse manure, dried	1.1	1	1.6
Horse manure, fresh	.5	.35	.3
King crab, dried	10	.25	.06
Lobster shell	4–5	3–4	
Molasses, residue			5.34
Manure, cow, fresh	.3	.25	.1
Manure, cow, dried	1.2	1	1.5
Seaweed			5
Poultry manure, fresh	1–3	1–1.3	.6–1
Poultry manure, dried	5	1.5–2	1.3

Nutrient percentage by weight to be found in a few organic fertilizers.

used organic fertilizers. So, even when the pound-for-pound cost is similar, which it rarely is, the chemicals offer more nutrients for less money. Some of the organic fertilizers are very high in nutrients, as for example burned bone meal. But the cost of this material is so high that, despite its concentration of phosphorus, it is still more expensive than its straight chemical counterpart.

Types of organic fertilizers. For simple classification and discussion we can divide the organic fertilizers into two groups: the hard and the soft. The hard organic group includes substances such as lobster shells, hoof and horn powder, bone meal. They are high in nutrients, low in bulk, and very slow acting. Years pass before they have given up all their nutrients to the soil. The soft organics, like the manures and plant ashes, release their plant food much more quickly. The manures most rapidly of all.

Selection. Your choice of organic fertilizer will probably be more limited by availability and price than any other factor. One organic fertilizer is no better than another, but some contain the nutrient that you require in a form that is rapidly assimilated by the plants. Others may contain a greater percentage but in far less soluble form and therefore not readily available to the crops.

For example, bone meal contains at least 20 times more phosphorus than dried cow manure. However, bone meal releases its nutrients very, very slowly. It is estimated that one application of bone meal will remain in the earth, releasing phosphorus for some 15 years. Cow manure will release its phosphorus in one season. Therefore, to get the same *first year* results we must add approximately 15 times more bone meal than cow manure to our soil to achieve the same results the following season.

If you can purchase ground bone meal at a price that makes it competitive with dried cow manure, or bone meal ash, which has an even higher phosphorus content, it may be advisable to do so. But remember, we grow soil by mulch-organic farming as well as crops. There is no need to invest phosphorus in your soil's future crops because in a few years no fertilizer will be needed.

Another factor to consider besides the need for specific nutrients and their costs per pound of organic fertilizer is the volume of the fertilizer you are purchasing. Bone meal ash, for example, being almost 35 percent phosphorus, has very little body per pound of nutrient. Dried cow manure, on the other hand, has 35 times the weight, on a pound of phosphorus basis, and several times again the volume, because it is composed of vegetable matter, straw, hay, and the like.

If, for example you are purchasing phosphorus because your tests indicated that was the nutrient your soil needed, you are better advised to purchase the dry manure than the chemical or even the bone meal because the manure has the important advantage of adding humus to your soil. We are assuming, of course that the cost of the desired nutrient in manure form is reasonably similar to its cost in chemical or organic form. But even if the nutrient in manure form were to cost several times more than it did in hard organic form (bone meal, horn and hoof dust) or straight chemical form, this farmer would opt for the manure, using less manure if necessary to save money.

The ruminants provide the best manure for our purpose. The manures of the cow, horse, and sheep and other cud-chewing animals contain lots more vegetable matter than that of poultry, for example. Poultry manure has lots more power; in fact poultry manure will explode under proper condition, but when we need to loosen our soil as well as fertilize it, ruminant manure is the better choice.

Three forms. The manures may be used in any of their three agricultural forms: fresh, composted, and dried. If you are lucky enough to live near a stable, very often you can get all the manure you want for the labor of hauling. Obviously this is fresh manure. Composted manure is manure that has been treated by our bacterial friends.

The practice of composting requires that the manure be exposed to the air for a period of time during which it is turned over to cool and air it. Bacterial action can raise the temperature inside a pile of manure to 175°F or so. This is doubly bad. The heat converts the "solid" nitrogen to its gaseous form, whereupon it is forever lost to the atmosphere. The heat also destroys most of the bacteria; so the all-important process of bacterial decomposition is slowed down, and composting takes considerably longer. When the manure no longer heats up of its own (bacterial) accord, composting is fairly well completed. Incidentally, never add lime to manure compost, as the lime also acts to turn the fixed nitrogen back to its gaseous form and so wastes it.

All ruminant manures should be composted. Where and how will be discussed shortly. All the manures contain nitrogen, phosphorus, and potash, but the ruminant manures also contain straw and similar plant material. When the bacteria attack the manure, and they always do, they consume much of the nutrients to manufacture protein in their bodies. Therefore, if you add fresh ruminant manure to your garden, you will lose nitrogen and phosphorus until the bacteria complete their life cycles, whereupon the food they have collected in their little bodies is added to that present in the manure.

In addition, fresh, ruminant manure is bulky and rough with hay and straw. In its fresh form it is difficult to mix evenly into the soil and makes for a ragged mass. If you try to sow fine seeds in this mixture, you will have a lot of difficulty, and the seeds will not germinate properly. Seeds like smooth, level soil. Composting breaks the manure down into a soft, granular mass that is easily mixed.

Dried manure sold for garden use is almost always composted first. Try for the dry mixtures when buying. The wet mixtures are half water, and water isn't something anyone usually cares to buy.

APPLYING CHEMICAL FERTILIZERS

It is best to attend to your soil's pH needs in the fall and add chemical fertilizers in the spring. If and when you add lime or sulfur, take into account the nature of the chemical fertilizers that you will apply in the spring. If you don't know whether they are acidic or basic, use a little less pH corrective just to be certain you don't use more than needed.

If you must add lime or sulfur in the spring along with chemical fertilizers, apply the fertilizer first. Let a week at a minimum go by, and then add the pH correctives.

Phosphorus must be mixed into the soil to a depth of at least 8 inches for most vegetables and more for crops such as potatoes with deep-ranging roots. The mixing must be carefully done, as phosphorus doesn't move about and plant roots are incapable of seeking nutrients. They will grow toward water but not toward food. Nonmigrating nutrients such as phosphorus must be in the root's path to be absorbed.

If you are adding a "complete" fertilizer which contains phosphorus, you must also mix it thoroughly in to get the phosphorus to the plant roots. The other fertilizers will dissolve and move downward into the soil, but even with soluble fertilizers it is much better to work them into the earth.

Conserving chemical fertilizer. Various schemes are used to make chemical fertilizers go farther. One used when farmers set out small plants consists of digging a foot-deep, foot-across hole in the earth. Some fertilizer is sprinkled over the bottom of the hole and mixed with the topmost layer of soil. More soil is placed on top, and then the green pepper or cucumber plant or what have you is planted in the hole. The plant's roots do not make direct contact with the fertilizer, and little of the chemical goes to feed unwanted weeds that may grow nearby.

When a row of seeds is to be planted, a shallow ditch is dug, and its bottom is covered with a light layer of fertilizer. Some soil is added, and the two are mixed. This is followed by more soil, and finally the seeds are planted. Again, the purpose is to confine the fertilizer to a small area.

By the same token the fertilizer will not be spread over walks and garden paths, even though some gardeners annually dig up their paths in an effort to keep their plants in different soil each year. In this way some portion of the garden lies fallow each season.

Side dressings. When fertilizer is applied to growing plants, the process is called side dressing. To avoid having the chemical fertilizer contact the plant's roots, the fertilizer is spread in a circle around the plant some 8 or more inches from its stalk. If there is a row of plants, the fertilizer will be spread in a line alongside the plants, again a distance from the plant's stalks.

A very small amount is used, just a little more than a light dusting. If the plants you are feeding have surface roots, just sprinkle the chemical, and let it be. If the roots are below the surface, you can work the fertilizer a few inches into the soil, bearing in mind that you do not want the fertilizer to touch the roots (since it will "burn" them). Additionally, you do not want to injure the roots by digging about.

APPLYING ORGANIC FERTILIZER

Except for fresh manure, which should not be permitted to contact seeds, roots, or stems of plants, you can apply all the organic fertilizers wherever you wish.

Best results will be obtained when you work the fertilizers down to the same depth as the root systems of crops you plan to raise. But if you are in a hurry and are willing to settle for something less than maximum, you can confine your spade work to the top 8 inches of soil. At the very least, the organic fertilizer should be mixed into the top few inches.

The hard forms of organic fertilizers, such as the bone and hoof meals, must be thoroughly worked in. They dissolve so slowly that unless the fertilizer particles are well dispersed and near the roots, they do little good. The manures, which are far more soluble, need not be mixed in as thoroughly, but for best results, mix away with a will. Remember the phosphorus will not move but will remain in place.

Chemical values. To estimate the quantity of any organic nutrient you may require for your farm, simply use the figure given in the table for organic fertilizers. If, for example, you are going to use oven-dried poultry manure, which is 5 percent nitrogen, you use the 5 percent just as you would if you were going to add an inorganic fertilizer having the same nitrogen percentage.

Composting. Fresh manure must be rotted, or composted as it is called down on the farm. This is best accomplished right in the soil that is going to be fertilized. If you leave a pile exposed to the weather, one-half to two-thirds of the contained nutrients will be lost in a few months. The highly soluble elements will be leached away. Gaseous nitrogen and carbon dioxide, two valuable by-products of decomposition, will be gone on the winds.

Composting fresh manure in a compost heap is more efficient, but still a goodly portion of the manure's plant food will escape. For maximum return the best place to compost manure (and other organic material) is right in the earth itself and not behind the barn or in a compost heap some distance away. The procedure is easy enough. Just don't lime the soil either before or immediately after you add the manure. Wait until the manure is fully composted before making your pH test and possibly adding lime.

The manure is spread evenly over the soil and worked into the top 8 inches of soil. Care is taken either to do this several months before planting, or if done afterward, to keep the fresh manure clear by several inches of all growing plants and seeds.

Spreading the manure and mixing it in with the soil helps lower its decomposition temperature. This speeds bacterial action and reduces gas loss. Mixing also helps aerate the manure, and as our little microbiotic friends need air, this too helps speed decomposition. At the same time, the manure acts as humus (which it shortly will become) and does all the good things for the earth that humus does.

The layer of earth atop the fresh manure traps the nitrogen and carbon dioxide, not completely, but to a large extent. The carbonic acid thus formed combines with the soil to release plant nutrients.

Quantity. It is almost impossible to apply too much manure to any soil. Once the manure has rotted, it makes an excellent soil for many crops, especially strawberries. Too much is hardly ever a problem. However, to be certain, take a pH test, and see where you are chemically.

Most of us will find that too little is the more common difficulty. Purchased by the bagful, manure is quite expensive. However, you can do far better with say

$5.00 worth of dry manure than you can with an equal expenditure for chemical fertilizer.

Conserving organic fertilizer. Whereas with chemical fertilizers the best you could do with safety was to spread a little near the plant, with an organic like dried manure you can mix the fertilizer and the soil together.

For example, if you are planting or rather setting out green pepper plants, dig a hole 1 foot deep and about as much across. Remove the soil, discard about half, and mix the remainder with dry manure. Replace the soil in the hole, and set your plant in it. You couldn't do this with chemical fertilizer because you would burn the plant.

The pepper starts out in loose, friable, rich soil and quickly establishes itself. By the time its roots have gone past the enriched soil, the plant is strong and vigorous and is able to more or less fend for itself.

The same can be done for a seed row. A shallow trench is scooped out of the ground. The removed soil is mixed with the fertilizer and replaced. The seeds are planted in the fertilizer-soil mix.

Fertilizer tonic. Steep horse or cow manure in water for several days. Remove the liqueur and pour it around the roots of your growing plants. Tomatoes are particularly partial to this brew.

Odor. Some of the organic fertilizers do have a distinctive, strong smell. However, the smell soon goes away when the fertilizer is mixed with earth or stands for a few days. There is no substance to the belief that the odor penetrates some of the sensitive vegetables. You do have to wash your hands, though.

Free fertilizer. If you follow my practice and toss all the kitchen leftovers, excepting meat and fish, into the garden you will be visited by countless birds, many of whom will instantly change the bread crumb into high-potency organic fertilizer. Birds will eat anything—vegetables, bread crumbs, noodles, soup, what have you. It isn't messy because it all disappears in a day or two.

GREEN MANURE

This is the name often used to describe crops sown and grown for the sole purpose of enriching and improving the soil. The plants most frequently sown for this purpose belong to the legume family. These include vetch, clover, alfalfa, soybeans, etc. The legume family of plants are those that collect nitrogen at their roots with the aid of various bacteria. However, nonleguminous plants such as winter wheat, spring wheat oats, and barley are also used for this purpose.

The general procedure is to sow the green manure immediately after the crop has been harvested in the fall. The rye or wheat, let us say, manages to grow a few inches before the frost begins. The plant varieties selected for this purpose are capable of surviving the winter. When spring comes, they resume their growth, but are not harvested in the normal way. Instead, they are cut down and plowed under before maturity.

The plant's body adds roughage and humus to the soil. Whatever nutrients the plant has absorbed are thereby returned to the soil. Whatever nitrogen has been collected at the plant's roots is a bonus. In this way, planting and turning a crop under utilizes what would otherwise be wasted growing time and increases both the humus and the nutrient content of the soil.

The practice is sound and widely used. Unfortunately there are obstacles in the way of backyard farming use. Generally a backyard farm is not a one-crop activity.

Therefore, the entire plot, of whatever size it may be, is not available at one time at the end of the season. Another, even more important, obstacle is that turning under a stand of wheat or vetch is hard work for a man armed with only a shovel. If all the green manure is not turned before it matures, some seeds will remain, and these will plague you with wild vetch or wheat for years on end. Still another obstacle is that we do not want to turn our soil over, and the only practical way to utilize green manure is to turn the soil over—atop the plant's roots and stalks. For these good reasons, green manure is not a practical source of fertilizer for the backyard farmer.

FOLLOW-UP TESTING

It is advisable to test your soil carefully for nutrients and pH at least once a year, preferably during the same week each year. And if your crop is not all that you hoped it would be, it is advisable to send a soil sample to the nearest lab for detailed examination.

Neither a generous application of chemical fertilizers nor an abundance of organic fertilizers can be depended on to supply all the many nutrients and trace elements that plants need. If you are applying mulch procured from a field deficient in one or more elements, the mulch will often be equally deficient. If you are applying too much chemical fertilizer, you may also be producing a nutrient deficiency by virtue of a chemical imbalance. If you are using no chemicals at all, there is a chance that you are losing valuable plant growth waiting for your mulch to supply the need.

So there is the possibility of much to be gained by regular, annual soil testing. And if results are still poor, at least you will have eliminated one possible factor.

CHAPTER TEN

Amendments

A N AMENDMENT IS any substance mixed in with the earth to improve its tilth, and make the soil more friable, loose, and granular. Many substances are used as amendments. Some are chemical, such as lime. Some are disintegrated rock such as sand, silt, or clay. And some are organic such as humus or manure.

The choice of amendment depends on the nature of the soil to be improved, the availability of the necessary or desired amendment, and its cost.

The reason for adding an amendment to the soil was discussed some chapters back, but we will repeat it for the sake of continuity here. If the soil is so much sand that water runs right through, an amendment must be added to make it hold water. On the other hand, if your soil is so much clay that you can go into the pottery business, you need to loosen it up so that plant roots can make their way.

TYPES OF AMENDMENTS

There are three types of amendments: chemical, mineral (disintegrated rock), and organic. No one of them is best. We use what is necessary and what we either have or can secure with the least trouble and expense.

Chemical amendments. When ground limestone is mixed with clay, an electro-chemical-physical reaction occurs known as flocculation. In theory and as seen under an electron microscope, each particle of lime attracts eight particles of clay. The lime and clay particles form granules and crumbs which help make the clay friable and loose. This is called a chemical reaction, which is why limestone is considered a chemical amendment, though it is also a kind of rock or mineral amendment.

It takes a lot of finely ground limestone to do the job, as much as 50 pounds on a 10 × 10-foot plot when the soil is heavy and clayey. This much lime usually drives the soil too far up the alkalinity scale. However, the alkalinity can be corrected without adversely affecting the soil's structure by adding powdered sulfur. The relation between limestone, pH, and sulfur is discussed in Chapter 7. Incidentally, if the soil's pH is far above neutral, adding sulfur to reduce it also acts to loosen clay. Clay is most friable (if it is ever friable) when it is near neutral.

The lime (and/or the sulfur) must be carefully worked into the soil to the depth of interest, and its pH tested at least a month afterward and before planting.

Note that the use of a chemical amendment does not eliminate or affect whatever additional amendments may be desirable or necessary.

Mineral amendments. These include sand, silt, and clay. If your soil is sandy, you can improve its cohesion by adding and mixing clay with it. If your soil is clayey, you can improve its tilth by adding and mixing sand with it.

The addition of a mineral amendment is an excellent way of improving tilth, and when either the quantity necessary is not too great or you can purchase the amendment in bulk and rent power equipment for mixing it in, mineral amendments are practical. It is a one-time expense and effort and remains with the soil forever.

The quantities required for even a small plot, however, are considerable: much more than you might imagine by just looking at the field. For example; assume that the soil is clay loam, which means it is 25 percent clay, with the remainder sand and silt. Assume further that you wish to convert a 10 × 10-foot plot to loam, which is an ideal soil mixture and consists of 50 percent sand, 40 percent silt, and only 10 percent clay. Ten by ten feet of soil to a depth of just 1 foot works out to 100 cubic feet (3.7 cubic yards). If the soil is clay loam that 100 cubic feet contains 25 cubic feet of clay (25 percent). To reduce this to 12½ percent to a depth of 1 foot you need 125 cubic feet of sand (4.6 cubic yards.)

Practical solution. However, there is another way of skinning this cat. If raising the level of the soil is not objectionable (doing so usually provides better drainage), the same approximate degree of soil improvement can be obtained with far less sand and effort. Mix roughly 50 cubic feet of sand with the top few inches of soil. By doing so you can bring the clay percentage down to the desired 12½ percent or lower by virtue of increasing the ratio of added sand to soil.

As a rule of thumb, add ½ cubic foot of sand to every square foot of land to be improved, and work it down into the top 6 or 8 inches.

As stated previously, if you can purchase the sand by the truckload and rent a Roto-tiller (power soil-tiller), improving tilth by adding sand is not impractical. But be advised that just mixing a few bags of sand into the field is a waste of time.

You need less clay to improve sand, but still far from an inconsiderable amount. To convert pure sand to sandy loam you need to add at least 25 percent clay and/or silt. Therefore, working with the same 10 by 10-foot plot you would need 25 cubic feet of clay if you mixed it in with the top 6 or 8 inches of soil, as described for adding sand. However, the task would be more difficult, as clay is not a substance that readily lends itself to mixing.

As can be seen, a lot less clay is required to improve sand than sand is needed to improve clay. However, the quantity is not insignificant. And, whereas sand is a

The second most valuable crop your land produces is the leaves that fall from your trees and the grass clipping left over from cutting the grass. Both these organic materials provide free fertilizer and soil amendments.

standard commodity to be found at all masonry supply yards, no one stocks garden-grade clay. So, to add clay to your sandy soil, you need to find a supply, dig it up, and haul it home. Quite a job. Fortunately there are less exhausting alternatives.

Organic amendments. Anything that was once alive can be used as a garden soil amendment. The list includes everything from coffee grounds to grass clippings.

There are two general sources of organic amendments. The first is far more practical than the other. The first is simply to scrounge fallen leaves, grass clippings and similar garden trash from all neighboring fields and gardens. The price cannot be beat. The alternative is to purchase peat, peat moss, humus, or a ruminant manure, dry or wet.

As you know, grass, leaves, and twigs break down to humus. In this form they occupy less space, but are in a much more permanent form. Foliage breaks down into humus in anything from a few weeks to a year. But humus remains in the earth for a dozen years or so before it is completely digested by the earth creatures and disappears. So, when we discuss the use of an organic amendment for improving the earth's tilth, we will consider all of them in their humus form.

Pound for pound, humus is several dozen times more effective in loosening soil than sand is. Whereas a bag of sand will disappear in clay, humus will not. Just how much humus should be added to any plot is difficult to say, except that you cannot add too much. One thing you might try is a measured test: Add a quantity of humus, say a level pailful, to 4 square feet of earth, and dig it in to a depth of one foot. Then check the feel of the amended soil with your hands. This will give you a rough measure of how much humus you require for your entire farm, and just how much change can be expected.

When forced to purchase humus or an organic amendment, bear in mind that the manures are your best bet. They contain fertilizers as well as "body." So even if you pay a little more on a pound basis, you are getting more than if you purchased peat or peat moss or straw.

COMPOSTING

The term probably comes from the word decomposition. To compost in the larger sense means to collect organic waste and speed its decomposition by one means or another, generally with the aid of a compost heap. And for years composting and the compost heaps have been a source of mild amusement to nonfarmers. Not as funny as someone collecting bits of string, but worth a snicker. And to be reasonably honest, the sight of a pile of leaves topped off with an unfinished dinner, fruit peels, and left over soup, does remind a viewer of the eccentric Collier brothers who never threw anything away. Their home was packed solid from floor to ceiling with trash and an old automobile or two.

Yet the last laugh has always been and will remain with the composter, for compost is a farmer's only free source of fertilizer. When organic matter is decomposed, it turns to humus which is a wonderful soil amendment and a low-grade (low concentration) fertilizer.

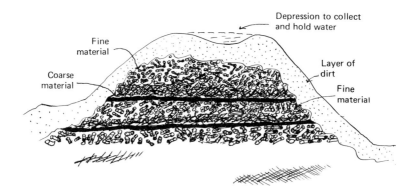

Compost heaps need not be complicated to be effective. Merely pile alternate layers of fine organic material, coarse material, and a layer of soil to make the heap. Top with a concave layer of earth, and wait for results.

The method most often used for composting is the compost heap. Very simply, the organic debris is formed into a pile and ignored for a year or so, during which time our friendly little soil people chew it up for us and convert it to humus.

The simple pile method works fine but is very slow. More speed can be secured by dusting a little dirt onto the pile as you build it up. The dirt contains the microorganisms, and thereby conversion or breakdown is accelerated.

Still better (meaning faster) results can be obtained by alternating layers of plant remains with manure, and covering the sides of the pile and top with a layer of dirt. The top should be made into a shallow dish to help retain rainwater.

If you don't have a horse or cow on hand to supply the manure but do have rough debris such as cornstalks, the pile is made of alternate layers of fine material such as leaves and grass clippings and coarse stuff such as plant stalks, dusted throughout with soil to inoculate the pile.

Some soak their compost heaps as they build them. However, the quantity of water is limited to that which the pile can absorb.

Still other farmers throw a little nitrogen in with the soil to help feed the bacteria while they chomp away on the greenery.

Another method consists of sprinkling dirt and nitrogen on the pile as you build it, wetting it down, and then covering it all with a plastic sheet that reaches to the ground and is held there by rocks. The proponents of this technique say it works beautifully.

A few of the organic substances that can be usefully composted:

Straw	Shredded twigs
Peat moss	Shredded bark
Sawdust	Buckwheat husks
Kelp	Cottonseed husks
Salt hay	Blood meal
Corn cobs	Animal waste
Packing material (if it is organic and not plastic)	Ground horns and hooves
	Coffee grounds
Leaves	Shredded corn stalks
Grass clippings	Pine needles
Cottonseed husks	Nut shells (excepting walnut)
Seaweed	Fish wastes

Both the complete top and side dirt layer and the all-encompassing plastic sheet have the advantage of retaining most of the carbon dioxide released by the microorganisms. The carbon dioxide combines with the moisture to form carbonic acid which dissolves a lot more rock particles than the water alone. Therefore both these methods produce more fertilizer in the final heap than any of the others. They are also both faster. However, the microbic digestive process, especially if there is fresh manure present, raises the temperature within the heap very high. Sometimes so high that the organic material is burned—carbonized into a form of charcoal. Which isn't a complete waste, but isn't humus.

To preclude this possibility, and also to speed decomposition because excessive heat destroys the bacteria, all compost heaps should be turned over once a month or so during the warm months. The "covered" heaps *must* be turned over this often if you are not to lose the humus. If the compost is dry when you turn it over, wet it down, but don't wash it away with excess water. Don't mix fresh wood ashes into the heap, as they will form a lye that will kill the bacteria.

And speaking of bacteria, don't waste your money on special strains of active bacteria. They will give you a little more speed in cold weather but not much more. Use a little black topsoil or humus to help things get started. Pure mineralized soil has very few bacteria.

The breakdown or rate of decomposition in a heap depends on the nature, surface area, and moisture content of the material, the temperature of the heap, oxygen available, and external moisture. Green leaves and young stalks are decomposed first. Dry twigs and branches take much longer. As decomposition works from the outside in, the larger-diameter material takes longer. So if you want smoothly textured humus, keep the sticks and logs out of your pile. The thick pieces can be converted in a pile of their own.

Now the surprising fact—surprising in view of all the years and effort expended on compost heaps and our own little discourse on the subject—the compost heap is not the best means of converting organic waste and debris to humus. It is wasteful.

Wasteful of nutrients and wasteful of labor. A goodly portion of the nutrients produced in the best engineered compost heap always escapes to the air in the form of gas, and a quantity of the soluble nutrients is always leached away by rain. Wasteful in labor in that the organic debris must be carried and formed into a pile, watered, covered, mixed, and watered, covered, and mixed again. Afterward the debris has to be transported a second time to the fields where it is to be added.

Much of this waste is eliminated by mulch-organic farming. Stated briefly, the organic debris is composted directly in the soil that it is going to enrich. All the nutrients remain in place; you haul the organic load just once to your field, dig it in, and forget it.

Now for another surprise; even if you do farm the mulch-organic way, you should maintain a compost heap on your farm preferably close to your kitchen door. During the spring, winter and late fall you can dump your kitchen remains right on the land. But during the growing season it will be awkward to dump things between the plants and it is a pity not to collect kitchen grease, leftovers and the like. Even fish and meat scraps can be placed on the heap. If you keep a shovel nearby and cover these things with a little soil, there will be no odor and no midnight visitors.

It is not as messy as it sounds, and saving food leftovers, peels, and similar organic remains is important. You are conserving important energy (saving the power needed to manufacture fertilizer), keeping the greases and oils out of the drain pipes, and easing the town's garbage collection load.

The humus that results from your composting can be used as a soil amendment, and/or as a minor source of fertilizer. It cannot be used as a mulch for the control of weeds because weed seeds falling on the humus will take root. In itself, humus is an excellent soil.

This brings up a point that perhaps requires clarification. Some gardeners hesitate to compost their garden wastes in the belief that weed seeds and insects thus collected will be returned to the soil. This is not so. Well-composted garden debris contains no seeds and no insect life. The heat and acids generated by composting and the bacteria themselves destroy all the seeds and all the insects originally in the leaves and grass.

The fresh manures and some of the manures that have been merely dried and not composted will contain a quantity of wild seeds and sometimes insect eggs. This can cause you additional work if you merely spread these manures. However, if you work them into the soil, they should cause very little trouble.

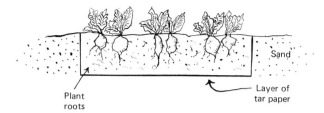

To grow crops in pure sand, trench the plot to a depth of about 1 foot. Line the bottom with tar paper, and then replace the sand. Paper keeps water from running off.

IMPROVING SANDY SOIL

If you can and do want to go to the trouble and work of mixing clay into your sand, fine. The results will be excellent. If, like most of us, you prefer to avoid the cost and effort, there is one trick you might try. It is usually successful.

Outline your garden plot. Remove the sand to a depth of 1 foot or so, making a flat-bottom pit the size of your intended plot. Line the bottom of the pit with 15-pound tar paper, taking care to have each sheet overlap its neighbor by a few inches. Replace the sand.

The impervious tar paper prevents water from running right down through the sand to the bottom of the world. Without this barrier, most plants have to be watered every day. Without the barrier the constant downward travel of the water removes all soluble minerals by leaching. Therefore it is almost a complete waste of time and money to add chemical fertilizers to soil that is all sand. The organics fare but little better. Humus mixed with pure sand will retain water, but much of its nutrients will be washed down into the earth. However, with the barrier to slow downward water movement, reasonably normal growth and plant food retention does take place.

When you go to harvest, do not pull the plants out. Instead, cut them off at the surface of the earth and let the roots remain. In time the tar paper will disintegrate, but by then you will have a mass of roots holding the sand in place and effectively retaining water.

WORKING WITH CLAYEY SOIL

The first step is to go the limestone route. After you have carefully worked the finely ground limestone in, examine your soil. If you are not satisfied with its tilth, your best bet is to add an organic amendment.

If you have time (and we are speaking of 6 months or so) you can make your own humus via composting. If it is spring and you want to sow your crops, your best bet is to add humus that you can purchase in the form of peat, peat moss, or a ruminant fertilizer. Of these, the best choice is the fertilizer if it doesn't cost too much.

There are no guidelines as to how much humus is necessary per square foot. The only thing you can do is to measure out a bucket of humus and mix it carefully into, say 4 square feet of garden. You can check the results by feeling the soil with your fingers. This will give you an approximation of just how much you will need for the entire plot. If you are going to plant shallow-rooted vegetables you can confine your humus and clay mixing to the top 6 inches. If your plants are deep rooted, you had better work down to 12 inches.

You can conserve your humus or fertilizer by confining the area to which you apply it. For example, if you are setting out pumpkins, you can dig a hole about 1 × 1 foot, mix a fairly large quantity of humus in with the soil, and plant your seeds there. If you are setting out a row of plants you can dig a trench and limit your amendment to the soil in that trench.

No matter what route you take to improve your soil, whether you completely rework the earth by adding sand or clay or lime, whether you improve your soil by mixing the top layer or horizon with a lower layer, it is a one-time job. Once the soil's tilth has been improved, it remains improved. There is no need to repeat any of this work, and with continued mulch-organic farming your soil will be further improved.

CHAPTER ELEVEN

Tilling the Soil

FOR CLOSE TO thirteen millennia people have tilled the soil. Century in, century out, they have bent their backs preparing the earth for seed by turning the soil over. Now it appears that most of this effort was unnecessary.

Tilling, the process of turning the soil over, breaking up the clods, and then raking the surface of the earth smooth, was and still is done for a number of reasons: Tilling, it is believed, discourages and to a great extent eliminates weeds, eases the planting and growth of seeds, and improves the tilth of the earth, making it more granular and improving aeration.

Pre-sowing tillage does reduce weed growth. Breaking the clods and smoothing the earth does make it easier to plant seeds, and seeds do germinate better and grow more vigorously in their early stages when the soil's surface is smooth. But plowing, turning the earth over, breaking clods and raking the lumps smooth—all that is directly implied by tilling—does not improve tilth. In many if not most soils, tilling can reduce tilth or soil friability.

There are some exceptions. Soils consisting of a clayey layer above or immediately below a sandy layer, or soils that have an otherwise uneven distribution of sand and clay, can be improved by mixing the two types of soil. Soils that support heavy stands of spring weeds or grass and are to be planted that season must be turned over or the weeds pulled out by hand if a crop is to be realized that fall.

Soils that do not comprise poorly mixed areas of sand and clay are harmed by tilling, and their granular structure is degraded. The greatest damage is done when the soil is wet; the least when it is dry. Unfortunately, the drier the soil, the more difficult it is to till. This has been stated many times in any number of agricultural publications; advising against working the soil when wet, warning against excessive tilling. However, to the best of this writer's knowledge no recognized agronomist has taken a published position that tilling is unnecessary, though this is always more or less implied. (But a recently concluded 12-year study by the Ohio Agricultural Research and Development Center found that greater yields of corn could be secured from unplowed fields than from plowed fields.)

So far, only two farmer-writers have flatly stated their opposition to ploughing and tilling. One is Edward H. Faulkner, who has published three books expounding his views: *Plowman's Folly,* 1938; *A Second Look,* 1946; and *Soil Development,* 1952 (all three published by the University of Oklahoma Press, Norman). He has proved his theory by taking a worn-out farm that could hardly grow beans and converting it into a highly productive piece of land without lime, fertilizer, soil amendments, or plowing. He accomplished all this by in-place mulching. Those plants that did grow he turned under with a disk harrow at the end of each season. *He did nothing more to improve fertility and tilth.* He did not plant special crops, and he did not return all the crop to the soil. He harvested each crop each season. Only the leaves and stems were left in place.

The other author is Ruth Stout, who doesn't even trouble to turn her plants under at the end of the growing season. Instead she simply mulches the entire area with several inches of straw. Her book is *How to Have a Green Thumb Without an Aching Back* (Exposition Press, New York, 1955).

The method used by this author and described herein differs only in that tilling is done as and when necessary to bring the soil quickly to a practical level of productivity.

Mr. Faulkner required a number of years to bring his soil to a level that exceeded that of neighboring farms. He was intent upon proving his point, and because he used no fertilizers or amendments the process required from 3 to 7 years. Fertility was good after 3 years, but it was not until the seventh that he could grow almost whatever crops he desired. Some crops are more sensitive to soil conditions than others.

Miss Stout began gardening the conventional way and year by year reduced her tilling and turning and eventually evolved her present method, which consists solely of mulching.

This too is our goal, to plant and harvest vegetables without any earth turning and tilling whatsoever; without the need and use for fertilizers, herbicides and pesticides; without the need for back-breaking, time-consuming weeding.

This goal has been reached by this writer and others. In my instance, working with a fourth-rate plot in terms of soil and sun, I have harvested some 100 pounds of vegetables a year with no more than 20 hours of work, total.

Except for weeds, and they are easily controlled by mulching, there is no self-evident reason why the soil should be turned over. Nature doesn't do it and yet gets by very well.

On the other hand, there are many reasons to try mulch-organic farming, including taking part in a giant experiment that is going to change many of farming's 13-millennia practices.

Obviously, it is impractical to economically sow wheat by this method. And obviously, if your soil is punk, if its pH is off, if it needs amendments, if it has little humus, you are not going to get a good crop this coming season just by sowing a few seeds. If you want rapid results, you are going to have to dig a little, or till the soil if you will. That is why there is a chapter on tilling in a book dedicated to eradicating tilling.

EQUIPMENT

The tool that is best for turning the earth is a long-handled shovel. But a shovel alone is not enough if you have more than a few minutes work. You also need heavy work shoes, the kind that are politely termed "turd ticklers." Without them you have no firm foundation for your feet and most of your energy will be wasted sliding around.

If you have earth moving to do you will need a wheelbarrow. There is a "gardening" type and a mason or contractor's type. Either will do, though the gardener's barrow with its wooden slats looks better.

You will also need a plain iron rake for smoothing the soil. (The new designs consisting of a number of plates bolted together don't work as well as the old-fashioned kind.) And lastly, you will need a gardener's trowel.

There are other tools you may need for other farming operations, but the few tools listed will take care of most if not all of your tilling and planting needs.

Next to a long-handled shovel, your best piece of equipment for tilling the field is a strong pair of work shoes.

There is nothing special about selecting any of the aforementioned implements except making certain they are sturdy. Some of the low-priced imports have pine handles, which makes them lighter. This is nice but the pine will not stand up. It will break before the season is over. So spend a little more and select tools with some heft. They don't have to be large, but they should be strong. Otherwise you are wasting your money. Garden tools should last long enough to be handed down to your grandchildren. The better ones do last that long.

EASY DOES IT

If you are familiar with the operating end of a shovel you can skip the next few paragraphs. If not, you won't be wasting your time to peruse the following.

The best way to break sod or tight soil with a long-handled shovel is to place its point straight down against the ground and stand on its edges. If your weight alone doesn't drive the shovel into the ground, try jumping up and down a few times. (This is where those heavy shoes come in.) With the shovel well into the ground, take hold of the end of the handle and pull it down. The leverage will enable you to easily break the soil and/or sod loose. Then bend over and grasp the handle with one hand just where it fastens to the shovel. Lift slowly and swing the load wherever you need to.

Since you are not going to be lifting very much weight, it doesn't much matter whether you use your back or legs for the lifting. What does matter is that you do all this slowly. No sudden jerks and swings. To reduce the effort required, do not lift the shovel and its load of dirt any higher than you need to. If you are merely turning the soil over and mixing, just keep the shovel clear of the ground. Any higher is a waste of effort.

To prevent blisters, which are calluses that break, keep shifting your hand positions. Work the shovel right-handed a while, then left-handed. If you need gloves, take them off every once in a while to permit your hands to cool and dry. Sweating hands become soft and are easily injured. Should you feel a sore spot developing on your hand, stop work. If you must continue, cover the spot with a large strip of tape. Putting the tape on the sore spot after the blister has broken is worse than putting locks on barn doors after you know what.

TILLING TIME

You till when you need to, bearing in mind that the drier the soil, the less you will damage its structure. The usual test is to try to form the soil into a ball. If it can be shaped this way, it is too wet and should be permitted to continue drying.

This is, of course, always a problem, at least in the East. If you continue to wait, it may rain again and the waiting will have been for nothing. But that is the farming game.

In any event, if planting time is pushing hard and the soil is wet and needs lime or fertilizer or amendments, it is better to turn it over and destroy some of its structure than to miss spring planting.

TECHNIQUE

To mix an amendment or anything else evenly into the soil, start by spreading it over the area you are going to mix. If the quantity you are going to add isn't very

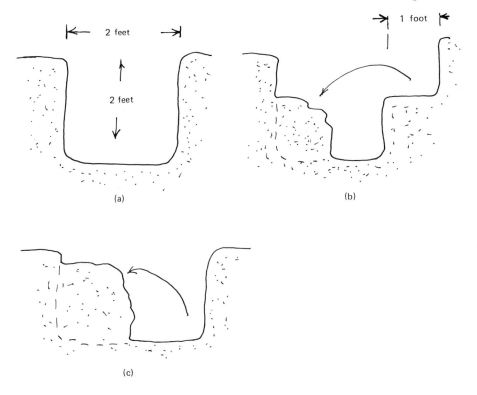

Double trenching. (a) through (c) Dig a trench about 2 feet wide by 2 feet deep. Now dig a 1 by 1-foot bench or shelf along one side. The soil moved from this area is placed alongside the bottom of the farther side. The soil remaining is placed on top. This is repeated until the entire area is dug up.

much, mix it with sand or dry soil. In this way you will be able to spread the material more evenly over the land.

If you are planning to go down about a foot or so, use the spit—shovel—face to guide you. Just push it down into the soil until the shovel's face is below the surface and then leverage it up and free. In this way you can control your digging depth without stopping to measure.

If you plan to go down 2 feet or so, it is best to use the trench method. Dig a trench 2 feet wide and 2 feet deep (or however deep you wish to go) across the width of your plot. Pile all the dirt you remove to your left (or right; it doesn't matter). Now dig a shelf along the right-hand side of the trench. Make this shelf 1 foot deep and 1 foot wide. Move the dirt that comprised the shelf to the bottom left-hand edge of your trench. Now remove the 1 foot of soil (that was below the shelf) from where it rests along the right-hand side of the trench, and place it atop the soil you just piled to your left. In this way, move your trench sideways to your left. First removing the top layer of dirt and then the under layer.

By doing it this way you never have to dig very deeply into the soil at any one point. You have an open space to one side where you can easily toss and turn the soil to mix it. And the top layer of soil is easily mixed with the lower layer.

Note that merely digging and turning doesn't mix the soil very much. If you are working phosphorus in (and this has to be well mixed), you have got to turn the soil over, shovel by shovelful several times, breaking the clods with the shovel's edge, and generally mushing things about.

When you uncover a rock larger than an inch or two, remove it. But don't go to the trouble of screening the soil or laboriously removing every little pebble you encounter. It isn't necessary; the plants will grow around them without complaint.

Should you encounter a tree stump or a log, remove it. But again, don't trouble to remove every root. They will slowly disintegrate by themselves and do no harm while they are about it.

If you have no natural collection point for the rocks and stones you gather, dig a hole somewhere and bury them. You can even bury them in the garden if you go below two feet and don't plant long-rooted plants on top.

DEPTHS

This brings us to the depth to which you should till the soil, either for adding an amendment or fertilizer: If drainage is good and you are not digging to mix an upper horizon with a lower soil horizon, there isn't much need to go down below a foot or so. This is where most plants do their feeding, though a number of vegetables do go down quite a ways.

Typically, spinach, celery, and radishes confine themselves to the top 1 foot. Potatoes remain above the 2-foot level. Corn, cotton, and tomatoes will go down to 4 feet and more if the soil is sufficiently open. Asparagus roots readily penetrate to 10 feet and even more. This is why some of the ancient agronomists suggested preparing asparagus beds by starting at a depth of 10 feet below the earth's surface. Cucumbers will grow laterally as much as 6 feet in all directions if water conditions favor them.

Raking. There isn't much to raking except to remember to keep changing hand positions. If you don't and you are unaccustomed to this exercise, you will work up blisters very quickly. Often they will develop and break before you feel any pain.

Use the tines to remove sticks and stones. Use the back side of the rake to smooth and level the soil.

CHAPTER TWELVE

Getting Started

T HE FIRST STEPS in getting started farming your land by the mulch-organic
method have been described. They are essentially no different from the steps
you need to take when farming by conventional techniques: Soil pH and nutrient
are tested and measured. If necessary, fertilizers and amendments are added.
These are properly worked in, and the soil is raked level and smooth.

These are not the steps that would be taken by an organic purist or an individual
bent on proving that soil can rebuild itself without artificial aids. These are
practical steps we take to ensure a good crop in the coming season and because we
know that chemical fertilizers are not harmful, merely limited.

START IN THE FALL

Mulch-organic farming is best started in the fall. However, as will be explained,
you can apply and benefit by some of the mulch-organic techniques whenever you
may pick up this book and decide to go this route.

Start by collecting or scrounging as much organic material as you can. The list of
suitable organic material is very long, but most of us are limited to leaves and grass
clippings, which will do fine. In addition, you can if you wish purchase any of the
commercially packaged organic material such as peat moss and salt hay. They are
all excellent, but spending money is contrary to our purpose, which is to produce
as much food as possible with as small an expenditure of money and effort as
possible.

When you work the organic debris into the soil, take care not to form a solid layer of leaves and clippings. Try to get a little bit of soil around each leaf or small clump of leaves and clippings.

Having amassed your debris, divide your collection into two piles. Pile one to contain all the green leaves and grass. Pile two to contain all the old, dried leaves and grass. If such a division entails work, simply make two piles and remove all the twigs from pile one. Twigs and branches do no harm, they are merely difficult to work into the soil.

If you have comparatively little organic matter, make just one pile, use it all for digging in, and worry about mulching material in the spring. On the other hand, if you have collected an enormous amount, don't make pile one so large that when you spread it over your field there are more than 5 inches of organic debris atop the earth. There is nothing wrong with digging tremendous quantities of organic material into the earth except that, as you increase the leaves and clippings, you increase the required effort a disproportionate amount. Don't worry about having too much in pile two; it is impossible to have too much mulch; besides it will lose considerable volume before spring. Hold the two piles in abeyance.

Next, spread about 5 pounds of nitrogen, which may be combined with other fertilizers, over every 100 square feet of your growing area. The nitrogen isn't essential, but it does speed decomposition. Now spread pile one over the same area. Disperse it as evenly as you can.

Then you take a strong grip on your shovel and work the fertilizer and organic debris into the top few inches of earth. Take great care to avoid matting the leaves and to make certain that you end up with a little dirt around each bit of organic material or at least each clump of material. And top it all off with an inch or two of dirt. The mixing is very important. At all costs you must avoid the formation of a leaf or grass mat extending horizontally across the earth. Such a mat, composed of a layer of packed debris, forms a moisture barrier that will stop the natural flow of subsoil water upward to the plant roots. This is exactly what a moldboard plow does and is one reason why plowing can be detrimental to plant growth.

The depth to which you work the trash into the soil, the separation between leaves and stalks, or what have you, are all unimportant. What you are striving for is a little dirt around each bit of organic matter. If that is impossible or impractical in terms of work, a little dirt around small clumps of organic matter will do.

When you finish, and it will take quite a bit of shoveling and turning to do the job properly, the surface of your ground will be lumpy and some bits of organic matter will stick out. Let it be. You can spend hours trying to cover each speck of leaf and stem with soil. It isn't necessary.

As you should restrict your turning and mixing to dry soil, for reasons discussed in the chapter on tilling, your soil will be or should be fairly dry. If so, take the hose and give it a thorough soaking. Moisture is necessary for decomposition. If the earth remains dry until the frost sets in, very little bacterial activity will take place before spring, and it is bacterial activity we are seeking.

The process of digging organic material directly into the soil is termed by this author "in-place composting." Its advantages are manifold. Authorities (always blame authorities) contend that upward of 50 percent of the nutrients are lost by leaching and gaseous waste in the average compost heap. Therefore, by confining our organic material to the very soil in which it is to be used, we eliminate this waste, if not completely, at least to a maximum possible extent. By in-place composting we save ourselves all the labor attending a conventional compost heap, which has to be constructed, covered with soil, wetted down, turned over once or twice, and again covered. By mixing our organic material directly into the soil we end up with a mix that is mainly soil, thereby preventing the organic material (and it can include fresh manure) from overheating. By in-place composting, our organic material protects our soil and its friendly creatures from heat and frost. The thermal rise that always accompanies decomposition works to our advantage, encouraging the growth and proliferation of bacteria, and to a small degree extending the growing season. In addition, in-place composting is a one-time job; we don't need to haul the debris to the pile and then haul the pile to our field.

After pile one has been mixed into the soil, pile two, if you have it, is spread over the field in a reasonably level layer. This layer becomes a mulch. It further protects and warms the soil through the winter.

To keep the leaves and what-have-you loose and prevent them from packing down, which would convert the leaves to a solid, water-repellent blanket, use your rake once in a while.

Now there is nothing to do until spring. Your fields are covered with a blanket. Underneath, the earth and its creatures are as warm and as snug as they can be. The condition you have created nearly duplicates that which nature itself creates when fields and forests are untouched by human intervention.

STARTING IN THE SPRING

It is inadvisable to start the growing season off by in-place mulching. Even if you start a month or two before seeding and transplanting, and even if you live fairly far South, there isn't sufficient time for the bacteria to do their stuff and break the organic matter down to an appreciable degree. Therefore, if you fill your

To save yourself the effort of turning over a plot of grass in order to plant a crop, just open up a trench for your plants. Turn the removed sod upside down alongside the trench. This will act as mulch.

soil with leaves and grass clippings before planting, the organic matter will physically interfere with small-seed planting and will do the same when the seeds begin to sprout.

If you can have your leaves and blades of grass ground up, if you have sawdust or a similar granular material to mix into the soil, you eliminate the physical barrier. However, there still is a chemical hurdle.

Granular organic matter poses a tremendous surface on which our little microscopic friends can work. Therefore, this type of material is decomposed comparatively rapidly. In turn, this means the microbes will be consuming far more nitrogen than they produce; so you *must* add nitrogen when adding granular organics. In addition, the little folk will be producing a lot of carbon dioxide and thus lots of carbonic acid. Thus, your soil will swing to a low pH.

The question arises of how much. Where will the pH go, and how much lime should be added to hold it within desired bounds? This is a question that is impossible to answer without full knowledge of all the parameters involved: soil, starting pH, temperature, moisture, nature, and quantity of amendment. And even with this knowledge, temperature and moisture never remain constant, so that it is impossible to advise on how much nitrogen and/or how much lime needs to be added.

The only suggestion this writer can make is that you add a generous quantity of nitrogen when adding the granular organic matter and that you wait a month, then take a pH test and figure the lime you may need from that point.

The wiser decision is, as stated previously; hold off on the in-place composting. Use whatever organic material you have, be it leaf or granular, as mulch. Dig it in after your crops have been gathered.

DO NOT START MIDSEASON

It is impossible to spade the earth without harming the roots of nearby plants. Their roots reach out for considerable distances, as for example the roots of cucumbers which can go sideways 4 or 5 feet when the soil is suitable. And even if you are not in-place composting next to cucumbers, you still are liable to injure root systems. Most of them are too fine to be seen by eye. Therefore, all in all, there is nothing to be gained except plant injury by trying to start mulch-organic farming while the fields are alive with crops. Use whatever organic material you have as mulch, and hold off with the digging in until fall.

MULCHING

We have used the words "mulch" and "mulching" quite frequently on pages back and perhaps it is about time the terms were fully explained.

Mulching is a farm term. It is the process of placing any material atop soil near growing plants to aid the growth of desired plants and discourage and stop the growth of undesired plants, namely, weeds.

Almost any material can be and probably has been used as a mulch: rocks, tar paper, plastic, wood in board and chip form, leaves, grass cuttings, salt hay, buckwheat hulls, peanut shells, sawdust, clamshells: The list is endless.

Mulch acts as a blanket. It encourages plant growth by protecting the soil against too much sun, increases soil temperature by retaining heat within the soil, conserves moisture, protects the soil against rain damage and wind erosion. Mulch discourages plants by the simple expedient of cutting off the sunlight. Thus to protect a young plant and at the same time eliminate the need for weeding, mulch is spread on the earth around the desired plant. The plant's leaves are up in the sunlight above the mulch, and it thrives. Nasty weed seeds are below the mulch, and therefore bereft of sunlight. They cannot get started, let alone thrive.

Another major plus for organic mulch is this: It decomposes and turns into humus, which enriches the soil and provides food and shelter for our little friends. The negative side of this vegetable coin is that when the mulch turns into humus, it can no longer act as weed-killing mulch because humus makes an excellent soil. Therefore, you have to continually cover the old organic mulch with a fresh layer every year.

Selecting a mulch. For our purpose every organic mulch is much like the others. The best is the cheapest, and this turns out to be leaves and grass clippings and the aboveground remains of last year's harvested crop. Organic kitchen waste, while very valuable in the compost heap, is much too messy for mulching.

Some backyard farmers use plastic film as a mulch. While it has a few advantages over leaves and clippings, it has a number of limitations and disadvantages.

The good thing about laying down mulch in a 5 or 6-foot wide roll is that it is easy, neat, and fast. A couple of stones hold it in place. A couple of holes permit your plants to come through and grow. The plastic acts as a kind of cold frame, trapping the sun's heat underneath. Farmers who have used it report an earlier crop.

Plastic sheeting is limited to perfectly level ground. If there is any pitch, the water will not find its way through the holes cut for your plants, but will run off. There must be uncovered soil to all sides of the plastic sheet; otherwise the soil beneath the sheet will dry out. In other words, the plastic-covered plot must be watered to a great extent from its sides.

The plastic does not contribute to the feeding of the plants or the soil's inhabitants. Instead it reduces the passage of air, thereby limiting bacterial activity and in-earth humus formation and soil production.

When the plastic sheet is removed, there is usually a vile smell produced by the anaerobic bacteria that have thrived underneath. If you use the plastic sheet method you must continue to chemically fertilize your soil because this method does not enrich and build soil.

An organic mulch does everything that the plastic film will do except that it will not raise the soil's temperature to the same extent, which while desirable in the early spring can be detrimental in the height of summer.

Planting through mulch. Our organic mulch, whatever it may be, is spread reasonably evenly across our plot. To plant a row of seeds, the mulch is pushed aside to clear a space several inches wide, and as long as the row of seeds we bury in the earth. To set out a plant, we form a circular opening in the mulch, dig our hole, and position the plant. That is all there is to it.

There are, however, several precautions to keep in mind. The mulch should never come right up to the plant. The lower portions of the plant's stem needs to be open to the air and dry. If the mulch is too close, a process called damping off takes place. This is caused by fungus growing at the base of the plant. It is very damaging to young growth.

The mulch should be kept loose and prevented from packing down into a more or less solid sheet. If it does, break the sheet up with your rake. Packed mulch prevents air and water movement.

Mulch is often criticized as furnishing a home for unwanted pests. This is true. However, the same mulch also furnishes room and board for pest predators. Should there be a host of slugs and similar creatures, turn the mulch over and expose the unwanted denizens to the birds and other enemies. A point worth repeating is that when the plants and insect life on a farm are in balance, there are always visible a few of each kind of insect indigenous to the area, and an infestation of any one particular species of bug always indicates an abnormal condition. For example, when potatoes grow normally, there are usually a few Colorado beetles on the plants. When there is a drought and the potatoes do not get sufficient water, the beetles for some unknown reason multiply like a computer and devour the aboveground portions of the plants.

Weeding. The purpose of mulch is to eliminate weeding completely, but unless you have a thick layer of mulch, there will always be a few weeds that poke through. If you have very little mulch, you may have lots of weeds, but never as many or as tough as if you had no mulch at all. In any case, wait until a heavy rainfall softens the soil. Then pull the weeds out and lay them atop the mulch or bare soil. Pulled weeds make as good a mulch as anything else.

AFTER THE HARVEST

When you have harvested your crop, cut the remaining vines and stalks off close to the ground. Do not pull them out by the roots. We want the roots to remain in the soil. If the stalks are heavily infested with bugs or fungus, toss them on the compost heap. The pests will not survive decomposition by the bacteria. If you have no compost heap, burn them or get rid of them some other way.

Now you have to decide whether to let your soil remain as it is or dig the layer of mulch into it. If you were satisfied with your crop, there is no good reason to do anything to the soil. Just spread your fall collection of leaves and grass clippings atop the old mulch and wait for spring. Your crop's remains can be added atop the new mulch.

If you are not satisfied with the season's crop or are merely desirous of improving the next one, repeat the pH and nutrient tests described in Chapters 7 and 8. Add whatever is required, taking care not to add lime if you have done so the year previous, unless the pH is off by two or more units. Wait until the soil is fairly dry, and do the in-place composting bit with the mulch. To use your crop remains you will have to cut them up into small pieces. (The compost heap solution is much easier.) After you have worked all the mulch into the soil, spread the current, fall collection of leaves and clippings on top.

By working your old mulch into the soil you speed soil development. However, if the soil is very sandy, it is usually better to let it be. Mixing it breaks up the in-place roots which helps hold it together. On the other hand, if your soil is tight and heavy with clay, it is much better to mix the mulch remaining on the soil in the fall directly into the soil instead of depending on plant roots alone to improve the soil.

As your second year's collection of mulching material will not be split in half—half mixed with the earth and half left on top—you will have roughly twice as much mulch the second year as the first.

There is nothing wrong with composting the mulch in place every fall, but after anywhere from 3 to 6 years, depending on the quantity of mulch and the original condition of the soil, there will be no further improvement and no point to the exercise. Therefore, as soon as you are satisfied with your crops, or as soon as you can see that the soil is rich with humus, you can stop in-place composting. Unless your soil is terribly deficient in nutrients, you can probably stop adding fertilizer after the first or second year.

As you can see, there are only a few steps to mulch-organic farming. In the fall organic debris and a little nitrogen are mixed into the soil. Following this, the earth is covered with a layer of organic mulch. In the spring the mulch is pushed aside, and seeds and plants are set out. In the fall the crop is harvested. The plants are cut down, their roots left in place. The mulch is worked into the soil and covered with another layer of mulch, and the earth sleeps until spring, when the process is repeated. After a few seasons there is no longer a need to work the mulch into the soil at autumn; all you do is add new mulch in the fall.

Using compost. Compost or humus is, as stated, an excellent soil and a good source of a large variety of plant nutrients in low concentration. It cannot be used as a mulch, but it makes an excellent soil amendment and a very inexpensive and safe fertilizer.

You can add it to your fall layer of organic debris and mix it into the soil along with your leaves and bits of grass. Or you can use the humus to enrich small, selected areas of your farm wherein to plant fine seeds or set out young plants. You can also use it as a midseason side dressing. Adding it close by, but not touching the stems of crop plants. In the latter case the humus would be placed underneath the leaf mulch, not atop it.

When you add humus taken from your compost heap, bear in mind its pH. On an average, such humus will exhibit a pH varying from 4 to 5. Incidentally, most composted, bagged ruminant manures have a pH of 7 or neutral.

WATERING

Water is the agent that disperses the protoplasm within each plant cell. Water is the means a plant uses to bring its nutrients up from its roots and disperse the results of photosynthesis to its entire structure. Without water in sufficient quantity, no plant can live and grow.

Most of the water absorbed by a plant is lost to the atmosphere by evaporation. That is the basic driving mechanism for getting water up from the roots. Typically a full-size tomato plant in a warm, dry climate will transpire (move from roots to leaves) as much as a gallon of water a day. It requires some 700 tons of water to produce one ton of alfalfa. And a field sown to corn will require some 13 to 15 inches of rainfall through the growing season to produce a full measure of golden ears.

At the same time, too much water can be harmful. Plant roots can "drown" for the lack of air. Roots need moisture, not submergence.

All this brings us to our backyard farm. When do we water, and how much? Obviously, we must water freshly set seeds to encourage their growth. And we must also water newly set plants to ensure their growth. But how much?

Seeds should be watered thoroughly with an ultrafine spray so as not to disturb them. Afterward, they should be rewatered sufficiently to keep the soil moist, but not slopping wet. Newly set-out plants should be thoroughly watered down at first, and then once a day until the plants have obviously taken hold as evidenced by new growth.

Guidance for watering a garden as a whole is not as easily specified. Some farmers water after a week has gone by without rain. Some water only after they have made an incision into the earth and have found it dry for a few inches. If the soil is arid to a depth of 5 or 6 inches, then 2 inches of water will soak the earth to that depth, which is good if the soil is dry that far down. You can measure your application of water by setting some straight-sided cans out. If you hose the garden down as evenly as you are able to, 2 inches of water in the cans indicates this much artificial rain.

In this farmer's opinion, the best method is to wait for wilt. No matter how much time passes after the last rainfall, unless the plants themselves show a lack of water by wilting a little, irrigation is withheld. There are several benefits to this method. You don't waste time and water. You do not overwater some plants and short others. And, most valuable, you force the plants to reach downward into the subsoil for their water and sustenance. This makes them more drought-resistant and helps loosen the subsoil. Should you water your plants as soon as surface moisture disappears, the roots will never reach into the depths of the earth. They have no need to do so.

CHAPTER THIRTEEN

Planning the Crop

P LANNING AND ANTICIPATING your crop is a large part of the pleasure of farming. But while you are dreaming of 50-pound pumpkins, 5-pound apples, and blueberries more than an inch across, give thought to the realities of farming. Give thought to selecting and positioning crops that are suited to your climate, soil, and available farming time.

Certain plants, certain climates and available water supplies go well together. Others do not. Some plants require a lot of care; some need but little. Some plants are companionable, others are solitary. Take the time, therefore, to assess all the factors involved, in addition to drawing sketches of where the corn and the rutabaga will go. Doing so will ensure a bountiful crop as much as anything can make a bountiful crop a certainty.

Most, if not everything, you need to consider when planning your crops is discussed in the following pages. You can, of course, ignore all this and imitate your neighbors. But that wouldn't be the scientific approach, and there is a good chance your neighbors' soil is different than your own. (Besides, if you have read this far, you probably know more about farming than they do.)

GROWING SEASON

The growing season begins just after the last killing frost in the spring and ends with the first killing frost in the fall. The word "killing" in this context means a temperature either low enough or sustained for a sufficient length of time to severely damage crop plants.

To find your approximate growing season refer to the accompanying two maps. The first gives the average or mean date on which you can expect the last frost of early spring (or late winter). To use it, find the heavy line nearest your neck of the woods. It will bear a two-digit number. The first is the month. The second is the day. Next, refer to the second map, same locality and same line. This map gives the average date of the first killing frost in the fall. The time between the two dates is

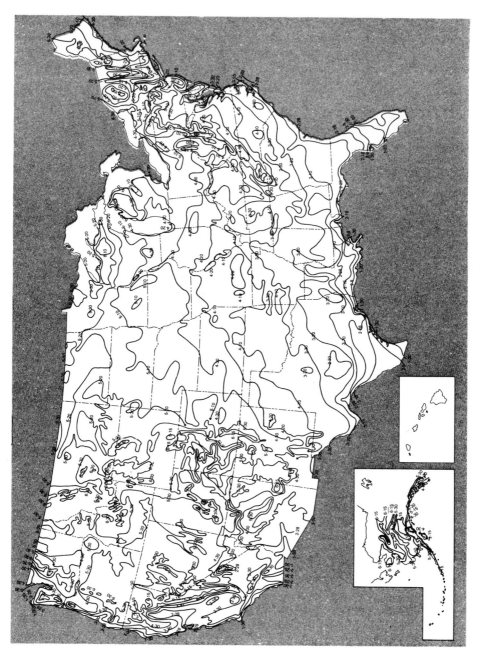

Average dates when the last killing frost in the spring can be expected. Figures on lines indicate month and day. (U.S. Department of Agriculture.)

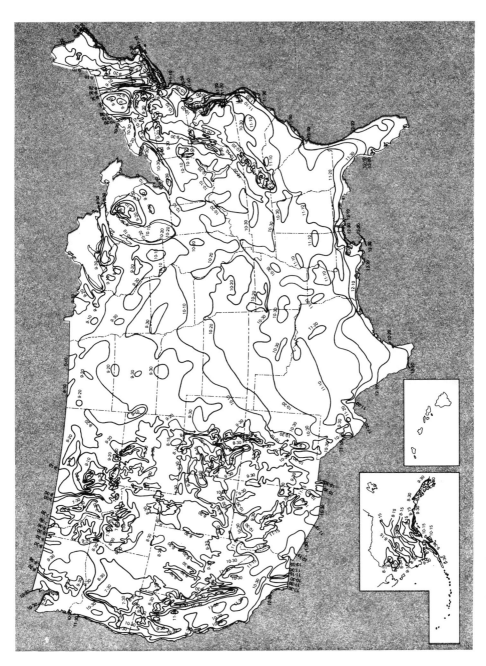

Average dates when the first killing frost in the fall can be expected. Figures on lines indicate month and day. (*U.S. Department of Agriculture.*)

your approximate growing season. If you are above sea level, the growing season will be a little shorter. If you are at sea level and near a large lake, the season will be a little longer.

The growing season's length is but a portion of the information you need. The other portion is the average temperature. This can only be provided by local authorities or experience. However, common sense and some of the information on seed packets and the detailed data on various crop plants in the following pages also help.

Briefly, to explain by example, northern Maine has a growing season stretching from May 30 to September 20, a time span of 110 days. Sweet potatoes require a growing season of 150. It would appear that you could grow sweet potatoes successfully in northern Maine if you started them indoors and then transplanted them. In practice, it doesn't work out very well, not because of the short time span, but because the average daily temperature is not high enough to make these tubers happy. Cabbage, on the other hand, some varieties of which require 120 days to mature, can be grown in northern climates because these plants prefer cool weather.

So when you match your plant to your growing season, consider the plant's temperature preferences as well as time to mature.

TIME TO HARVEST

The time required for a plant to go from seed to edible fruit varies with the plant and its variety. The difference between plant families can be almost five to one. Certain radishes will ripen in less than 30 days, for example. Some cauliflowers need 155 days to be ready for eating. Other varieties of the same plant are ready in only 60 days.

SIZE OF HARVEST

Although you can grow four or five successive crops of small radishes in the space of time it requires a cauliflower to ripen (assuming we are considering the 155-day variety), one good, large cauliflower weighs more than five batches of radishes grown in the same space. So when you are shooting for maximum food return, a "short time to harvest" is not the only yardstick. You have also to consider the relative weights and food values of the crops. Another example is tomatoes and green peppers. The same growing space will give you several more times the weight in tomatoes than in peppers.

LABOR

If you can spend an unlimited time with your garden, the following isn't germane, but if your time is limited, you need to evaluate the labor required for different plants. Returning to our radish-cauliflower example; small radishes cannot be easily mulched; therefore, you will have to weed them to some extent, in addition to planting them and harvesting them some four or five times over the summer. Not so with cauliflower.

Another example is strawberries. Of all the crops these plants require just about the most care. Picking is difficult; you have to get close to the ground. And, unless you can train your cat to guard the berry patch, you will be ripped off by the birds.

They will eat more than you will. In contrast, there are potatoes. They produce the most food per square foot of ground, when conditions are suitable. If you have mulched, care during the growing season is negligible.

HARDINESS AND TEMPERATURE REQUIREMENTS

In order to extend the growing season and secure the largest harvest from a given piece of ground, it is common to start various crop plants indoors and transplant them as early (or as late) as possible. The ability to withstand frost is termed "hardiness," and it varies from plant to plant and from one plant variety to the next.

Not too surprisingly, those plants that are most hardy are those that do best in cold and cool weather. They can be set out as early as a month before the last freeze-free day in the spring, and even earlier. Of course, the earlier you set out your plants, the greater the chance you will lose them. The weather shifts from year to year. Of course, you can to some degree copper your bet by protecting the young plants with wind breaks, plastic, paper shields, and the like.

The same plants that can be set out early will not thrive in midsummer. So, depending on where your farm is located, if you cannot get these plants going early in the year, your best bet is to set them out sometime shortly before the first freeze of winter. In this way these heat-sensitive plants are not exposed to midsummer heat. By the same token, it is quite practical to secure two crops a season from these plants, if you are far enough South.

The same holds true for plant seeds. Plants that can be safely put in the ground before all danger of frost is past have seeds that are also frost-hardy. Those that die when kissed by Jackie Frost have seeds that are just as delicate. These seeds must not be planted until the frost is well gone and the soil is warm. Beans, for example, will rot in the ground if the soil remains wet and cold too long.

SOIL AND pH PREFERENCE

According to the seed packets all plants desire rich, fertile loam, with only one or two willing to live in the suburbs—slightly clayey or sandy soil. Unfortunately, all farms are not composed of black, rich loam as soft as cream cheese. Most of our farmland is bereft of humus, light in color, and high in minerals. In a word, pauper soil.

Our problem, therefore, at the start of our farming career, is to find vegetables that can tough it out; make their way in hard, tight soils. As a general guide, you can count on the leaf crops and vines to do better than the tubers. If you stop to consider the difference in mechanical effort needed, you can easily understand why. A tomato plant has only to send its roots into the earth. A potato has to open a hole for itself. Imagine the force necessary to spread the earth wide enough to accommodate a 6 by 3-inch tuber.

Not all leaf and vine crops fare passably well on poor soil. Tomatoes will thrive where green peppers will not. Peas will falter where beans will get by. Spanish or black radishes will perform acceptably on soil that will stunt small radishes or the Icicles (long, white variety of radish). Both the black and the white will grow, but if the white doesn't grow quickly, it becomes very peppery and tough. Pepper in a Spanish radish is more acceptable.

Usually, "set-out" plants do much better in poor soil than seed. The reason is

RANGE OF EARLIEST DATES FOR SAFE, OUTDOOR SPRING PLANTING

	Planting dates for localities in which average date of last freeze is—						
Crop	Jan. 30	Feb. 8	Feb. 18	Feb. 28	Mar. 10	Mar. 20	Mar. 30
Asparagus*	....	....	....	....	Jan. 1–Mar. 1	Feb. 1–Mar. 10	Feb. 15–Mar. 20.
Beans, lima	Feb. 1–Apr. 15	Feb. 10–May 1	Mar. 1–May 1	Mar. 15–June 1	Mar. 20–June 1	Apr. 1–June 15	Apr. 15–June 20.
Beans, snap	Feb. 1–Apr. 1	Feb. 1–May 1	Mar. 1–May 1	Mar. 10–May 15	Mar. 15–May 15	Mar. 15–May 25	Apr. 1–June 1.
Beet	Jan. 1–Mar. 15	Jan. 10–Mar. 15	Jan. 20–Apr. 1	Feb. 1–Apr. 15	Feb. 15–June 1	Feb. 15–May 15	Mar. 1–June 1.
Broccoli, sprouting*	Jan. 1–30	Jan. 1–30	Jan. 15–Feb. 15	Feb. 1–Mar. 1	Feb. 15–Mar. 15	Feb. 15–Mar. 15	Mar. 1–20.
Brussels sprouts*	Jan. 1–30	Jan. 1–30	Jan. 15–Feb. 15	Feb. 1–Mar. 1	Feb. 15–Mar. 15	Feb. 15–Mar. 15	Mar. 1–20.
Cabbage*	Jan. 1–15	Jan. 1–Feb. 10	Jan. 1–Feb. 25	Jan. 15–Feb. 25	Jan. 25–Mar. 1	Feb. 1–Mar. 1	Feb. 15–Mar. 10.
Cabbage, Chinese			+				
Carrot	Jan. 1–Mar. 1	Jan. 1–Mar. 1	Jan. 15–Mar. 1	Feb. 1–Mar. 1	Feb. 10–Mar. 15	Feb. 15–Mar. 20	Mar. 1–Apr. 10.
Cauliflower*	Jan. 1–Feb. 1	Jan. 1–Feb. 1	Jan. 10–Feb. 10	Jan. 20–Feb. 20	Feb. 1–Mar. 1	Feb. 10–Mar. 10	Feb. 20–Mar. 20.
Celery and celeriac	Jan. 1–Feb. 1	Jan. 10–Feb. 10	Jan. 20–Feb. 20	Feb. 1–Mar. 1	Feb. 20–Mar. 20	Mar. 1–Apr. 1	Mar. 15–Apr. 15.
Chard	Jan. 1–Apr. 1	Jan. 10–Apr. 1	Jan. 20–Apr. 15	Feb. 1–May 1	Feb. 15–May 15	Feb. 20–May 15	Mar. 1–May 25.
Chervil and chives	Jan. 1–Feb. 1	Jan. 1–Feb. 1	Jan. 1–Feb. 1	Jan. 15–Feb. 15	Feb. 10–Mar. 10	Feb. 10–Mar. 10	Feb. 15–Mar. 15.
Chicory, witloof	....	....	....	....	June 1–July 1	June 1–July 1	June 1–July 1
Collards*	Jan. 1–Feb. 15	Jan. 1–Feb. 15	Jan. 1–Mar. 15	Jan. 15–Mar. 15	Feb. 1–Apr. 1	Feb. 15–May 1	Mar. 1–June 1.
Cornsalad	Jan. 1–Feb. 15	Jan. 1–Feb. 15	Jan. 1–Mar. 15	Jan. 1–Mar. 1	Jan. 1–Mar. 15	Jan. 1–Mar. 15	Jan. 15–Mar. 15.
Corn, sweet	Feb. 1–Mar. 15	Feb. 10–Apr. 1	Feb. 20–Apr. 15	Mar. 1–Apr. 15	Mar. 10–Apr. 15	Mar. 15–May 15	Mar. 25–May 15.
Cress, upland	Jan. 1–Feb. 1	Jan. 1–Feb. 15	Jan. 15–Feb. 15	Feb. 1–Mar. 1	Feb. 10–Mar. 15	Feb. 20–Mar. 15	Mar. 1–Apr. 1.
Cucumber	Feb. 15–Mar. 15	Feb. 15–Apr. 1	Feb. 15–Apr. 15	Mar. 1–Apr. 15	Mar. 15–Apr. 15	Apr. 1–May 1	Apr. 10–May 15.
Eggplant*	Feb. 1–Mar. 1	Feb. 10–Mar. 15	Feb. 20–Apr. 1	Mar. 10–Apr. 15	Mar. 15–Apr. 15	Apr. 1–May 1	Apr. 15–May 15.
Endive	Jan. 1–Mar. 1	Jan. 1–Mar. 1	Jan. 1–Mar. 1	Feb. 1–Mar. 1	Feb. 15–Mar. 15	Mar. 1–Apr. 1	Mar. 10–Apr. 10.
Fennel, Florence	Jan. 1–Mar. 1	Jan. 1–Mar. 1	Jan. 15–Mar. 1	Feb. 1–Mar. 1	Feb. 15–Mar. 15	Mar. 1–Apr. 1	Mar. 10–Apr. 10.
Garlic	+						
Horseradish*	....	....	....	....	....	Feb. 1–Mar. 1	Feb. 10–Mar. 10.
Kale	Jan. 1–Feb. 1	Jan. 10–Feb. 1	Jan. 20–Feb. 10	Feb. 1–20	Feb. 10–Mar. 1	Feb. 20–Mar. 10	Mar. 1–20.
Kohlrabi	Jan. 1–Feb. 1	Jan. 10–Feb. 1	Jan. 20–Feb. 10	Feb. 1–20	Feb. 10–Mar. 1	Feb. 20–Mar. 10	Mar. 1–Apr. 1.

Crop						
Leek	Jan. 1–Feb. 1	Jan. 1–Feb. 15	Jan. 15–Feb. 15	Jan. 25–Mar. 1	Feb. 1–Mar. 1	Feb. 15–Mar. 15.
Lettuce, head*	Jan. 1–Feb. 1	Jan. 1–Feb. 1	Jan. 15–Feb. 15	Feb. 1–20	Feb. 15–Mar. 10	Mar. 1–20.
Lettuce, leaf	Jan. 1–Feb. 1	Jan. 1–Mar. 15	Jan. 1–Mar. 15	Jan. 15–Apr. 1	Feb. 1–Apr. 1	Feb. 15–Apr. 15.
Muskmelon	Feb. 15–Mar. 15	Feb. 15–Apr. 15	Mar. 1–Apr. 1	Mar. 15–Apr. 15	Apr. 1–May 1	Apr. 10–May 15.
Mustard	Jan. 1–Mar. 1	Feb. 1–Mar. 1	Feb. 1–Mar. 1	Feb. 10–Mar. 15	Feb. 20–Apr. 1	Mar. 1–Apr. 15.
Okra	Feb. 15–Apr. 1	Mar. 1–June 1	Mar. 10–June 1	Mar. 20–June 1	Apr. 1–June 15	Apr. 10–June 15.
Onion*	Jan. 1–15	Jan. 1–Feb. 1	Jan. 1–Feb. 1	Jan. 15–Feb. 15	Feb. 10–Mar. 10	Feb. 15–Mar. 15.
Onion, seed	Jan. 1–15	Jan. 1–15	Jan. 1–Feb. 15	Feb. 1–Mar. 1	Feb. 10–Mar. 10	Feb. 20–Mar. 15.
Onion, sets	Jan. 1–15	Jan. 1–15	Jan. 15–Mar. 1	Jan. 1–Mar. 1	Jan. 15–Mar. 20	Feb. 1–Mar. 20.
Parsley	Jan. 1–30	Jan. 1–30	Jan. 15–Mar. 1	Feb. 1–Mar. 1	Feb. 15–Mar. 15	Mar. 1–Apr. 1.
Parsnip		Jan. 1–Feb. 1	Jan. 1–Mar. 1	Jan. 15–Mar. 1	Feb. 1–Mar. 15	Mar. 1–Apr. 1.
Peas, garden	Jan. 1–Feb. 15	Jan. 1–Feb. 15	Jan. 15–Mar. 1	Jan. 15–Mar. 15	Feb. 1–Mar. 15	Feb. 10–Mar. 20.
Peas, black-eye	Feb. 15–May 15	Feb. 15–May 15	Mar. 10–June 20	Mar. 15–July 1	Apr. 1–July 1	Apr. 15–July 1.
Pepper*	Feb. 1–Apr. 1	Feb. 15–Apr. 15	Mar. 15–May 15	Apr. 1–June 1	Apr. 10–June 1	Apr. 15–June 1.
Potato	Jan. 1–Feb. 15	Jan. 1–Feb. 15	Jan. 15–Mar. 1	Feb. 1–Mar. 1	Feb. 10–Mar. 15	Feb. 20–Mar. 20.
Radish	Jan. 1–Apr. 1	Jan. 1–Apr. 1	Jan. 1–Apr. 1	Jan. 1–Apr. 1	Jan. 20–May 1	Feb. 15–May 1.
Rhubarb*						
Rutabaga		Jan. 1–Feb. 1	Jan. 1–Feb. 1	Jan. 15–Feb. 15	Jan. 15–Mar. 1	Feb. 1–Mar. 1.
Salsify	Jan. 1–Feb. 1	Jan. 15–Feb. 20	Jan. 15–Feb. 15	Jan. 15–Feb. 15	Feb. 1–Mar. 1	Mar. 1–15.
Shallot	Jan. 1–Feb. 1	Jan. 1–Feb. 20	Jan. 1–Mar. 1	Jan. 1–Mar. 1	Feb. 1–Mar. 1	Feb. 15–Mar. 15.
Sorrel	Jan. 1–Mar. 1	Jan. 1–Mar. 1	Feb. 1–Mar. 10	Feb. 1–Mar. 10	Feb. 10–Mar. 20	Feb. 20–Apr. 1:
Soybean	Mar. 1–June 30	Mar. 10–June 30	Mar. 20–June 30	Apr. 10–June 30	Apr. 10–June 30	Apr. 20–June 30.
Spinach	Jan. 1–Feb. 15	Jan. 1–Mar. 1	Jan. 1–Mar. 1	Jan. 15–Mar. 10	Jan. 15–Mar. 10	Feb. 1–Mar. 20.
Spinach, New Zealand	Feb. 1–Apr. 15	Mar. 1–Apr. 15	Mar. 15–May 15	Mar. 20–May 15	Apr. 1–May 15	Apr. 10–June 1.
Squash, summer	Feb. 1–Apr. 15	Mar. 1–Apr. 15	Mar. 15–May 15	Mar. 15–May 15	Apr. 1–May 15	Apr. 10–June 1.
Sweet potato	Mar. 15–May 15	Mar. 20–June 1	Mar. 20–June 1	Apr. 1–June 1	Apr. 1–May 20	Apr. 10–June 1.
Tomato	Feb. 1–Apr. 1	Feb. 20–Apr. 10	Mar. 1–Apr. 20	Mar. 20–May 10	Mar. 20–May 10	Apr. 10–June 1.
Turnip	Jan. 1–Mar. 1	Jan. 1–Mar. 1	Jan. 10–Mar. 1	Jan. 20–Mar. 1	Feb. 1–Mar. 1	Feb. 20–Mar. 20.
Watermelon	Feb. 15–Mar. 15	Feb. 15–Apr. 1	Feb. 15–Apr. 15	Mar. 15–Apr. 15	Apr. 1–May 1	Apr. 10–May 15.

*These vegetables are not set out as seeds, but as plants.
†These vegetables are usually planted in the fall.
U.S. Dept. of Agriculture

RANGE OF EARLIEST DATES FOR SAFE, OUTDOOR SPRING PLANTING (Continued)

Crop	Planting dates for localities in which average date of last freeze is—						
	Apr. 10	Apr. 20	Apr. 30	May 10	May 20	May 30	June 10
Asparagus*	Mar. 10–Apr. 10	Mar. 15–Apr. 15	Mar. 20–Apr. 15	Mar. 10–Apr. 30	Apr. 20–May 15	May 1–June 1	May 15–June 1.
Beans, lima	Apr. 1–June 30	May 1–June 20	May 15–June 15	May 25–June 15	...	...	....
Beans, snap	Apr. 10–June 30	Apr. 25–June 30	May 10–June 30	May 10–June 30	May 15–June 30	May 25–June 15	May 15–June 15.
Beet	Mar. 10–June 1	Mar. 20–June 1	Apr. 1–June 15	Apr. 15–June 15	Apr. 25–June 15	May 1–June 15	May 15–June 15.
Broccoli, sprouting*	Mar. 15–Apr. 15	Mar. 25–Apr. 20	Apr. 1–May 1	Apr. 15–June 1	May 1–June 15	May 10–June 10	May 20–June 10.
Brussels sprouts*	Mar. 15–Apr. 15	Mar. 25–Apr. 20	Apr. 1–May 1	Apr. 15–June 1	May 1–June 15	May 10–June 15	May 20–June 10.
Cabbage*	Mar. 1–Apr. 1	Mar. 10–Apr. 1	Mar. 15–Apr. 10	Apr. 1–May 15	May 1–June 15	May 10–June 15	May 20–June 1.
Cabbage, Chinese	†	†	†	Apr. 1–May 15	May 10–June 15	May 10–June 15	May 20–June 1.
Carrot	Mar. 10–Apr. 20	Apr. 1–May 15	Apr. 10–June 1	Apr. 20–June 15	May 1–June 1	May 10–June 1	May 20–June 1.
Cauliflower*	Mar. 1–Mar. 20	Mar. 15–Apr. 20	Apr. 10–May 10	Apr. 15–May 15	May 10–June 15	May 20–June 1	June 1–June 15.
Celery and celeriac	Apr. 1–Apr. 20	Apr. 10–May 1	Apr. 15–May 1	Apr. 20–June 15	May 10–June 15	May 20–June 1	June 1–June 15.
Chard	Mar. 15–June 15	Apr. 1–June 15	Apr. 15–June 15	Apr. 20–June 15	May 10–June 15	May 20–June 1	June 1–June 15.
Chervil and chives	Mar. 1–Apr. 1	Mar. 10–Apr. 10	Mar. 20–Apr. 20	Apr. 1–May 1	Apr. 15–May 15	May 1–June 1	May 15–June 1.
Chicory, witloof	June 10–July 1	June 15–July 1	June 15–July 1	June 1–20	June 1–15	June 1–15	June 1–15.
Collards*	Mar. 1–June 1	Mar. 10–June 1	Apr. 1–June 1	Apr. 15–June 1	May 1–June 1	May 10–June 1	May 20–June 1.
Cornsalad	Feb. 1–Apr. 1	Feb. 15–Apr. 15	Apr. 1–June 1	Apr. 15–June 1	May 1–June 1	May 1–June 15	May 15–June 15.
Corn, sweet	Apr. 10–June 1	Apr. 25–June 15	May 10–June 15	May 10–June 1	May 15–June 1	May 1–June 15	....
Cress, upland	Mar. 10–Apr. 15	Mar. 20–May 1	Apr. 10–May 10	Apr. 20–May 20	May 1–June 1	May 15–June 1	May 15–June 15.
Cucumber	Apr. 20–June 1	May 1–June 15	May 15–June 15	May 20–June 15	June 1–15	....	....
Eggplant*	May 1–June 1	May 10–June 1	May 15–June 10	May 20–June 15	June 1–15	....	....
Endive	Mar. 15–Apr. 15	Mar. 25–Apr. 15	Apr. 1–May 1	Apr. 15–May 15	May 1–30	May 1–30	May 15–June 1.
Fennel, Florence	Mar. 15–Apr. 15	Mar. 25–Apr. 15	Apr. 1–May 1	Apr. 15–May 15	May 1–30	May 1–30	May 15–June 1.
Garlic	Feb. 20–Mar. 20	Feb. 20–Mar. 15	Mar. 15–Apr. 15	Apr. 1–May 1	Apr. 15–May 15	May 1–30	May 15–June 1.
Horseradish*	Mar. 10–Apr. 10	Mar. 20–Apr. 20	Apr. 1–30	Apr. 15–May 15	Apr. 20–May 20	May 1–30	May 15–June 1.
Kale	Mar. 10–Apr. 1	Mar. 20–Apr. 10	Apr. 1–20	Apr. 10–May 1	Apr. 20–May 10	May 1–30	May 15–June 1.
Kohlrabi	Mar. 10–Apr. 10	Mar. 20–May 1	Apr. 1–May 10	Apr. 10–May 15	Apr. 20–May 20	May 1–30	May 15–June 1.

Crop					
Leek	Mar. 1–Apr. 1	Mar. 15–Apr. 15	Apr. 1–May 1	Apr. 15–May 20	May 1–15.
Lettuce, head*	Mar. 10–Apr. 1	Mar. 20–Apr. 15	Apr. 1–May 1	Apr. 15–May 15	May 20–June 30.
Lettuce, leaf	Mar. 15–May 15	Mar. 20–May 15	Apr. 1–June 1	Apr. 15–June 15	May 20–June 30.
Muskmelon	Apr. 20–June 1	May 1–June 15	May 15–June 15	June 1–June 15	....
Mustard	Mar. 10–Apr. 20	Mar. 20–May 1	Apr. 1–May 10	Apr. 15–June 1	May 20–June 30.
Okra	Apr. 20–June 15	May 1–June 1	May 10–June 1	May 20–June 10	....
Onion*	Mar. 1–Apr. 1	Mar. 15–Apr. 10	Apr. 1–May 1	Apr. 10–May 1	May 10–June 10.
Onion, seed	Mar. 1–Apr. 1	Mar. 15–Apr. 1	Mar. 15–Apr. 15	Apr. 20–May 15	May 10–June 10.
Onion, sets	Mar. 1–Apr. 1	Mar. 20–Apr. 1	Mar. 10–Apr. 10	Apr. 20–May 15	May 10–June 10.
Parsley	Mar. 10–Apr. 10	Mar. 20–Apr. 20	Apr. 1–May 1	May 1–20	May 20–June 10.
Parsnip	Mar. 10–Apr. 10	Mar. 20–Apr. 20	Apr. 1–May 1	May 1–20	May 20–June 10.
Peas, garden	Feb. 20–Mar. 20	Mar. 10–Apr. 10	Mar. 20–May 1	Apr. 15–June 1	May 10–June 15.
Peas, black-eye	....	May 10–June 15	May 15–June 1	....	....
Pepper*	May 1–July 1	May 10–June 1	May 15–June 10	May 20–June 10	....
Potato	Mar. 10–Apr. 1	Mar. 15–Apr. 10	Mar. 20–May 10	Apr. 1–June 1	May 15–June 1.
Radish	Mar. 1–May 1	Mar. 10–May 10	Mar. 20–May 10	Apr. 1–June 1	May 15–June 1.
Rhubarb*	Mar. 1–Apr. 1	Mar. 10–Apr. 10	Mar. 20–Apr. 15	Apr. 1–May 1	May 15–June 1.
Rutabaga	....	....	May 1–June 1	May 1–20	May 20–June 1.
Salsify	Mar. 10–Apr. 15	Mar. 20–May 1	Apr. 1–May 15	Apr. 1–June 1	May 20–June 1.
Shallot	Mar. 1–Apr. 1	Mar. 15–Apr. 15	Apr. 1–May 1	Apr. 10–May 10	May 10–June 1.
Sorrel	Mar. 1–Apr. 15	Mar. 15–May 1	Apr. 1–May 15	Apr. 1–June 1	May 10–June 10.
Soybean	May 1–June 30	May 10–June 20	May 15–June 15	May 25–June 10	....
Spinach	Feb. 15–Apr. 1	Mar. 1–Apr. 15	Mar. 20–Apr. 20	Apr. 1–June 15	Apr. 20–June 15.
Spinach, New Zealand	Apr. 20–June 1	May 1–June 15	May 1–June 15	May 10–June 15	May 1–June 15.
Squash, summer	Apr. 20–June 1	May 1–June 15	May 1–30	May 20–June 15	June 1–20.
Sweet potato	May 1–June 1	May 10–June 10	May 20–June 10	May 25–June 15	June 10–20.
Tomato	Apr. 20–June 1	May 5–June 10	May 10–June 15	May 15–June 10	June 15–30.
Turnip	Mar. 1–Apr.1	Mar. 10–Apr. 1	Mar. 20–May 1	Apr. 15–June 1	May 15–June 15.
Watermelon	Apr. 20–June 1	May 1–June 15	May 15–June 15	June 15–July 1	....

*These vegetables are not set out as seeds, but as plants.
†These vegetables are usually planted in the fall.
U.S. Dept. of Agriculture

Intercropping lettuce and cabbage. Lettuce and cabbage plants are set out and mulched with grass clippings.

The lettuce is almost ready to harvest. The cabbages are growing strong.

that germination and early growth are the most difficult period for a plant. By planting the seeds indoors in rich, friable soil, they are given a good start. By the same token, onion sets, which are tiny onions sold by the pound, will struggle along in almost any soil. You may not get full-size bulbs, but you will certainly show a profit by having many more pounds of onions at the end of the season than at the start. It is customary to set these small onions close to one another and then to pull alternates early in the growing season and use them as a kind of large scallion. To harvest large, mild onions, however, it is necessary to grow them in highly fertile, friable loam.

In general, your best approach to a first season with poor soil is to plant those crops that are most popular in your area. Usually, when a type of plant has found continuous acceptance in one area year after year it is a toughie. In my area tomatoes, beans, and cucumbers are standard, and they have never failed to give me good to excellent returns, though I still cannot grow peas, and my green peppers are just beginning to form good-sized fruit.

In addition to sowing the standard, local favorites, try a few that you and your family will enjoy, but with the understanding that it is in the nature of an experiment; that you are not going to lose hope just because one or two vegetables don't take.

In the matter of pH, match the plants to the soil if it is spring and you are naturally anxious to get your crops under way. At the same time don't let pH limit you. Each group of plants performs best within a narrow pH range. This is true, but they are all tolerant, some more than others no doubt, but given a choice of, let us say, planting potatoes in acidic soil (which they love) or beans in the same soil, I'd plant the beans if the soil was poor and tight. The beans will do better even though they prefer a pH of 5.6 to 6.8, and potatoes do best from 5.0 to 5.6.

COMPANION PLANTS

There are a number of plants that can be grown together if not without mutual benefit, at least without harm. For example, pumpkins thrive in partial shade. They can be planted between rows of pole beans or sweet corn. Cucumbers can be grown on the same trellis as tomatoes. Cucumbers aren't mad for shade, but they will put up with it. On the other hand, string beans should not be grown with tomatoes; they will fight the tomatoes for sunlight, growing over and in front of them. (One or two strings per trellis do little harm and help hold the tomatoes to the trellis.) Tomatoes appear to profit by a nearby planting of marigolds. Squash likes nasturtium.

The reason appears to be some sort of fluid exuded by the roots of the various plants. Called "auxins," the substances are a form of plant hormones, and are as yet not thoroughly understood. But there is no doubt that certain plants stimulate the growth of other types planted next to them.

INTERCROPPING AND SUCCESSION PLANTING

Intercropping is the technique of planting alternate rows of different kinds of plants, or one type of plant between two other kinds. The purpose is both to stimulate their growths and to make better use of the soil.

An example, perhaps not the best, is the practice of growing cucumbers and beans on the same trellis with tomatoes. The tomatoes form the major crop, the

RANGE OF LATEST DATES FOR SAFE, OUTDOOR FALL PLANTING

Crop	Planting dates for localities in which average dates of first freeze is—					
	Aug. 30	Sept. 10	Sept. 20	Sept. 30	Oct. 10	Oct. 20
Asparagus*	···	···	···		Oct. 20–Nov. 15	Nov. 1–Dec. 15
Beans, lima	···	···	···	June 1–15	June 1–15	June 15–30
Beans, snap			June 1–July 1	June 1–July 10	June 15–July 20	July 1–Aug. 1
Beet	May 15–June 15	May 15–June 15	June 1–July 1	June 1–July 10	June 15–July 25	July 1–Aug. 5
Broccoli, sprouting	May 1–June 1	May 1–June 1	May 1–June 15	June 1–30	June 15–July 15	July 1–Aug. 1
Brussels sprouts	May 1–June 1	May 1–June 1	May 1–June 15	June 1–30	June 15–July 15	July 1–Aug. 1
Cabbage*	May 1–June 1	May 1–June 1	May 1–June 15	June 1–July 10	June 1–July 15	July 1–20
Cabbage, Chinese	May 15–June 15	May 15–June 15	June 1–July 1	June 1–July 15	June 15–Aug. 1	July 15–Aug. 15
Carrot	May 15–June 15	May 15–June 15	June 1–July 1	June 1–July 10	June 1–July 20	June 15–Aug. 1
Cauliflower*	May 1–June 1	May 1–July 1	May 1–July 1	May 10–July 15	June 1–July 25	July 1–Aug. 5
Celery* and celeriac	May 1–June 1	May 1–June 1	May 15–July 1	June 1–July 5	June 1–July 15	June 1–Aug. 1
Chard	May 15–June 15	May 15–July 1	June 1–July 1	June 1–July 5	June 1–July 20	June 1–Aug. 1
Chervil and chives	May 10–June 10	May 1–June 15	May 15–June 15	+		+
Chicory, witloof	May 15–June 15	May 15–June 15	May 15–June 15	June 1–July 15	June 1–July 1	June 15–July 15
Collards*	May 15–June 15	May 15–June 15	May 15–June 15	June 15–July 15	July 1–Aug. 1	July 15–Aug. 15
Cornsalad	May 15–June 15	May 15–July 1	June 15–Aug. 1	July 15–Sept. 1	Aug. 15–Sept. 15	Sept. 1–Oct. 15
Corn, sweet	···	···	June 1–July 1	June 1–July 1	June 1–July 10	June 1–July 20
Cress, upland	May 15–June 15	May 15–July 1	June 15–Aug. 1	July 15–Sept. 1	Aug. 15–Sept. 15	Sept. 1–Oct. 15
Cucumber	···	···	June 1–15	June 1–July 1	June 1–July 1	June 1–July 15
Eggplant*	···	···		May 20–June 10	May 15–June 15	June 1–July 15
Endive	June 1–July 1	June 1–July 1	June 15–July 15	June 15–Aug. 1	July 1–Aug. 15	June 1–July 1
Fennel, Florence	May 15–June 15	May 15–July 15	June 1–July 1	June 1–July 1	June 15–July 15	July 15–Sept. 1
Garlic	+	+	+	+	+	+
Horseradish*	+	+	+	+	+	+
Kale	May 15–June 15	May 15–June 15	June 1–July 1	June 15–July 15	July 1–Aug. 1	July 15–Aug. 15
Kohlrabi	May 15–June 15	June 1–July 1	June 1–July 15	June 15–July 15	July 1–Aug. 1	July 15–Aug. 15
Leek	May 1–June 1	May 1–June 1	+	+	+	+
Lettuce, head*	May 15–July 1	May 15–July 1	June 1–July 15	June 15–Aug. 1	July 15–Aug. 15	Aug. 1–30

Crop					
Lettuce, leaf	May 15–July 15	May 15–July 15	June 1–Aug. 1	July 15–Sept. 1	July 15–Sept. 1
Muskmelon	· · ·	May 15–July 15	May 1–June 15	June 1–June 15	June 15–July 20
Mustard	May 15–July 15	May 15–July 15	June 15–Aug. 1	July 15–Aug. 15	Aug. 1–Sept. 1
Okra	· · ·	May 1–June 10	June 1–20	June 1–July 15	June 1–Aug. 1
Onion*	May 1–June 10	May 1–June 10	†	†	†
Onion, seed	May 1–June 10	May 1–June 10	†	†	†
Onion, sets	May 1–June 10	May 1–June 15	June 1–July 15	· · ·	· · ·
Parsley	May 15–June 15	May 1–June 15	May 15–June 15	June 15–Aug. 1	July 15–Aug. 15
Parsnip	May 15–June 1	May 1–June 15	June 1–July 15	June 1–July 10	†
Peas, garden	May 10–June 15	May 1–July 1	June 1–June 20	· · ·	†
Peas, black-eye	· · ·	· · ·	May 1–July 1	· · ·	· · ·
Pepper*	· · ·	· · ·	June 1–Aug. 15	June 1–July 1	June 1–July 1
Potato	May 15–June 1	May 1–June 15	Sept. 15–Nov. 1	May 15–June 15	June 1–July 10
Radish	May 1–July 15	May 1–Aug. 1	June 1–July 1	July 15–Sept. 15	June 15–July 15
Rhubarb*	Sept. 1–Oct. 1	Sept. 15–Oct. 15	Oct. 1–Nov. 1	Oct. 15–Nov. 15	Aug. 1–Oct. 1
Rutabaga	May 15–June 15	May 1–June 15	June 15–July 15	June 15–July 15	Oct. 15–Dec. 1
Salsify	May 15–June 1	May 10–June 10	May 20–June 20	May 20–June 10	July 10–20
Shallot	†	†	†	†	June 1–July 1
Sorrel	May 15–June 15	May 1–June 15	June 1–July 1	July 1–Aug. 1	†
Soybean	May 15–July 15	May 1–June 15	June 1–July 15	June 1–25	July 15–Aug. 15
Spinach	May 15–July 1	June 1–July 15	July 1–Aug. 15	Aug. 1–Sept. 1	June 1–July 5
Spinach, New Zealand	· · ·	· · ·	May 25–June 10	June 1–July 15	Aug. 20–Sept. 10
Squash, summer	June 10–20	June 1–20	May 15–July 1	June 1–July 15	June 1–Aug. 1
Squash, winter	· · ·	· · ·	May 15–July 1	June 1–July 1	June 1–July 20
Sweet potato	· · ·	· · ·	May 20–June 10	May 20–June 10	June 1–July 1
Tomato	June 20–30	June 1–20	June 1–20	June 1–20	June 1–15
Turnip	May 15–June 15	June 1–July 1	July 1–Aug. 1	July 1–Aug. 1	July 15–Aug. 15
Watermelon	· · ·	· · ·	May 15–June 1	June 1–June 15	June 15–July 20

*These vegetables are not set out as seed, but as plants.
†These vegetables are usually planted in the spring.

RANGE OF LATEST DATES FOR SAFE, OUTDOOR FALL PLANTING (Continued)

Crop	Planting dates for localities in which average date of first freeze is—					
	Oct. 30	Nov. 10	Nov. 20	Nov. 30	Dec. 10	Dec. 20
Asparagus*	Nov. 15–Jan. 1	Dec. 1–Jan. 1	· · ·	· · ·	· · ·	· · ·
Beans, lima	July 1–Aug. 1	July 1–Aug. 15	July 15–Sept. 1	Aug. 1–Sept. 15	Sept. 1–30	Sept. 1–Oct. 1
Beans, snap	July 1–Aug. 15	July 1–Sept. 1	July 1–Sept. 10	Aug. 15–Sept. 20	Sept. 1–30	Sept. 1–Nov. 1
Beet	Aug. 1–Sept.1	Aug. 1–Oct. 1	Sept. 1–Dec. 1	Sept. 1–Dec. 15	Sept. 1–Dec. 31	Sept. 1–Dec. 31
Broccoli, sprouting	July 1–Aug. 15	Aug. 1–Sept. 1	Aug. 1–Sept. 15	Aug. 1–Oct. 1	Aug. 1–Nov. 1	Sept. 1–Dec. 31
Brussels sprouts	July 1–Aug. 15	Aug. 1–Sept. 1	Aug. 1–Sept. 15	Aug. 1–Oct. 1	Aug. 1–Nov. 1	Sept. 1–Dec. 31
Cabbage*	Aug. 1–Sept. 1	Sept. 1–15	Sept. 1–Dec. 1	Sept. 1–Dec. 31	Sept. 1–Dec. 31	Sept. 1–Dec. 31
Cabbage, Chinese	Aug. 1–Sept. 15	Aug. 15–Oct. 1	Sept. 1–Oct. 15	Sept. 1–Nov. 1	Sept. 1–Nov. 15	Sept. 1–Dec. 1
Carrot	July 1–Aug. 15	Aug. 1–Sept. 1	Sept. 1–Nov. 1	Sept. 15–Dec. 1	Sept. 15–Dec. 1	Sept. 1–Dec. 1
Cauliflower*	July 15–Aug. 15	Aug. 1–Sept. 1	Aug. 1–Sept. 15	Aug. 15–Oct. 10	Sept. 1–Oct. 20	Sept. 15–Nov. 1
Celery* and celeriac	June 15–Aug. 15	July 1–Aug. 15	July 15–Sept. 1	Aug. 1–Dec. 1	Sept. 1–Dec. 31	Oct. 1–Dec. 31
Chard	June 1–Sept. 10	June 1–Sept. 15	June 1–Oct. 1	June 1–Nov. 1	June 1–Dec. 1	June 1–Dec. 31
Chervil and chives	†	†	Nov. 1–Dec. 31	Nov. 1–Dec. 31	Nov. 1–Dec. 31	Nov. 1–Dec. 31
Chicory, witloof	July 1–Aug. 10	July 10–Aug. 20	July 20–Sept. 1	Aug. 15–Sept. 30	Aug. 15–Oct. 15	Aug. 15–Oct. 15
Collards*	Aug. 1–Sept. 15	Aug. 15–Oct. 1	Aug. 25–Nov. 1	Sept. 1–Dec. 1	Sept. 1–Dec. 31	Sept. 1–Dec. 31
Cornsalad	Sept. 15–Nov. 1	Oct. 1–Dec. 1	Oct. 1–Dec. 1	Oct. 1–Dec. 31	Oct. 1–Dec. 31	Oct. 1–Dec. 31
Corn, sweet	June 1–Aug. 1	June 1–Aug. 15	June 1–Sept. 1	· · ·	· · ·	· · ·
Cress, upland	Sept. 15–Nov. 1	Oct. 1–Dec. 1	Oct. 1–Dec. 1	Oct. 1–Dec. 31	Oct. 1–Dec. 31	Oct. 1–Dec. 31
Cucumber	June 1–Aug. 1	June 1–Aug. 15	June 1–Aug. 15	July 15–Sept. 15	Aug. 15–Oct. 1	Aug. 15–Oct. 1
Eggplant*	June 1–July 1	June 1–July 15	June 1–Aug. 1	July 15–Sept. 1	Aug. 1–Sept. 30	Aug. 1–Sept. 30
Endive	July 15–Aug. 15	Aug. 1–Sept. 1	Sept. 1–Oct. 1	Sept. 1–Nov. 15	Sept. 1–Dec. 31	Sept. 1–Dec. 31
Fennel, Florence	July 1–Aug. 1	July 15–Aug. 15	Aug. 15–Sept. 15	Sept. 1–Nov. 15	Sept. 1–Dec. 1	Sept. 1–Dec. 1
Garlic	†	Aug. 1–Oct. 1	Aug. 15–Oct. 1	Sept. 1–Nov. 15	Sept. 15–Nov. 15	Sept. 15–Nov. 15
Horseradish*	†	†	†	†	†	†
Kale	July 15–Sept. 1	Aug. 1–Sept. 15	Aug. 15–Oct. 15	Sept. 1–Dec. 1	Sept. 1–Dec. 31	Sept. 1–Dec. 31
Kohlrabi	Aug. 1–Sept. 1	Aug. 15–Sept. 15	Sept. 1–Oct. 15	Sept. 1–Dec. 1	Sept. 15–Dec. 31	Sept. 1–Dec. 31
Leek	†	†	Sept. 1–Nov. 1	Sept. 1–Nov. 15	Sept. 1–Nov. 1	Sept. 15–Nov. 1
Lettuce, head*	Aug. 1–Sept. 15	Aug. 15–Oct. 15	Sept. 1–Nov. 1	Sept. 1–Nov. 15	Sept. 15–Dec. 31	Sept. 15–Dec. 31

	Col 1	Col 2	Col 3	Col 4	Col 5	Col 6	Col 7
Lettuce, leaf	Sept. 15–Dec. 31	Sept. 15–Dec. 31	Sept. 1–Dec. 1	Sept. 1–Nov. 1	Aug. 15–Oct. 1	Aug. 25–Oct. 1	Aug. 15–Oct. 1
Muskmelon	⋯	⋯	⋯	⋯	July 1–July 15	July 15–July 30	July 1–July 15
Mustard	Sept. 15–Dec. 1	Sept. 1–Dec. 1	Sept. 1–Dec. 1	Sept. 1–Dec. 1	Aug. 15–Oct. 15	Aug. 15–Nov. 1	Aug. 15–Oct. 15
Okra	Aug. 1–Oct. 1	Aug. 1–Oct. 1	June 1–Sept. 20	June 1–Aug. 15	June 1–Aug. 10	June 1–Aug. 20	June 1–Aug. 10
Onion*	Oct. 1–Dec. 31	Oct. 1–Dec. 31	Oct. 1–Dec. 31	Oct. 1–Dec. 31	⋯	Sept. 1–Oct. 15	⋯
Onion, seed	Sept. 15–Nov. 1	Sept. 1–Nov. 1	Sept. 1–Nov. 1	Sept. 1–Nov. 1	⋯	⋯	⋯
Onion, sets	Nov. 1–Dec. 31	Nov. 1–Dec. 31	Nov. 1–Dec. 31	Nov. 1–Dec. 31	Aug. 1–Sept. 15	Oct. 1–Dec. 1	Aug. 1–Sept. 15
Parsley	Sept. 1–Dec. 31	Sept. 1–Dec. 31	Sept. 1–Dec. 31	Sept. 1–Dec. 31	†	Sept. 1–Nov. 15	†
Parsnip	Sept. 1–Dec. 1	Sept. 1–Dec. 1	Sept. 1–Nov. 15	Aug. 1–Sept. 1	Aug. 1–Sept. 15	†	Aug. 1–Sept. 15
Peas, garden	Oct. 1–Dec. 31	Oct. 1–Dec. 31	Oct. 1–Dec. 31	Oct. 1–Dec. 1	Aug. 1–Sept. 15	Sept. 1–Nov. 1	Aug. 1–Sept. 15
Peas, black-eye	July 1–Sept. 20	July 1–Sept. 20	July 1–Sept. 10	July 1–Sept. 1	June 1–July 20	June 15–Aug. 15	June 1–Aug. 1
Pepper*	Aug. 15–Oct. 1	Aug. 15–Oct. 1	June 15–Sept. 1	June 1–Aug. 15	July 20–Aug. 10	June 1–Aug. 1	June 1–July 20
Potato	Aug. 1–Sept. 15	Aug. 1–Sept. 15	Aug. 1–Sept. 15	Aug. 10–Sept. 15	July 20–Aug. 10	July 25–Aug. 20	July 20–Aug. 10
Radish	Oct. 1–Dec. 31	Aug. 1–Sept. 15	Sept. 1–Dec. 31	Sept. 1–Dec. 1	Aug. 15–Oct. 15	Sept. 1–Nov. 15	Aug. 15–Oct. 15
Rhubarb*	⋯	⋯	⋯	⋯	Nov. 1–Dec. 1	⋯	Nov. 1–Dec. 1
Rutabaga	Oct. 15–Nov. 15	Oct. 1–Nov. 15	Sept. 1–Nov. 15	Aug. 1–Sept. 1	July 15–Aug. 1	July 15–Aug. 15	July 15–Aug. 1
Salsify	Sept. 1–Oct. 31	Aug. 15–Oct. 15	Aug. 15–Sept. 30	July 15–Aug. 15	June 1–July 10	June 15–July 20	June 1–July 10
Shallot	Sept. 15–Nov. 1	Sept. 15–Nov. 1	Aug. 15–Oct. 15	Aug. 15–Oct. 1	†	Aug. 1–Oct. 1	†
Sorrel	Sept. 1–Dec. 31	Sept. 1–Dec. 15	Sept. 1–Nov. 15	Aug. 15–Oct. 15	Aug. 1–Sept. 15	Aug. 15–Oct. 1	Aug. 1–Sept. 15
Soybean	June 1–July 30	June 1–July 30	June 1–July 30	June 1–July 30	June 1–July 15	June 1–July 25	June 1–July 15
Spinach	Oct. 1–Dec. 31	Oct. 1–Dec. 31	Oct. 1–Dec. 31	Oct. 1–Dec. 1	Sept. 1–Oct. 1	Sept. 15–Nov. 1	Sept. 1–Oct. 1
Spinach, New Zealand	⋯	⋯	⋯	June 1–Aug. 15	June 1–Aug. 1	June 1–Aug. 15	June 1–Aug. 1
Squash, summer	June 1–Oct. 1	June 1–Sept. 15	June 1–Sept. 1	June 1–Aug. 20	June 1–Aug. 1	June 1–Aug. 15	June 1–Aug. 1
Squash, winter	Aug. 1–Sept. 1	Aug. 1–Sept. 1	July 15–Aug. 15	July 1–Aug. 1	June 10–July 10	July 15–Aug. 10	June 10–July 10
Sweet potato	June 1–July 1	June 1–July 1	June 1–July 1	June 1–July 1	June 1–15	June 1–July 1	June 1–15
Tomato	Sept. 1–Nov. 1	Aug. 15–Oct. 1	Aug. 1–Sept. 1	June 1–Aug. 1	June 1–July 1	Sept. 1–Oct. 15	Aug. 1–Sept. 15
Turnip	Oct. 1–Dec. 31	Oct. 1–Dec. 1	Sept. 1–Nov. 15	Sept. 1–Nov. 15	Aug. 1–Sept. 15	Sept. 1–Nov. 1	Aug. 1–Sept. 15
Watermelon	⋯	⋯	⋯	⋯	July 1–July 15	July 15–July 30	July 1–July 15

*These vegetables are not set out as seed, but as plants.

†These vegetables are usually planted in the spring.

cucumbers a secondary crop, and the string beans are there merely to intertwine with the rest of the plants and hold them in place. The single trellis simplifies garden construction and cost for the farmer. The intertwining simplifies the work of tying the vines in place. It doesn't eliminate it, but it helps. The entire grouping makes a pleasing array; however, from a maximum production point of view it has some drawbacks. For one, the pH preferences of the three plants are somewhat different, and for another, the string beans will fight the tomatoes for sunlight. Yet, all in all, in terms of labor and material, the return is good.

Another example is the practice of planting lettuce, which matures quickly, between slower-growing tomato or potato plants. The lettuce is harvested before the other plants come up to full size. Even if the lettuce is a little late, the other plants are not troubled too much by partial shade.

VARIETIES

Each year our actively experimenting seedmen produce new varieties of our old species. There must be dozens of new faster, bigger, and better-tasting vegetables and fruits patented and marketed each year. Choosing your particular variety can be a lot of fun, but bear in mind that the perfect plant is yet to be bred. The largest vegetable is not always best suited to your particular climate and soil. Then too, the largest does not always have the flavor and keeping qualities you may be accustomed to or prefer. The variety with the shortest time span to maturity is not always fastest onto the table.

I believe it is safe to assume that the old standard varieties probably give the best all-around performance in regard to crop quantity, drought resistance, bug resistance, heat and cold hardiness, and blight resistance. If the old "standard" variety is still listed in the catalogs, there must be good reason. Those varieties that have been surpassed are no longer grown and sold.

So don't limit your selection to the "amazing new giant, two-week wonders," but try some of the older, established varieties as well, keeping careful record of the species, variety, and planting conditions.

An example that comes to mind demonstrates several points just made. I have two apricot trees. One has been producing well for some 10 years. The fruit is small but very tasty with a lovely odor. My second apricot is a new variety. It has been in the ground about 2 years, which makes the tree's total age about 7. Last year it produced a small number of very large, beautiful, juicy apricots. They are the size of lemons. They are easily twice or thrice the circumference of the apricots produced by the old tree; but no one in my family cares for their flavor. Whether the total annual production of the two trees will be near equal when the young tree is fully grown remains to be seen. On the basis of the larger fruit, it would appear that the second tree would produce at least twice as much, but will it? And if it does, no one, including myself, cares to eat the fruit.

The second point I wish to make with this example is that I didn't trouble to record the name of the first variety of apricot nor the second. Now, if I go to purchase a third tree, I will not know what to buy. The picture tag on the first tree showed apricots as large as or larger than those that actually appeared on the second tree.

Some agronomists believe that the new hybrid varieties are not really better plants, in the full sense of the word, but only new species that thrive better in

THE MORE COMMON VEGETABLES CLASSIFIED ACCORDING TO THEIR RESISTANCES TO HEAT AND COLD

Cold-hardy plants for early-spring planting		Cold-tender or heat-hardy plants for later-spring or early-summer planting			Hardy plants for late-summer or fall planting except in the North (plant 6 to 8 weeks before first fall freeze)
Very hardy (plant 4 to 6 weeks before frost-free date)	Hardy (plant 2 to 4 weeks before frost-free date)	Not cold-hardy (plant on frost-free date)	Requiring hot weather (plant 1 week or more after frost-free date)	Medium heat-tolerant (good for summer planting)	
Broccoli	Beets	Beans, snap	Beans, lima	Beans, all	Beets
Cabbage	Carrot	Okra	Eggplant	Chard	Collard
Lettuce	Chard	New Zealand spinach	Peppers	Soybean	Kale
Onions	Mustard	Soybean	Sweet potato	New Zealand spinach	Lettuce
Peas	Parsnip	Squash	Cucumber	Squash	Mustard
Potato	Radish	Sweet corn	Melons	Sweet corn	Spinach
Spinach		Tomato			Turnip
Turnip					

U.S. Department of Agriculture.

highly mineralized soil that is artificially fertilized. Their argument is that the standard varieties, developed over centuries, are superior to the new types when grown in suitable soil, meaning soil high in humus.

One new family of garden plants is the miniature plants. You can now purchase seeds for tiny carrots, tiny cabbages, lettuce, and so on. There is no doubt that they are useful if you want to play at gardening and if you want to have a variety of vegetables in a flower box. But when you match labor against crop volume, they are almost a waste of time. I was given some cherry tomato plants one season, and to avoid insulting my neighbor who gave them to me, I planted them. They grew well and formed large clusters of pretty tomatoes, but they took so long to pick, and their bushes took up as much space as full-size tomato plants, that there was no practical return. A couple of pounds of cherry tomatoes required a half hour of my time. I picked that much weight in tomatoes while merely passing by my full-size plants.

This is true of all the miniature plants. They are pretty and cute, but if you are seeking to fill the garden basket, plant one full-size plant in place of a half-dozen pip-squeaks.

SEEDS

So far as my experience goes, I have found the seeds of one seedsman no better or worse than that of another, but they do of course present different varieties of the same species.

Some of the seed companies are now offering seeds on a strip of cloth. They cost a little more but are worth the money when you are buying small seeds such as lettuce seeds. The tape or strip permits you to space the seeds evenly without overcrowding. Usually it is hard to drop fine seed into the soil at anything resembling regular intervals. Most of the time they just spill out of your hand. The tape disintegrates very rapidly, and so that is no problem. Incidentally, the first seed tape was patented June 22, 1915, by one W. N. McComb. What took it so long to come to market? (Birds pull the strip out—which is one reason, I recently discovered, why the strips took so long to come to market.)

You will note that most of the seed packets carry a date, usually reading "Packed for 19—." Don't let this bother you. If you have kept unused seeds dry, don't discard them if you still have them on hand a year, two, or even three years later. Just use more seeds, and then thin them out later on.

To be more scientific: Leek, onion, corn, salsify, parsley, parsnip, and rhubarb seeds usually will not germinate after 2 years. Asparagus, bean, cabbage, carrot, Brussels sprouts, cauliflower, kale, celery, lettuce, okra, peas, spinach, radish, turnip, and watermelon seeds are usually good for 3 years and sometimes as long

A LIST OF COMMON GARDEN VEGETABLES, THEIR COMPANIONS AND THEIR ANTAGONISTS

Vegetable	Likes	Dislikes
Asparagus	Tomatoes, parsley, basil	
Beans	Potatoes, carrots, cucumbers, cauliflower, cabbage, summer savory, most other vegetables and herbs	Onion, garlic, gladiolus
Pole beans	Corn, summer savory	Onions, beets, kohlrabi, sunflower
Bush beans	Potatoes, cucumbers, corn, strawberries, celery, summer savory	Onions
Beets	Onions, kohlrabi	Pole beans
Cabbage family (Cabbage, cauliflower, kale, kohlrabi, broccoli, Brussels sprouts)	Aromatic plants, potatoes, celery, dill, camomile, sage, peppermint, rosemary, beets, onions	Strawberries, tomatoes, pole beans
Carrots	Peas, leaf lettuce, chives, onions, leek, rosemary, sage, tomatoes	Dill
Celery	Leek, tomatoes, bush beans, cauliflower, cabbage	
Chives	Carrots	Peas, beans
Corn	Potatoes, peas, beans, cucumbers, pumpkin, squash	
Cucumbers	Beans, corn, peas, radishes, sunflowers	Potatoes, aromatic herbs
Tomato	Chives, onion, parsley, asparagus, marigold, nasturtium, carrot	Kohlrabi, potato, fennel, cabbage
Eggplant	Beans	
Peas	Carrots, turnips, radishes, cucumbers, corn, beans, most vegetables and herbs	Onions, garlic, gladiolus, potato
Squash	Nasturtium, corn	

A LIST OF COMMON GARDEN VEGETABLES, THEIR COMPANIONS AND THEIR ANTAGONISTS (Continued)

Vegetable	Likes	Dislikes
Onion (including garlic)	Beets, strawberries, tomato, lettuce, summer savory, camomile (parsley)	Peas, beans
Leek	Onions, celery, carrots	
Lettuce	Carrots and radishes (lettuce, carrots and radishes make a strong team grown together), strawberries, cucumbers	
Radish	Peas, nasturtium, lettuce, cucumbers	
Parsley	Tomato, asparagus	
Potato	Beans, corn, cabbage, horseradish (should be planted at corners of patch), marigold, eggplant (as a lure for Colorado potato beetle)	Pumpkin, squash, cucumber, sunflower, tomato, raspberry
Pumpkin	Corn	Potato
Soybeans	Grows with anything, helps everything	Potato
Strawberries	Bush bean, spinach, borage, lettuce (as a border)	Cabbage
Spinach	Strawberries	
Sunflower	Cucumbers	Potato
Turnip	Peas	

Taken from *The Basic Book of Organically Grown Foods,* by the editors of Organic Gardening and Farming, Rodale Press Book Division, Emmas, Pa., 1972.

as 5 years. The seeds of beets, cucumbers, eggplants, muskmelons and tomatoes are viable for more than 5 years if kept dry.

GROWING YOUR OWN SEED

You can if you wish let plants like radishes, onions, and cabbage go to seed and use the seeds for planting the following season. You can also, if you wish, dry tomatoes, cucumbers, muskmelons, and the like, and extract their seeds for future use. Whether or not the crop that results will match the original depends on whether or not the parent plant was cross-pollinated. Plants have no sexual inhibitions. They fool around a lot. When they do, their progeny, their seeds, show the effects of living it up. Some plants, as, for example, corn, cucumbers, melons, squash, pumpkin, cress, mustard, kohlrabi, kale, spinach, onion, radish, beet, and turnip readily cross-pollinate with plants of their own family. (Few vegetables do not.)

The result may be a wonderful new variety. More likely, the result will be an undesirable plant. One common example is radishes. If you do not pull radishes when they mature but let them go to seed, that is to say, let them form blossoms and later seeds, your garden will be plagued with wild radishes that are little better than weeds.

Intercropped lettuce, cucumber, string beans, and tomatoes. The lettuce is cut and used early in the season. The cucumbers and tomatoes do not trouble one another. The strings, however, do compete with the tomatoes for sunshine; so you have to limit the string beans you plant. The string beans help hold the tomato plants to the trellis.

Eggplant, pepper, tomato, carrot, celery, and chives do not cross-pollinate much. String beans, peas, okra, lettuce, muskmelon, and watermelon even less. However, the last two listed are the only ones that you can safely replant without much concern over developing a new, unwanted strain. Still, with two varieties of the same family close by each other, the seeds are usually not worth saving.

Therefore, unless you have time and farm space in which to experiment, don't trouble to save and dry vegetable seeds. The results will be unsatisfactory.

ANNUAL VS. PERENNIAL

There are advantages and disadvantages to both. The annuals produce more for any given space. The perennials require less work. For example, asparagus can't be harvested the first year, but will produce without very much attendance for as many as 50 years. At the same time asparagus returns aren't much to speak of. The

SUGGESTIONS FOR INTERCROPPING AND SUCCESSION PLANTING

Set early lettuce between tomato or potato plants.
Set early black radish between bean poles; plant more radish in the fall.
Follow beans with kale.
Follow beans with turnips.
Follow carrots with Chinese cabbage.
Follow early beets with escarole.
Follow mustard and Chinese cabbage with kohlrabi.
Follow early peas with cabbage or Brussels sprouts.
Interplant corn with pole beans.
Interplant corn with pumpkin or squash.
Mix pole beans and cucumbers on the same trellis.
Follow early peas with beans or late cabbage, celery, carrots, or beets.
Follow early corn with cabbage, broccoli, or lettuce.

Note: To stretch your double cropping or succession planting, start the second crop in seed flats and transplant when needed. Every plant that grows can be successfully transplanted, even corn.

U.S. Department of Agriculture bulletin recommends a row 50 to 75 feet long or 20 feet square for a family of five or six persons—providing the soil is well enriched. That is a lot of space to permanently give up to a single-crop-per-season vegetable. But once planted, that is it for 50 years. If you have the space (remember we stated that the bigger gardens are better), fine. If you are short on space and big on family, better think twice about tying up space with perennials.

Everbearing. Everbearing strawberries, everbearing raspberries, and so on are Jim Dandy when you have a lot of plants going for you. In place of a single crop ripening within a week or two, you have fruit ready to pick most of the season. However, a plant is not a machine. It cannot grow any more fruit over the season than it can at one time. Therefore, if you haven't set sufficient plants out, you will be picking a fraction of the total harvest at a time. This can be quite a nuisance, and if you don't pick enough for a meal, or at least enough for one bowl with cream for the farmer, it hardly seems worthwhile.

How much? You can't plant too much. You may make yourself and your family unhappy by planting more of one fruit than another, but don't hesitate to farm all your land.

Bear in mind you are growing soil as well as crops. Therefore, you are not removing soil nutrients when you sow. And whether you harvest your crop or not, and even if you forget about it in the middle of the growing season, your soil is benefiting by the growth of the plants, and even by whatever weeds may sneak in.

The more ground you put to seed, the less care you need take with any individual plant; the more you can lose to the weather and bugs and furry thieves and still harvest bountifully.

If you believe you may have too many vegetables at one time and want to stretch the harvest period out, there are several steps you can take.

One method is to plant a variety of each vegetable, taking care to select types with varying growth spans. For example, there is corn that ripens in 60 days, and corn that ripens in 80 days. There is squash that requires 90 days to mature, and squash that requires 120 days before it is ready for harvest.

Another method is to sow but a portion of your crop at a time. For example, if you are planning to sow twenty poles worth of string beans, sow five poles a week

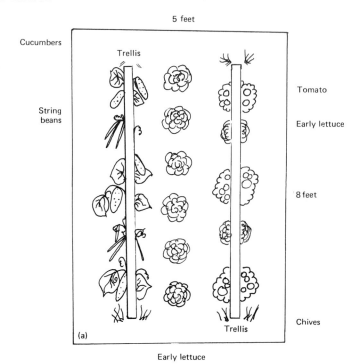

5 feet

Cucumbers

Trellis

Tomato

String
beans

Early lettuce

8 feet

Chives

(a)

Trellis

Early lettuce

Suggested layout for a small garden. By the time the plants growing on the trellises reach out, the lettuce will be harvested.

over a 4-week period. That will stretch your bean harvest over a like period. The same can be done with any plant that can be planted late and still mature.

Still another approach is to sow heavily and pick early. For example, plant Chinese radishes closer together than normal. Pick alternate radishes early, say when they are only 1 or 2 inches long. In this way, you thin the crop and harvest more over a longer period of time.

Another method you will probably use without thinking about it is to plant more than one vegetable. A variety of vegetables will in themselves spread your harvest over many weeks.

Should you be fortunate and reap a really huge harvest, you'll have no trouble in giving it away. Fresh farm fruits and vegetables are a most appreciated gift.

You may also give thought to the new marketing procedure rapidly becoming popular with small farmers on the fringe of cities. They do not pick and sell; they permit the customer to pick his own. It cuts down labor, helps keep the produce fresh to the last minute and, surprisingly, most people enjoy going into the fields and gathering their own. Farmers employing this sales method report that their customers are very careful not to harm the plants.

Vine vs. bush. Lima beans, string beans, and peas can be had in either bush or pole varieties. Some farmers believe that the bush varieties produce more per acre than the vine varieties. This may be true. However, it is difficult to mulch the bush

16 feet

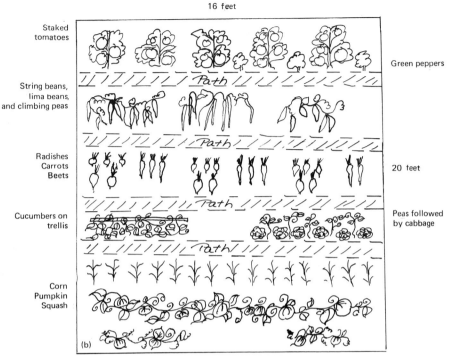

Staked tomatoes

Green peppers

String beans, lima beans, and climbing peas

Radishes
Carrots
Beets

20 feet

Cucumbers on trellis

Peas followed by cabbage

Corn
Pumpkin
Squash

(b)

Suggested layout for a 16 by 20-foot garden.

types because you have to mulch a lot of small bushes. And the bush type requires considerable bending. The vines are easily mulched and save you a lot of knee work. But they require poles. And when you have set out a lot of poles in your backyard, people may say you live in the sticks. (This is how the term originated.)

WHAT GOES WHERE

Run your rows north and south if you have an all-day sun. Doing so will prevent the rows from shading each other.

Plant your cool weather crops in the shaded portions of your land if you do not have sunlight all day long.

When you must run your rows east and west, plant the heat-loving crops such as corn and tomatoes to the western side of the land. This will give them more exposure to the afternoon sun, which is hotter than the morning sun.

Plant your perennials where there will never be any need to move them. Each time they are replanted, you lose one or two crops.

Keep like plants together. Most (corn especially) do best in their own company. Grouping also makes caring for them easier.

Plant your quick-growing crops in your best soil. The others may be placed elsewhere with usually less loss of flavor and texture.

QUICK GUIDE TO CROP SELECTION

Cool weather crops for spring and fall
  Broccoli
  Lettuce
  Radish
  Spinach
  Turnip
  Pea
Maximum yield for space and labor
  Tomatoes
  Bush snap beans
  Lettuce
  Zucchini
  Carrots
  Beets
  Onion sets
Easiest to grow
  Bush beans

Beets	Radish
Corn	Rutabaga
Cucumbers	Squash
Leaf lettuce	Swiss chard
Pumpkin	Turnip

Seeds to be started indoors (in Northern areas)
  Peppers
  Tomatoes
  Broccoli
  Cabbage
  Cauliflower
  Eggplant
  Head lettuce
Quickest crop

Radish—22 days	Bush snap beans—48 days
Scallions—40 days	Summer squash—50 days
Loosehead lettuce—40 days	Early peas—55 days
Spinach—42 days	Kohlrabi—55 days
Turnip—45 days	Swiss chard—60 days

Window box crops
  Tomato
  Leaf lettuce
  Bush snap beans

Plant chives and other herbs in borders and empty corners.

Plant squash and pumpkins alongside a lawn. Let them wander onto the grass during the growing season. In this way the plants will get the growing space they need while utilizing very little bare-earth space.

CHAPTER FOURTEEN

Growing Aids

T HERE ARE ANY number of gadgets and devices you can make to help your plants grow. The most useful and probably therefore the most common is a trellis. A formal trellis can be quite a bit of work, but the kind we use in our garden doesn't have to be more than a gridwork of sticks.

MAKING TRELLISES

Almost any material can be used: furring strips from the lumber yard, garden poles purchased from a garden supply shop, tree branches, poles and string, poles and wire screen, pipe and wire, and anything else you can think of.

If you have to purchase your material from a lumber yard, first check whether they have oak or hickory strips for sale. Yards that cut a lot of oak often save the 1 × 1 or 1 × 2 strips for sale to backyard farmers. Oak isn't the most rot-resistant wood, but of all the species of wood usually available, it is the best compromise between cost, resistance, and strength. California redwood and cypress are more rot-resistant, but the redwood is very expensive, and the cypress is too soft.

If the yard doesn't have leftover strips for sale at reduced prices, ask for furring. This is rough-cut fir and just about the least expensive lumber you can buy. Use 1 × 3 for the vertical pieces and 1 × 2 (inches) for the horizontal strips. Drive the vertical strips in with their flat sides parallel to one another. Position them about 6 to 8 feet apart. Make a series of notches on each vertical strip's sides about 1½ feet

Cutting fir for use in making a trellis. This is the least expensive wood at the present time. If you paint the portion that enters the ground, the wood will last half a dozen years or so.

Using 2 and 4-inch fir to make a trellis. Notches cut in vertical members support crossbars. One nail will hold them in place. Vines can be guided up between crossbars.

The easiest way to join wood for making garden trellises and the like is by wiring the pieces together. Wired sticks are also much easier to take apart than nailed sticks.

apart on alternate edges. Rest the horizontal pieces in these notches, and hold them fast with a single, long, galvanized finishing nail partially driven in. This makes it easy to take the trellis apart for the winter.

As an alternative, paint the lower 1½ feet of the vertical strips before you drive them into the earth. This will reduce their proclivity to rot. Any paint will help; none will prevent rot.

Pulling the trellis out of the ground each year will extend its life by a number of years. It also makes for a neat-appearing farm. If you leave your trellis in place, the bottoms will rot away in 3 or 4 years. When they do, drive a short length of whatever wood you have alongside, and nail the extension onto the old board.

Assuming that furring strips are not available and you have to make your purchase at a garden shop, be advised that oak is easily recognized by its coarse pores and sour smell. Also that pine isn't too bad a material for making a growing aid, but that maple is positively terrible. Maple is a very hard wood with an attractive grain having small pores. As hard as it may be, it will rot right through before a single growing season is over, and your trellis and plants will fall down.

Pine can be nailed fairly easily; just hold a flat stone behind the boards (backup) when you try to nail them together. Oak is the very devil to nail. The better method with oak is to wire it together. Use medium-weight galvanized iron wire (baling wire to farmers) and a pair of pliers. A couple of turns and a twist will do it.

The same technique is useful for making a trellis or anything else out of branches. Each branch is chopped free of side arms, and if you want to splice two lengths together, cut a flat on the mating surfaces first.

The trellis illustrated and described has a space up between the horizontal members through which the plants can be guided. It saves some tying, but as stated, it should be removed from the earth each fall.

The tent-shaped trellis is another design that has the advantage of not requiring that its poles be driven into the earth. It is made of two wood grids which are angled one against the other to form a flat-sided tent with an angle of about 20° where the two sides meet. The tops of the poles can be tied together. The assembly just rests on the earth. However, if you are in high-wind country, drive a few stakes into the earth, and wire the trellis legs to the stakes.

The disadvantage of the narrow trellis first described is that the plant can grow only along its width. If you are growing tomatoes, you have to guide the arms back to the trellis. If they are permitted to extend directly out from the support, the plant's arms will fall down and fold. This cuts off the plant's circulation, and that section stops growing.

The disadvantage of the tent trellis is that the space nearest the bottom is too much for the young plants to reach; so with this design you have to use short stakes with each plant. Though, if you are growing cucumbers or squash, you can set out two rows, one under each side of the trellis.

Both trellis designs are made to stand about 6 feet high when in place.

STAKING ARRANGEMENTS

The single stake is common enough. It is simply pointed at one end and driven into the ground for a foot or so. When you are working with branches, drive them into the ground upside down: that is, with their thin ends pointing downward. By doing so you will find it is easier to pound them in.

The single stake is fast and economical. Unfortunately, when it is used for tomatoes, you end up with a hanging plant. The tie support is directly under each limb, and the limbs or branches just hang down. You will get more tomatoes from a plant on a trellis than on a single stake. You'll get even more if you let the plant raggle all over the earth, but unless you support the individual fruit, each will rot where it touches the ground.

Tent trellis used for tomatoes. Plants are set along both sides of the "tent." Some farmers use a large bolt at the apex of the triangle so that the trellis can be folded for storage over the winter.

An alternative to the single stake is the teepee arrangement. Three or four stakes are driven into the earth around the circumference of a circle about 2 feet in diameter. The tops of the stakes are brought together and tied. A single tomato plant can be placed in the center. The teepee design provides a better spread for the plant's arms and is much sturdier.

A strong wind following a heavy, earth-softening rain will often topple single stakes burdened by a mass of growth. Under the same adverse conditions, the cluster of stakes will remain standing. You can use much thinner stakes with the cone arrangement than you can with the single stake alone. Each stake in the group supports its fellows.

STRING SUPPORTS

When you don't have enough stakes to take care of all your climbing creatures, use string. Drive two or more stout stakes into the earth about 6 feet apart. Run a heavy string or wire from the top of one stake to the next. Then tie string at 6-inch intervals to the horizontal string. Let the tied-on strings hang down to the earth. When completed you will have a curtain of string, each about 6 inches from its neighbors. Now sow your beans, or what have you, along a line between the stakes. When the beans emerge, tie each string lightly to each plant. The plants will climb up on their own.

It is good practice to tie the tops of all single stakes, standing a distance apart, together with strong string. This provides additional climbing room for the vines and serves to brace the stakes against the wind.

WIRE MESH SUPPORTS

Wire mesh is wire screen with large openings. The type most useful for farming has fairly heavy wire, with openings about 3 inches square, and is available with a dipped rubber covering. It has a multitude of applications.

You can use the screen for vine crops. In which case the screen is stood on edge and tied to stakes driven into the earth. The vines just climb right up. Used this way you can have a bean vine every 6 inches of horizontal length of screen. For vines, the screen should be about 6 feet wide, making for a 6-foot height. If this width is unavailable, use two narrow widths.

For use with tomatoes or peppers a length of screen is rolled into a tube, and the tube is stood on end with the plant at the center of the opening. As the plant grows, it stretches its limbs through the openings in the screen. For peppers use screen that is about 3 feet wide, making a 3-foot-high tube. For tomatoes use wider screen. To make a 1-foot-in-diameter tube and provide some overlap, you need about 4 feet of screen.

The tubed screen will prevent the plants from falling down and being blown over by the wind, but you must fasten each screen to the earth with a stake to prevent the wind from lifting the plant and the screen.

WALKS

The practical, easy-does-it approach is to simply confine your steps to one path in the hope that doing so will discourage grass and weeds. If you have plenty of mulch, you probably won't be troubled by weeds in your paths. If you don't have

Self-supporting trellis made of wire mesh rolled to make a cylinder. One or two tomato vines planted within the cylinder will make their own way without much assistance. *(Courtesy W. Atlee Burpee Co.)*

any mulch to spare on your paths, you can cover the path with whatever flat stones you can scrounge. Or, to be neat but not economical, you can pave your walk with 2-inch concrete block. These are 2 inches thick by 6 by 18 inches in outline. Or you can lay down a layer of roofing. The best for the purpose is known as "starter." It is a 1-foot-wide roll of heavy tar paper which will last a year or two and keep your paths clear without attention.

BORDERS

Vegetable-bed borders will help you conserve mulch and help you keep track of your seed when you first plant it. You won't need to lay down string or other guides to keep you from walking accidentally over everything.

The simplest and least expensive way is to make them of furring strips. Use 1 by 3-inch or 1 by 4-inch material. Cut the boards to length, and nail them together to make rectangles. Lay the rectangles on the earth. Remove whatever soil is necessary to make the wood forms lie flat along their entire perimeters. Next cut a number of 1-foot-long stakes. Drive them into the soil alongside the wood frames. Nail the stakes to the frames, and then cut the stake tops flush with the top edges of the frames. Lying on the earth this way, a wood frame will last 3 or 4 years before it rots so badly that it has to be replaced.

Making garden borders from furring strips.

Completed border. Note peg at corner that holds border in place.

An expensive alternative is to make the borders from either concrete block or common brick. Start by laying out the border with stakes and string. Dig a trench alongside the string. Set the blocks or bricks in the trench. Line them up neatly with the aid of the string. Fill in with earth, and tamp firmly in place. The block and brick will not remain perfectly aligned for more than a season or two. But they won't rot, and crooked or straight, they look attractive.

CHAPTER FIFTEEN

Direct and Indirect Planting

Y OU CAN PLACE your seeds directly within the earth of your farm and let nature take them from there, or you can start your seeds in temporary beds, and when the seeds have germinated and grown to suitable size, they are moved to their permanent homes.

Seeds are sown directly when their time to maturity will comfortably fit within the growing season and when a large number of plants are desired. There's lots less work to sowing seeds directly. The per-seed return is higher, and harvests are identical with those produced by like seeds indirectly planted.

When the desired plants cannot complete their harvest cycle outdoors, or when two successive crops are to be fitted within a growing season that can chronologically accommodate little more than one, the indirect method is used. That is, the seeds are started under cover and later transplanted.

The indirect method, starting seeds indoors and then transplanting the seedlings, requires a lot more time and effort. However, there is no other practical way of securing the same results; so that is the way it is done.

DIRECT PLANTING

This procedure is simple enough. The mulch remaining on the surface of the earth after winter has passed is pushed aside. If you are going to plant a row of seeds, open a space about 3 inches wide and as long as your planned row of seeds. If you are going to plant a single seed or a group, clear a space about 3 inches in diameter or 3 inches larger in diameter than your group of seeds. Very simply, you do not want the mulch up against your plants but you do want about 2 to 3 inches of clear space around each growing plant.

Seed depth is more or less based on seed size. The exact depth varies with soil condition, seed type, and the agronomist you are reading. When the soil is light, you can plant your seeds a little deeper than usual. When the soil is tight, it is better to plant the seeds closer to the soil's surface. Some books advise that the seeds be planted four times their diameter; others that the seeds be planted no more than two times their diameter. Personally, I find the seeds do best in my soil when planted to a depth of approximately two times their diameter. There are, however, certain exceptions. Tomato seeds are more than a quarter of an inch in diameter (across the flat side) but no more than paper thin. Such seeds are always planted at a depth of no more than a quarter of an inch—just enough soil to hide them from the light.

When you need to hold seed depth to a quarter of an inch, scratch a shallow groove in the soil, drop the seeds in the specified distance apart, and cover them by letting dry soil sift down from between your fingers upon them.

Afterward the soil is gently tamped firm with a small block of wood or your palm. The purpose of the tamping is to make the soil contact the seed firmly so that water from the soil readily enters the seed. The soil is not packed hard.

Seeds having eyes, as for example beans, do best when they are buried with their eyes down. But, if you have lots of bean seeds to plant, don't trouble to turn each one eye down. It doesn't make that much difference.

Place the individual seeds and the rows of seed just as far apart as recommended. Generally the individual spacing is calculated to account for those plants that will be removed during the thinning out process, and for those plants that will be lost to bugs and other creatures and the few seeds that will not germinate. In any event, it is better to sow a few more seeds than necessary just to cover all contingencies and still have the number of plants you want.

When sowing instructions call for the seeds to be placed in a "hill," plant them in a circle about 6 or so inches across. Do not literally form the earth into a little hill and seed the hill. This may have been done in the past, but unless you have a moist growing period, the little hill of soil will quickly dry out, and the seeds will be bereft of water.

When planting very fine seeds such as those of the onion, mix the seeds with some sand to help you sow them evenly.

The standard practice is to water the freshly sown seed as soon as they are covered. A very fine spray must be used, or the seeds will be washed out of the earth. An alternative, and possibly a better method, is to soak the soil thoroughly before sowing. If you water after planting, you have to water ever so gently, especially with fine seed covered with only a sift of soil. This limits the quantity of water you can lay down at one time, and so you have to water several times the first day to make certain that the rest of the earth will not soak up most of your water.

INDIRECT PLANTING

When seeds are started in one place, as for example indoors or in a cold frame, and then moved into the field, the method is called indirect planting.

There are two problems that almost always attend indirect planting. They are damping off and watering. Both can be solved with a little care.

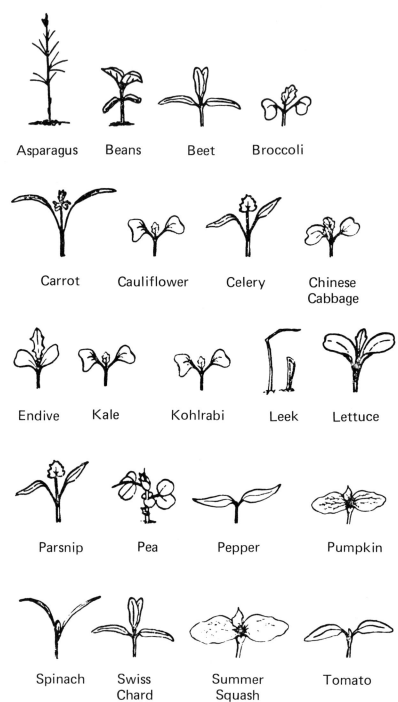

Asparagus   Beans   Beet   Broccoli

Carrot   Cauliflower   Celery   Chinese Cabbage

Endive   Kale   Kohlrabi   Leek   Lettuce

Parsnip   Pea   Pepper   Pumpkin

Spinach   Swiss Chard   Summer Squash   Tomato

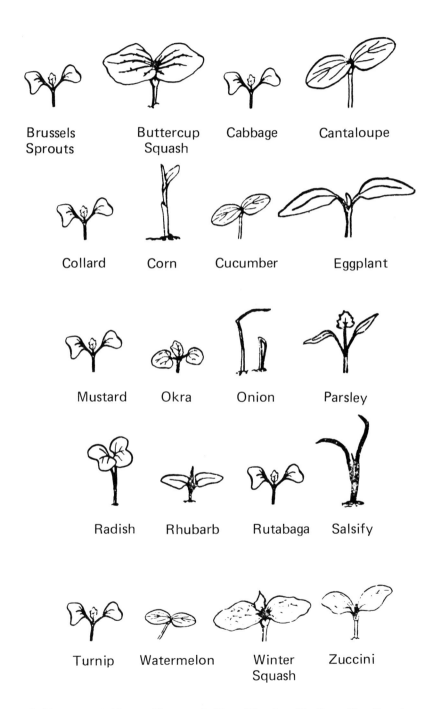

Brussels Sprouts   **Buttercup Squash**   **Cabbage**   **Cantaloupe**

Collard   **Corn**   **Cucumber**   **Eggplant**

Mustard   **Okra**   **Onion**   **Parsley**

Radish   **Rhubarb**   **Rutabaga**   **Salsify**

Turnip   **Watermelon**   **Winter Squash**   **Zuccini**

Guide to vegetable seedling recognition. *(Courtesy Northrup King Corp.)*

Planting pea seeds directly in the field where they will remain for the season.

Damping off is a farm term used for the damage done seedlings by fungus. Fungi, as you may know, are present everywhere. Their seeds or spores travel on the wind. There is no escaping fungus in this atmosphere. Fertile soil, as is to be expected and as is necessary, is rife with it. When seeds send out their young, thin shoots, the fungus attacks near the surface of the soil. The plant's hair-thick stem shrivels in a narrow band near the ground. The plant topples over and dies; there is no cure.

Outdoors, under the driving power of the sun, which forces the young plant or seedling to grow quickly and which inhibits the growth of fungus, damping off is not a problem. Indoors, where the young seedlings are thin, weak, and spindly, even with the aid of sun lamps, fungus can completely ruin crop after crop of seedlings. The plants emerge fine, but droop and die soon afterward.

There is no cure, but prevention is fairly easy: Eliminate the fungus, or reduce it to an insignificant factor. This is done by sterilizing the earth in which the seeds are planted or substituting a sterile medium such as sand, vermiculite, or sphagnum moss. There are also commercially compounded mixtures that may include all three mentioned substances including the moss, which is generally chopped up into fine particles. If you use a commercial starting mixture, make certain it is a seed starter and not potting soil, which is simply ordinary, but fertile soil.

The difficulty you may encounter with watering is keeping the starting medium moist but not wet. To eliminate the daily attention that would otherwise be necessary, cover your pots or flats with a sheet of clear plastic of the kind used in the kitchen. This will prevent moisture loss. The cover can be left in place until the seedlings touch the plastic with their tops. Or you can make some holes in your pots or flats, and set them in larger pans having an inch or so of water.

STERILE GROWING MEDIUMS

Ordinary sand or vermiculite, both of which can be purchased in a mason supply yard (vermiculite is used as an insulator) can be used as a starting soil or medium if you sterilize it by placing it in a 400° oven for an hour or two and mixing the material frequently to make certain everything is hot. After cooling, store the soil in tightly closed plastic bags to keep the fungi out. Sphagnum moss needs no treatment. It appears to be able to inhibit the growth of fungi by some chemical method without assistance. The chopped form is best for starting seeds.

To make starting soil, which has a special value that will shortly be discussed, mix one part light, fertile soil to about three parts sand or vermiculite or a mixture of the two. Sterilize by the aforementioned heat treatment, and store in a sealed container until needed. Or mix a little soil with a lot of moss after the soil has been sterilized.

Two-step starting. A container is filled to the depth of an inch with a level layer of sand, vermiculite, or moss. Then water is added to a level of about ½ inch from the

Emerging tomato plants. These will have to be pricked out and thinned. (*Courtesy Ferry-Morse Seed Co.*)

Pricking out cucumber seedlings.

bottom. The seeds are sown about 1 inch apart and covered with just enough of the growing medium to completely hide them. A cover is placed over the container to retain the moisture. So long as the cover is in place, no water has to be added.

When the seeds have germinated and the seedlings have grown to a height of about 1 inch, they are "pricked" out with a small, flat stick and moved to a second home. This must be done before the seedling exhausts all the energy remaining in its seed. There is very little nutrient in the water; if you let the seedling remain in the sterile, empty sand or vermiculite (or moss), it will grow weak and die.

The seedling's second home can be standard, light, and fertile soil, or it can be a starting mixture, which makes for easier and faster growth. The soil is kept moist by careful watering. The second flat or pot should have soil to a depth of 2 inches or thereabouts.

In their second home the seedlings are permitted to grow large enough to be transplanted safely outdoors. This point in time is not at all critical. So long as each plant has at least four leaves, it is large enough to be moved; but you can let it grow as large as you wish or until it is convenient for you to commence the transplant operation.

About a week before this time, use a spatula or a knife to cut the soil around the seedlings (assuming they are not in separate containers) into squares: one to each plant. This forces the roots to head downward and makes it easier to separate the plants later on. At the same time the process of hardening off is begun. This consists of reducing the quantity of water supplied to the plants and placing them outside in the sun for longer periods of time each succeeding day. Doing so literally hardens the plants and makes them better able to withstand the transition to their permanent home in the fields.

One step-starting. The seeds are sown in the starting mixture previously discussed; that is to say a combination of sterile soil, sand, vermiculite, and/or sphagnum moss. The seeds are no more than covered but spaced far enough apart

Summer squash seedlings being separated with a knife to force their roots to head back and down.

Summer squash seedlings ready for transplanting.

to enable them to grow large enough for transplanting without interference from their neighbors. There should be at least 2 inches of soil in the container; but there is no need for more than 3.

Keep the growing mixture moist by either covering the container with a cover of some sort or by making holes in its bottom and placing it in a larger container with about ½ inch of water.

When the seedlings have grown to size, divide the earth that they share into equal portions, and give them a week or so of hardening off. Then transplant.

The single-step system has the advantage of less plant handling and therefore less labor and plant damage. However, each plant must be furnished with its own glob of sterilized starting mixture, which goes into the earth with the plant. With the two-step method you can get by with an inch of sterile sand. When you are starting a lot of plants each season, it can be an important saving.

A few pointers. The temperature of the starting medium, whatever it may be, must be suited to the seeds you are starting. Although the seeds of plants that are cold-hardy, as for example onion and lettuce, will germinate in cool soil, they will do so very slowly. It is best to keep the soil with these seeds up around 70°F. The seeds of plants that are cold-sensitive such as tomato and lima bean require a higher starting soil temperature. These seeds should be in soil around 75 to 80°F, with hybrid tomato seeds at 80°F preferably. If you allow lima bean seeds to remain in soil below 70°F, they will germinate so very slowly that they may rot because of fungi spores on their surface, even if there are no spores in the sterile growing medium.

The germinating seeds may be kept in the dark until they germinate and send forth tendrils. At this time they should be placed in direct sunlight, if possible, and if only for a few hours. An electric sun lamp is a useful substitute, but not as good.

If you are starting seeds for the first time, sow heavily and be prepared for failure. It takes a little time to learn when to water, when to prick out, and how to do it without damaging the seedlings.

STARTING CONTAINERS

A variety of different containers are used for starting and growing seedlings. They include fiber pots or planters, soil pellets, flats, and flowerpots. Each type has its own good reason for being used.

Fiber pots are made of material that is supposed to decompose rapidly once it is beneath the soil. Therefore, there is no need to remove a plant from a fiber pot: The entire pot may be planted, with only the plant and its stem emergent. This saves plant handling and plant damage.

Fiber pots can be purchased in garden supply shops in sizes ranging from 1½ inches upward. The pots have a number of advantages in addition to the one just discussed. As the pots are fibrous, they are easily watered by setting them in a pan of water. You don't have to watch their water level very carefully, and as the water is absorbed from below, damping off is discouraged.

On the other hand, there is the cost of the one-time-use pots, which can mount up, and the need to start more than one seed in each pot to make certain you have the desired number of healthy plants, or to start more pots than you need.

Also, despite literature to the contrary, fiber pots do restrict root growth. You will find that your transplants do better if you remove them from the fiber pots before you set them out. The fiber is definitely a root and moisture barrier.

Tomato seedlings grown in fiber containers. Setting them in a plate makes it easier to keep them watered.

Cucumber seedlings grown in soil pellets. It is advisable to cut the plastic net holding the pellet together before transplanting.

Soil pellets are small, flat buttons composed of compressed fiber, nutrients, and other substances. Each pellet is designed to accommodate a single seed. The pellet is placed in water and permitted to soak up as much as it will. Then the seed is dropped into the hole on top, and a little fiber is pulled over. The seed sprouts and sends its roots through the swollen pellet. When a lot of roots are exposed, it is time to plant the pellet, seedling and all. The pellets are excellent, but they aren't cheap and you cannot stall with transplanting. Once a lot of roots are outside the bundle of fibers, the plant must be set out. If you work with fair-sized pots you have a lot more time, if you wish it, before setting the plants out.

A flat is simply a shallow container. It can be made of wood, metal, or plastic. You can purchase plastic flats designed and constructed for growing seedlings, or you can use whatever plastic dishes you have handy, or you can fabricate your own flats from scrap lumber or even cardboard. There is little difference in growing results. The only difference is that the plastic flats last longer.

Generally a flat is about 2 to 3 inches high (depth) and 12 by 18 inches in size, but you can make your own flats any size you find convenient.

Each flat holds a considerable number of seeds, and if this is your first try, it is advisable to sow the seeds in neat rows. Otherwise you may not be able to differentiate between crop plants and weeds. It is also advisable to sow many more seeds than you need the first time around. In following years when you are better able to estimate your losses you need not overplant as much.

Thinning out. When you have garnered a little experience, you will not need to overplant very much and so will have to do very little thinning out in the flats. But at first, you may have to. Do it so soon as you are certain which plants are growing strong. Then do not pull the unwanted plants out if they are close to their neighbors, but cut them short with your thumbnail.

Just how much space you should leave depends on when you plan to transplant. If you are transplanting early and are going to use small plants, a couple of inches or less between individual plants is all you need. If you plan on transplanting relatively late, leave more space between plants. The exact amount is unimportant; just bear in mind that a little more space does no harm; too little will force you to damage a lot of roots when you transplant.

Hardening off. A week or more before you transplant [and you should not do this before each plant has at least four leaves (two true leaves)], reduce the quantity of water you are supplying the plants and move them outdoors, preferably into the sun, for a few hours each day. This toughens the plants, gets them accustomed to the cooler air, and accelerates their growth. At the same time, use an old knife or spatula to cut the flat into little squares; one square to each plant. Doing so separates the roots of the individual plants and reduces the shock that each plant suffers when it is moved from its warm indoor home outdoors into strange, cold soil and air. Each cut in the soil of the flat also acts as a root barrier and forces the plant to turn its roots downward and inward and confine them to its own individual square bit of earth. Plants grown in pellets and pots, of course, do not need to be cut apart, but they too must be hardened before setting out.

The amount of time that the plants spend outdoors isn't critical. The less temperature difference that exists between indoors and out, the shorter the hardening period. A week for the most abrupt change is probably sufficient. Just be certain you don't forget them and the frost does them in. And if you are running late and the weather is fine and you have extra plants, you can skip the hardening period and chance you will lose no more than a few.

You can make your own growing flats from a cardboard box by cutting it and giving it several coats of varnish.

To protect young plants against cold weather and the wind, paper and plastic bags, often called hotkaps, are sometimes placed over them. These act like tiny greenhouses and keep the plants safe through mild frosts.

WHEN TO SOW, WHEN TO TRANSPLANT

There are no hard and fast rules as to indirect sowing time. Just bear in mind that if you are using the two-step method you will probably lose a week of growing time while the diminutive plant becomes accustomed to its new home.

The general rule is to allow 6 to 8 weeks for germination and seedling growth. Therefore you must time your indoor sowing date from the first day in the season that you believe will be safe for the specie you are growing. If you are growing tomatoes, for example, which are cold-sensitive, you will want to have your seedlings ready about one week after the last day of spring frost. For other plants with other proclivities, other seed starting days are easily computed.

The growth of your seeds will depend on seed variety and species and soil temperature. Most seeds germinate well at soil temperatures between 70 and 80°F, and most seedlings do best between 60 and 75: the cold-hardy species preferring the lower temperature range, and the warm-weather crops preferring the higher temperature range. So, if your basement or cellar is cold, you can expect the plants to take the full 8 weeks and more to come to transplanting size. If it is warm, figure on less time.

One point to bear in mind when timing your seedlings is that only the cold-hardy plants will grow appreciably in cool and cold weather. The others will just hang in there. So there is little point to risking crop loss by rushing the season too much.

TRANSPLANTING

A hole is dug in the soil where each plant is to be set out. The hole should be large enough and deep enough to easily encompass the roots and accompanying soil of each plant. The spaces between the plant's block of soil and the side of the hole are filled, and all is tamped firm. Then the plant's roots are given a good soaking, and if the ground is moist, that is all there is to it. If there hasn't been a fair amount of rain recently, it is advisable to rewater each plant thoroughly every day afterward until it does rain.

To facilitate watering it is good practice to set the plants a few inches deeper than they were when in the flats and then to form a cuplike depression in the soil around each stem. In this way you can provide each plant with half a quart of water each time you take the watering can or hose to it.

Some old-timers let their tomato seedlings go to a height of 2 feet or more. Then they submerge the plant in a foot-deep hole. The theory being that the deep-rooted tomato plant will never run out of water. It doesn't work out that way. Dig these deep-plant tomatoes up in the fall, and you will find that the plant has reduced its underground stem to a couple of inches: The deep-planted tomato's roots look like those of a normally planted tomato.

Another theory for improving one's tomato crop requires that the lower half of the entire plant be buried at an angle. Tilt-planting supposedly produces a long, horizontal main root from which more smaller roots than usual can and do grow. The tilted, aboveground portion of the plant soon straightens itself up. Whether or not this technique produces a better tomato crop cannot be proven by this farmer, but many backyard farmers swear by it.

Some gardeners believe they can help their transplants survive the shock of moving by watering them with a weak solution of fertilizer dissolved in water. This too is a moot question, but you might want to try it on a few plants. Use about 1 tablespoon of mixed fertilizer to a gallon of water. My thinking is that the use of a rich soil for starting eliminates this need and provides just the right amount of plant food without any danger of fertilizer burn or shock.

COLD FRAMES AND HOTBEDS

A cold frame is a low, glass-topped structure that serves as a way station for seedlings on their way from the flats to their permanent home in the outdoor ground. In a large sense a cold frame is a small greenhouse. A hotbed is not an arena for sexual activists but merely a cold frame with steam heat, or any other source of heat.

You can convert a wooden garden border into a cold frame by covering it with a sheet of plastic. A couple of laths and nails will hold the plastic in place.

Cold frame construction. A cold frame is easily constructed from four pieces of wood and either a transparent sheet of plastic or a window sash, which is a wood frame fitted with glass. The boards are fastened together to form a square or rectangle with a sloping top. The sash or sheet of plastic is fastened by a hinge to the high-ended side. The frame is set a few inches into the earth, preferably backed up against the south side of a wall or fence for wind protection. If you have a choice, use cypress, redwood, chestnut, or oak, in that order, for the frame. Use boards at least 1 inch thick, but better they be 2 inches thick; they will last that much longer. Make the high side of the frame about 1½ feet high and the low side about 1 foot high. Cut the board lengths to make a square or rectangle that is a fraction of an inch smaller than the covering sash or plastic sheet.

Some farmers replace the soil found inside the cold frame with a thick layer of gravel topped by soil suitable for starting plants. The gravel is there to provide adequate drainage. Some let the original soil be.

Using the cold frame. In the spring, plants started indoors in a flat or pot are brought out to the cold frame for further growth and hardening. Either the entire flat is laid inside the cold frame or the plants themselves are moved from the flats and planted in the soil inside the frame.

While the temperature within the cold frame is usually higher than that of the surrounding air, it is not always higher. Cold-frame temperature is dependent on sunlight and earth temperature. In all the states excepting Alaska, subsoil temperature is always higher than surface temperature, and so a little warmth enters the cold frame from below. Sunlight entering through the glass or plastic is trapped inside and adds tremendously to the heat. It is not unusual to have 70°F inside the frame and 30° or lower outside. However, should a number of sunless days go by with the air temperature much below freezing, it is quite possible for the temperature within the frame to also go below freezing.

The point of all this explanation is to point out that you cannot assume that a cold frame always has an inside temperature above freezing. It is a good practice to install a thermometer inside the frame for quick reference.

During sunny days the cold frame cover is lifted an inch or so to admit air and release moisture. After sunset the cover is closed to conserve heat. As no rain falls inside the frame, the plants, whether in flats or growing in the base soil itself, must be watered. However, since there is little air circulation, it is best to go easy on the water.

In midsummer and later, the cold frame can be used for starting and growing plants that are to be set out in the fall. During this time the frame's cover should be kept open all the time to prevent overheating the winter-hardy plants.

During the winter months the cold frame can be used to store root crops such as carrots and potatoes. The bottom of the frame is covered with a layer of straw or leaves. The vegetables are placed on top and covered with another layer of insulating material.

A hotbed is used exactly the same way as a cold frame. It differs only in that it is provided with some form of artificial heat, which makes it independent of air temperature and ensures a frost-free interior.

Various methods and gimmicks can be used to provide the heat. When horses were in favor, the common method was to excavate the frame to a depth of a couple of feet and fill the space with fresh manure. As the manure decomposed it produced considerable heat.

Today you can heat your cold frame with electricity. You can purchase a cold frame complete with a thermostatically controlled electric heating element. You can rig up your own thermostat and some heating wire, or simply place a couple of 100-watt bulbs inside the frame and turn them on at night.

A less costly method of providing heat consists of backing the cold frame up to a basement window. Heat escaping from the house warms the cold frame and converts it into a hotbed.

Hotbed use. Since the temperature within a hotbed is always above freezing, you can start your seeds inside, no matter (almost) what the air temperature may be. Since the seedlings will be exposed to direct sunlight, they will grow faster and stronger than they would if grown indoors.

Hotbeds can also be used to grow short-term plants such as radishes to maturity during the cold months and without transplanting. However, if you are seriously thinking of family-size winter harvests, you have to have a fairly large hotbed, which then becomes a greenhouse. This is not a criticism of hotbeds, but a touch of reality. You can't grow very much under the usual 2 by 4-foot window sash, but it is fun to grow what little you can.

Practical considerations. If you have a basement or a windowsill where you can grow a flat or two of seedlings, there is really little need for a cold frame or even a hotbed.

CHAPTER SIXTEEN

The Vegetables

THE VEGETABLES AND their culture described in the following are by no means all the vegetables grown in the United States for food and flavor, and very possibly do not include some of your favorites. But they are those most popular with backyard farmers and are fairly easy to grow.

The vegetables are discussed in alphabetical order for reference convenience and no other reason.

Farm supply companies that will be glad to send you free catalogs for the asking:

Geo. W. Park Seed Co. Inc., Greenwood, S.C. 29647
W. Atlee Burpee Co., 300 Park Ave., Warminster, Pa. 18974
Kelly Bros. Nurseries, Inc., Dansville, N.Y. 14437
Stark Bros. Nurseries, Louisiana, Missouri 63353
Jackson & Perkins Co., Medford, Oreg. 97501
Van Bourgondien Bros., 245 Farmingdale Rd., Rt. 109, Babylon, N.Y. 11702
Lakeland Nurseries Sales, Hanover, Pa. 17331
Spring Hill Nurseries, Tipp City, Ohio 45371
Joseph Harris Co., Inc., Moreton Farm, Rochester, N.Y. 14624

Asparagus

Cold-hardy perennial.
pH 6.4 to 7.6.
Highly fertile, sandy loam.

Start with one-year old crowns (roots).
Plant 6 weeks before last spring frost 8 inches deep, 18 inches apart.
Yields about 1 pound per year per plant.
Mary Washington is the preferred variety.

Asparagus can be started from seed, but as crowns are readily available in nurseries and each plant lasts for decades, their cost is nominal.

Asparagus prefers cold winters, and best yields will be secured in the northern states. It also prefers well-fertilized sandy loam, but the plant is tough and will grow in almost any soil that isn't water-logged and sour.

Generally the plants are set out in a single, long row. However, they will do as well in a number of short rows if the rows are 4 feet apart (center of one plant to the next). If space is limited, the plants can be set closer, but never less than 18 inches apart.

Planting and cultivation. Dig a trench about 10 inches deep and 14 inches wide. Take the soil you have removed, and mix it with well-rotted manure—as much as you can afford. Spread and firm a 4-inch-thick layer of the mixed soil along the bottom of the trench, thus, reducing the trench depth to 6 inches or so. Set out the plants, crowns up and roots outstretched like resting octopi, and cover them with an inch or two of the manure-soil mix. Tamp lightly, and water. When the crowns send up shoots, add more soil mix and cover them. Repeat as the shoots ascend until the trench is completely filled.

If you have compost (humus) and no manure, use it the same way. If you have neither compost nor manure, dig the trench to a depth of only 6 inches. Set out the plants as before, and cover them with an inch or so of soil. Then mix 5-10-10 fertilizer with the remaining soil at a rate of about 5 pounds for every 75 feet of trench. As the shoots grow, cover them with the fertilizer-soil mix.

If you have no fertilizer, humus or manure, just use good old, plain dirt. The plants will still grow, but until you build up your soil, your harvest will be small.

Cultivation consists of mulching the asparagus patch, nothing more.

Harvest. The first year you will see nothing more than a few spindly, weak imitations of asparagus spears making their way up through the soil. Let them be, and they will grow into fern-leafed plants. In the fall, when they become frost-damaged, cut them off near the ground.

With the onset of the spring of the second year, you will see a number of fat spears emerging from the ground above the asparagus roots. These may be cut. When the spears become thin and spindly, it is time to stop cutting and let the spears form the plant's leaves, which replenish the food reserves the roots utilized to form and produce the spears you cut. You cannot continue harvesting, or the plant will die.

Thick spears should be cut before they are over 6 inches long and while their tips are still compact and firm. Let the spears grow much longer, and they will become fibrous and tough. Like sweet corn and sweet peas, asparagus changes flavor rapidly after it has been harvested. So, for best taste, set your pot aboiling before you begin cutting.

You can use an asparagus cutter, which looks somewhat like a weed cutter, or an ordinary knife. Some farmers cut the spears at an angle an inch or two below the surface of the soil. The better way is to simply cut them flush with the top of the dirt. You get a little less spear this way, but you run no risk of damaging the roots.

String beans ready for picking.

Beans, String

Cold-sensitive
pH 5.6 to 6.8.
Loam.
Plant well after last frost, or start indoors:
  1 to 2 inches deep, 2 to 3 inches apart in rows 2 feet apart;
  Or in hills, five seeds to a hill, thinned to three plants and supported by poles 3 feet apart.
Harvest in 50 to 60 days.
Yields about ⅛ pound per bush plant; 1 pound per pole plant.
So many excellent varieties of string beans are available that it is hard to list any preferred types: Kentucky Wonder, King of the Garden, Romano, Green Isle, and Tendergreen Bush are just a few.

Most of us still call green beans "string beans," although the string was removed about 100 years ago by Calvin N. Keeny and his new variety was first marketed in

1896 by W. Atlee Burpee. The correct name is therefore "green beans" or "snap beans."

No matter their name, they are easy to grow, and like all seed crops are loaded with vitamins A, B, G, and protein. Since they are legumes, they increase the nitrogen content of the soil. However, the nitrogen is fixed by soil bacteria that gather round the plant's roots. If you have grown beans in that spot the year before, the necessary bacteria are probably there waiting for more bean roots to which to attach themselves. If there were no beans there the year before, you can ensure nitrogen fixation by shaking the bean seeds in bacterial powder, which is available at many garden supply shops.

Planting and cultivating. All beans—wax, snap, bush, pole, etc.—are similarly planted and cultivated. So whatever type and variety you select, these are the general instructions to follow.

Beans prefer a rich, fertile loam, but they will do well in any soil that is not water-soaked and alkaline. You don't need to fertilize the soil to grow beans, but if you do so, be especially careful with chemical fertilizer, as beans are particularly sensitive to fertilizer burning. The far better choice is composted manure or humus. With either material, a handful mixed into the soil where you are going to plant the seeds is all that you need.

Beans are sensitive to cold. They are easily frozen, and if you plant your seeds before the earth is thoroughly warm and fairly dry, the seeds will not germinate; they will rot.

One way to speed germination is to start the beans indoors in flats. An additional time jump can be secured by soaking them in water overnight before planting. However, the soaking softens their skins, and you have to be very careful not to injure the seeds when planting.

Bush beans are simply planted in one or more rows, with each seed 1 to 2 inches deep and 2 to 3 inches apart from its neighbor. Rows should not be less than 2 feet apart. The seeds are covered, tamped in place, and watered. When the seeds have sprouted and grown to the height of a foot or so, you can bring the mulch fairly close, but always leave some space for air circulation around the stems.

Pole beans are planted in hills (circles) about 5 to 6 inches across. Sow five or six seeds, and later thin to the best three plants. Set the single pole in the center of the hill before you plant. If you use a tepee arrangement of three poles tied together at the top, you can let three plants per pole grow. Mulch just as you would for the bush beans.

To prevent your entire bean crop from ripening on the same day, spread your planting over a succession of weeks, but make certain that your last batch of seed goes into the ground early enough to ripen before the first frost.

Harvest. Actually, beans do not ripen all at once but over a period of weeks. There is no best time for harvesting. The very small beans are no more flavorsome than the full size beans. However, when they go over 6 inches or so in length, they tend to toughen up somewhat. If you fail to pick them at this point, let them remain on the plant where they will dry, and you can later shell them easily and store them for winter use.

One most important point to bear in mind about harvesting—don't go among the plants when they are wet with dew or rain.

Special varieties. To grow beans for dry use, plant White Kidney, Red Kidney, White Marrowfat, or Navy Pea-Bean.

Should you be interested in upping your protein intake without increasing your consumption of beef, try raising edible soybeans. They are heavy with vitamins A, B, and G, plus a touch of vitamin C. Soybeans have more iron than spinach and more calcium than milk and about twice the protein content of an equal weight of lima beans.

Soybeans are planted and cultivated exactly like ordinary beans. Green Giant, one variety that is popular, is ready for picking in 80 days. Higan, another variety, requires 110 days and is better suited to the South. To shell soybeans you have to steam them or boil them for a few minutes first, and then squeeze the beans out the end of the pod.

Beans, Lima

Cold-sensitive.
pH 5.6 to 6.8.
Moderately fertile soil.
Plant well after last frost, or start indoors:
   1 to 2 inches deep, 10 to 12 inches apart, in rows 3 feet apart;
   Or in hills, five seeds to a hill, thinned to three plants, and supported by poles 3 feet apart.
Harvest in 65 to 75 days.
Yields about ½ pound per bush plant and about 1½ pounds per pole plant.

Three pole varieties are most popular. King of the Garden takes about 88 days to mature. Pods are about 5½ inches long and will contain four or five large flat beans. Good for eating or freezing. Carolina or Sieva has smaller pods, takes only 88 days to harvest, and is sometimes called butter bean. Burpee's Big Six forms pods up to 7 inches long and 1 inch wide containing six large beans. Maturity occurs in about 90 days, and the beans differ from others in that they retain their green color very well during cooking. This variety is probably the heaviest producer, its vines growing very tall.

Among the bush limas the following are most often selected by small-area farmers: Henderson Bush, matures in only 65 days, produces small curved pods with three or four flat, small beans that turn white when dry. This type of lima bean is usually called baby lima. Burpee's Fordhook is ready for picking in 78 days. The pods grow up to 5 inches long and 1½ inches wide. The beans are fat and thick, and many people consider this variety to have the best flavor. Plants grow to a height of around 20 inches and spread out some 2 feet. Fordhook 242 forms pods up to 4 inches long with three or four large thick beans. Each bush can produce up to 50 pods per bush. It is ready in about 85 days. Burpee's Improved is a very heavy producer with pods up to 6 inches long, each holding four to six large beans. Time to maturity is about 75 days.

Lima beans were so named by young Captain John Harris, U.S. Navy, because he secured them in the city of Lima, Peru, sometime in the year 1824. The name stuck, though the same beans were already under cultivation in our Southern states at the time.

Limas are the most cold-sensitive members of the bean family. Their seeds rot quickly in cold soil, and though once grown, they can survive a light frost, cool weather slows their growth. Therefore, if you live in a Northern state, it is best to start limas indoors although you may have the frost-free time span necessary.

Soils for limas cannot be heavy or crusted, or the seed bean will be unable to force its heavy cotyledons (the seed bean itself, which forms the seed leaves) up to the sun. For the same reason limas should be planted with their eyes downward so that the bean is correctly positioned for ascension.

The beans are planted 1 to 2 inches deep. Bush varieties are spaced about 12 inches apart in rows or furrows 3 feet apart. Pole varieties are planted in a circle about 6 inches across. Start with five beans and thin to three or two. Lima vines are heavy; so make certain that you have stout poles, driven firmly into the earth.

When the plants have grown to about 1 foot or so, bring the mulch close, but not in contact with the stem. If the vine hasn't found its own way, guide it up the pole or trellis. This is all you have to do until harvest time.

Harvest. Pods can be picked as soon as the beans can be felt inside, but for maximum returns you have to wait until the pods and beans are fully formed. If this occurs near fall, harvest isn't at all critical. However, if you are in the deep South and your beans have matured in mid or late summer, don't let them remain on the vines too long or they will become mealy and lose some flavor. On the other hand, if you want dry beans, you can let them be until the pods brown out and harden.

Beets, Root

Cold-hardy.
pH 6.0 to 7.2.
Moderately fertile, sandy loam or loam.
Plant as soon as the ground can be worked, ½ inch deep, 1 inch apart; thin to 3 inches apart, in furrows about 2 feet apart.
Yields about 10 pounds for a 12-foot row.
Matures in 50 to 70 days.

Actually two kinds of beets are grown in the United States. The type we call beet is known as beetroot elsewhere and is cultivated primarily for its root. The other type, called Swiss chard, belongs to the same family, *Beta vulgaris,* but is grown for its broad stalks and luxuriant leaves.

One of the best globular beetroots is Asgrow Wonder, which is ready in 7 or 8 weeks. Detroit Dark Red needs another 10 to 14 days. Both beets have a good dark red color and are excellent for eating or canning. Long Smooth Blood is an older variety. It grows partially above the surface, has roots 10 inches long, and requires 90 days to mature. It is still a favorite for winter storage.

Red Ball needs but two months to reach its prime. Its smooth red ball is about 3½ inches in diameter. Burpee's White is known for its white flesh and sweetness. Its top makes an excellent green.

Planting and cultivation. Whether grown for roots or tops, beets remain root vegetables, and as such they require loose soil, for they must grow rapidly if they are to be tender and succulent. If the soil is tight, the roots will be deformed, tough, and peppery.

Beets can be planted very early; weeks before the last spring frost, just so soon as the earth is dry enough to work. And you can sow beets continuously through the summer if you are up North, and if you wish, up until a week or two before the first frost of winter. In the deep South, it is best not to plant beets in midsummer.

In the spring, when the earth is relatively moist, seed can be sown ½ inches deep. In the late summer and fall when the earth is relatively dry, it is better to increase seed depth to 1 or 2 inches to ensure moisture.

Beet seeds germinate very slowly; so mark the row with a string, or add some quick-growing radish seeds to the row to mark it. Each beet seed is actually a small, dried fruit containing two to six seeds; so when the seeds germinate you will see clusters of tiny plants. Cut them off with your thumbnail, leaving a single plant every 2 inches. When the plants have grown to the size of small radishes, thin them out to one every 3 inches, and use the small beets exactly as you would the large ones. In this way you can extend the harvest.

Beets are fairly tough and not particularly troubled by weeds. However, if some weeds do show between your mulch and the plants, simply pull them up. Do not let the mulch touch the beet roots.

Harvest. As stated, beets can be harvested any time you wish up until a week or more after they have reached full maturity. You will know that this point has been reached when the tops of the beet roots extend an inch or so above the surface of the earth. It is inadvisable to let the beets remain in the earth much past this moment. Pull the plant. Cut the top off an inch above the top of the root. Eat or store the root in a cool place. Use the tops for salad, or prepare as you would spinach, if you prepare spinach.

Swiss chard midseason, mulched with grass clippings.

Planting a cabbage seedling.

Beet, Leaf

Chard or Swiss chard, which is a beet developed and grown for its leaves rather than its root, is planted and cultivated almost exactly like the root beet just discussed. The differences are covered here.

While chard is listed as being as cold-hardy as beets, chard can withstand summer heat, but beets cannot. While beets are a one-time crop—once you have pulled your beet, you have had it—chard is not. When the plant comes to maturity, you remove its outer leaves only, which of course, is the reason you are cultivating the plant. In due time more leaves grow to size and can be removed. Thus, once the plant has grown, you have a constant supply of chard the summer through.

Another difference is the nature of the soil that the two plant species desire. Both prefer light soil, but chard needs a richer, more fertile soil than beets. And the last important difference is that chard is thinned to individual plants about 6 inches apart instead of 3.

Some of the better known varieties include Lucullus, named after a Roman general, known for setting a fine table. This variety has crumpled, green-yellow leaves and broad green stalks. Another, Dark Green, has smooth leaves and light green stalks or chards. Fordhook Giant has white stalks and crinkled, dark green leaves.

Broccoli

> Very cold-hardy.
> pH 6.0 to 7.2.
> Fertile loam, high in nitrogen and potassium.
> Start indoors, and transplant for a spring crop, or outdoors for a late fall or following spring crop.
> Sow the seeds ¾ inch deep, spaced 18 inches apart, in rows 30 inches apart.
> Yields about ¾ pound per plant.
> Harvest in 75 to 85 days.

Broccoli, like the cabbage and cauliflower, is a member of the Brassica family. Broccoli is believed to have resulted when a wild cabbage married a cauliflower. Actually, broccoli is closer to cauliflower than cabbage because we eat the flower of both the cauliflower and the broccoli, whereas the edible portion of a cabbage plant is its leaves.

There are several varieties of broccoli. One is a type of very late-maturing cauliflower, only grown commercially. The other is called by a number of names: Italian, Calabrese, and Sprouting, and comes in three colors: green, purple, and white. The green Italian or green Sprouting broccoli is best suited to small-farm cropping, and that is the one we will discuss.

Green Comet, Calabrese, Waltham 29, and De Cicco are the best-known varieties. The De Cicco takes about 75 days to mature but is edible even sooner. The Calabrese requires 85 days. It has a larger head, with bluish-green buds, all in all as much as 6 inches in diameter. As with other varieties, the Calabrese forms side branches and heads after the main flower has been cut off.

Planting and cultivation. Broccoli likes cool weather and moist conditions; therefore, for best results you need to time your plantings so as to harvest in the spring or late fall.

For a spring harvest, start the seeds indoors about 6 weeks before you expect the frost to be out of the ground. At this time, the plants are moved outdoors and spaced about 18 inches apart in rows about 30 inches apart. For a fall crop, set the seeds directly in the soil, but sow more than you want: say, two to three seeds in groups about 9 inches apart. When the plants are about 5 inches high, thin them out, leaving the best ones. Do your fall planting a little after the midsummer heat, say at the end of August, and depending on temperature and weather, you may harvest some before the snow falls. And if you protect the plants with some mulch, you may harvest broccoli in the following spring.

Brussels Sprouts

> Very cold-hardy.
> pH 6.0 to 7.2.
> Fertile loam.
> Start indoors early, and transplant for spring crop, or outdoors for a late fall crop.
> Sow seeds ¾ inch deep, transplant to 18 inches apart, in rows 30 inches apart.
> Yields about ¾ pound (1 quart) per plant.
> Harvest in 80 to 120 days.

Brussels sprouts are miniature cabbages about 1 to 2 inches in diameter when ready to eat. They grow in the axils (armpits) of the leaves that form on the plant's long stalk. Brussels sprouts are yet another member of the tribe developed from the

Cabbage seedling before mulching.

wild cabbage. In seedling form the seven species, which include cabbage, cauliflower, broccoli, kale, kohlrabi, and collards, can hardly be told apart. So if you plant more than one member of the wild cabbage family, be certain to mark your seeds carefully.

Long Island is one of the better-known varieties. It matures in about 90 days and the plant grows to 26 inches in height. It is also called "Long Island Improved."

Planting and cultivating. The seeds are sown ¾ inch deep, 3 or 4 inches apart in the flats. As Brussels sprouts are very cold-hardy and prefer cold weather, start your seeds early enough to be able to set them out as soon as the frost is out of the ground. In their permanent home they are usually spaced about 18 inches apart in rows 30 inches apart or a little less. As Brussels sprouts are slow growers, you can interplant with companionable vegetables that mature rapidly.

If you mulch, there is little to be done to the plants during the growing season.

Harvest. The little green balls ripen from the bottom of the stalk upward; so these are first removed by cutting with a sharp knife. When the growing little cabbages begin to press against the leaf stems, some farmers cut the lower leaves off, taking care not to damage the stalks of the plants themselves. The terminal or top leaves are always left in place to foster growth.

Brussels sprouts are not harmed by mild frost. Some people even believe that frost improves the flavor of the little cabbages. But when a hard frost is on its way, pull the entire plant, leaving a ball of dirt on its roots; and store roots, stalk, dirt, and all in a cool, damp place. This will keep the remaining sprouts fresh for several months.

Cabbage

Very cold-hardy.
pH 6.0 to 7.2.
Fertile loam rich in nitrogen and potassium.
Plant indoors, and transplant for spring crop, or outdoors for late fall crop.
Sow seeds ½ inch deep about 4 inches from each other; transplant 18 to 24 inches apart in rows 2 to 3 feet apart.
Yields up to 10 pounds per plant (depending on variety).
Matures in 60 to 120 days.

There are several hundred different varieties of cabbage, which divide into a number of distinct types. There are small- and large-headed varieties, early, midseason, and late ripening; cone-shaped, oval, globe, green, red (purple), smooth-leafed and wrinkled-leafed. There are also varieties grown for their resistance to a disease known as cabbage yellows. This is a fungus infection (*Fusarium*) that often attacks cabbages in the Eastern half of the United States.

No matter what the variety, the planting and cultivation are the same. The heads that are picked and consumed are giant buds consisting of a compressed stem and leaf. Cabbage is a biennial. It buds (heads) the first year and goes to seed the second if not harvested. Sometimes a cabbage will go to seed the first year. If one of yours appears to be doing so, extending a stalk through spread leaves, pull it out, and discard it on the compost heap. The seeds that develop will most likely produce wild cabbages, which can be as troublesome as any weeds.

There are many popular varieties. Early Jersey Wakefield, for example, forms conical heads about 7 inches long and is ready in only 65 days. Golden Acre takes about 63 days. The heads are about 6 inches in diameter, round and solid, weighing up to 4 pounds. This variety can be planted closer than the others. Stein's Dutch flat produces heads as much as 9 inches across and weighing 6 pounds each. Maturity comes after about 83 days. Resistant Golden Acre is resistant to cabbage yellows and is a variety to plant where this fungus infection is a problem.

Premium Dutch Flat, Danish Roundhead, and Penn State Ballhead are three varieties suited to fall planting and winter harvest. They require up to 110 days to reach full growth. Dutch Flat heads can run to 10 pounds on the average.

Planting and cultivation. For spring harvest the seeds are started indoors about 6 weeks before the last frost of spring. You can sow the seeds two or so inches apart, and then transplant to a second flat when the seedlings have reached a height of about 3 inches. Second flat spacing should be about 4 inches between plants. Or you can start them 4 inches apart and save yourself the trouble. As soon as the earth is frost-free, you can set out your plants, but first give them a few hours outdoors in the shade to harden them. Although cabbage is very frost-hardy, the sudden change from indoors or cold frame to outdoors should be avoided.

Cabbages like the sun, but when you first set them out, protect them from direct sunlight by a cover of some sort. Space the early, quick varieties that do not produce large heads about 12 inches apart. The larger varieties are spaced about 2 feet apart in rows 3 feet apart.

Plant the young cabbages a little deeper in the soil than they originally were in the flats, and when you do, soak the earth around each plant thoroughly.

If your soil is rich and moist, the cabbages will head up nicely. If they don't head up, but produce sprawling leaves, the trouble can be too much heat (you planted too late in the spring or too early in the fall), lack of water, or infertile soil.

For a fall crop you can sow your seeds directly in the earth. Sow them closely together, and mark the rows. By overseeding you will be certain you have a good stand of healthy plants. As cabbage is a slow grower, you can intercrop with suitable quick-growing plants.

You don't need very much mulch around cabbages. Once their leaves reach out, they shade whatever else is trying to grow out of existence.

Chinese Cabbage

Cold-hardy.
pH 6.0 to 7.2.
Fertile, sandy loam or loam.
Generally planted outdoors as a fall crop.
Sow seeds ½ inch deep, 2 to 3 inches apart; thin to 8 inches, in rows about 18 to 25 inches apart.
Yields about a little more than ½ pound per plant.
Matures in about 50 to 80 days.

Chinese cabbage has been cultivated by the Chinese for at least 40 centuries. Although it is remotely related to the wild cabbage, and its Latin name is *Brassica pekinensis,* many call it celery cabbage because it tastes a little like celery. In appearance it is more like Swiss chard. Its outer leaves may be used as well as its crisp, mildly flavored, blanched heart for greens and salad.

The variety called Chihli or Hopei, stands about 15 inches high with its leaves tightly gathered, much like celery. It is possibly the best known variety. The Wong Bok is shorter and thicker, and the Pak choi does not form a solid head but grows much like Swiss chard.

Planting and cultivation. Chinese cabbage has a poor root system; therefore, it is rarely transplanted but is started outdoors in the space that it is going to occupy. Chinese cabbage is also sensitive to heat. Give it a warm spell, and it may rush through its growth and go right to seed. In this form it isn't particularly edible, and its seeds can become a nuisance in the garden by growing into a form of wild cabbage. So, if a plant of yours does run away, remove it immediately.

You have the choice of planting the seeds as early in the spring as the ground can be worked and hoping that the plants will ripen normally before they have a chance to go to seed. Or you can sow the seeds mid or late summer, timing the planting to allow 75 days before the first killing frost of the oncoming winter. Of the two possibilities, most farmers choose the latter course.

The seeds are planted about ½ inch deep a few inches apart in rows 18 to 25 inches apart. Later the plants are thinned to a space of about 8 inches for the Chihli variety and about 12 inches for the Wong Bok variety.

Like the rest of the cabbage family, this cousin is a leaf crop and should not be permitted to go dry. Mulching will conserve moisture and eliminate the need to weed.

Harvesting. Cut with a sharp knife at ground level when the head is full and firm. Use the dark outer leaves for greens.

Carrots

Cold-hardy.
pH 5.6 to 6.8.
Sandy loam or loam.
Plant 2 to 4 weeks before last frost of spring, ½ inch deep, about ½ inch apart, in rows 16 inches apart.

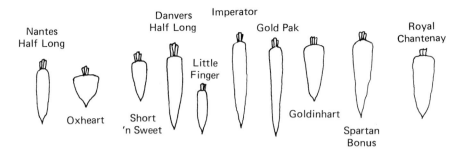

A few of the many varieties of carrots available.

Yields about 1 pound of carrots per linear foot of row.
Harvest in 70 to 75 days.

Although the carrot has been prized as a vegetable ever since the "French root" was brought to Rome two millennia ago, it wasn't until the mid-1800s that the varieties we now grow were developed. Reportedly, our smooth-rooted, succulent vegetable was developed from Queen Anne's Lace, a wild, roadside, bristly weed by one M. Vilmorin of Paris almost a century and a half ago. One aid he used in the conversion was rich, soft soil. It is still a necessity. If you don't have loose, fertile soil, you won't have much success with carrots.

Carrot seeds are slow to germinate, but once they do, they must grow easily and quickly. If the soil is heavy and tight, their growth and flavor are stunted.

Today there are countless varieties of Vilmorin's creation. The short types do better in heavy soil. The long thin types must have light soil to flourish.

The Oxheart is ready in 75 days. Its root reaches a length of 4½ inches or so, while its body may be up to 3½ inches across. It is the toughest of the bunch, good for late season growing and somewhat heavy soil.

Chantenay Red Core matures in 70 days, is deep orange, very sweet, and 5½ inches long by 2¼ inches thick.

Danvers Half Long matures in 75 days, and is 6 to 7 inches long with thick shoulders and a blunt end. It is a heavy producer.

Nante Coreless, ready in 70 days, has a very light top and almost no core; is smooth and fine grained; especially good for as-is eating and freezing.

Planting and cultivation. You face two immediate problems when you plant carrots: The seeds are so very small that it is difficult to space them properly. The seeds germinate so slowly and sprout so leisurely that other plants (weeds) have more than sufficient time to get their roots in.

The first problem can be solved by mixing the seeds with a little sand and a few radish seeds. Both the sand and the radish seeds provide more "body" to the carrot seeds, which enables you to space them better. In addition, the quick-sprouting and growing radishes mark the rows for you. Plus, through some magic of their own, radishes encourage and help the growth of carrots.

As an alternative, perhaps simpler, purchase your carrot seeds mounted on a tape. (Be certain to cover the tape completely with soil or the birds will pull it up.)

As for invasion by weeds, there is little you can do except to hand-nip the weeds after waiting long enough to make certain which are the weeds and which are the carrots.

The seeds are sown ½ inch deep, approximately ½ inch apart, in rows about 16 inches apart. When the plants come up and are definitely recognizable, they are thinned to about 1 inch apart. When the carrots have grown to where each is about three or so inches long, thin them out again. The "baby" carrots are delicious. The spaces between them should now be 2 to 4 inches wide, depending on whether you are growing fat or skinny carrots. For a continuous, summer-long harvest of carrots, space your planting out in successive batches about 2 weeks apart. Plant until you have approximately 80 days before the first killing frost of fall.

Harvest. Carrots are best when pulled young, but if it's size you are after, you can harvest anytime convenient, up to but not after maturity. If you harvest after the fernlike leaves begin to show yellow, if you harvest after the top of the root shows aboveground, you'll find the plant fibrous and tough. Most of its sweetness will be gone.

Although carrots are cold-hardy, do not let them remain in the ground during a frost. They will be damaged. Remove them, cut their tops short, and let them dry a while before storing them in a cool, damp place.

Cauliflower

Cold-hardy.
pH 6.0 to 7.2.
Very fertile, sandy loam.
Start indoors, ½ inch deep, 4 inches apart. Transplant as soon as frost is gone in spring, 20 inches apart, in rows 30 inches apart.
Yields up to 1 pound per plant.
Harvest in 50 to 100 days.

Cauliflower is more sensitive to cold and heat than the other members of the cabbage tribe. It is also less tolerant of poor soil and will only grow well in highly fertile, loose, and moist soil that is well drained. Many farmers believe the secret of cauliflower success is to make certain that the plant is well watered. If there is no rain for a week, they give each plant a thorough soaking, applying as much as 1½ inches of water.

Cauliflower seeds are difficult to produce, and there aren't too many varieties to select from. Of those available, Early Snowball is a good choice, as it matures in only 55 days, has a snow-white head, and is comparatively easy to grow. For fall planting, try Dry Weather and Danish Giant. They require more time to mature, but are more drought-resistant than the others.

Planting and cultivation. Start your seeds about 4 weeks before the last spring frost. Give the seedlings plenty of elbowroom in the flats, and transplant them when they are about 3 inches high and the frost is out of the ground. In the fields they are spaced about 20 inches apart, in rows about 30 inches apart. Outside of keeping the soil covered with mulch, all you need to do is blanch the head. This is done by tying the leaves loosely over the head when it is the size of a baseball. If you don't, the head will turn brown. And if you don't want to fool with tying leaves, plant Purple Head, which doesn't need blanching and supposedly tastes the same.

For a fall crop, time your seed planting so as to have the young plants ready for the field as close to the first frost of oncoming winter as possible. If your variety requires 90 days and the first frost is expected October 1, start the seed late in June. That will give them 90-days-plus growing time.

Harvest. Cut the head when it is full and firm. Do not let it remain on the plant, as its texture and flavor will quickly change, as will its color. Trim the leaves back to make an attractive display of your prize.

Sweet Corn

Not cold-hardy.
pH 5.6 to 6.8.
Fertile loam.
Plant seeds after earth is warm, ½ inch deep, 4 inches apart. Thin to 8 inches apart, in rows 12 inches apart.
Yields two or more ears per plant (depending on soil).
Harvest in 60 to 90 days.

Corn or maize has been cultivated by the American Indians for many thousands of years, but sweet corn appears to have been a very minor crop. It was grown by many tribes, but little importance was attached to it as a food staple. Even the settlers paid it scant attention. It is only in the past century that this variety was separated from the others and recognized with the dignity of a name; and it is only in the past 50 years or so that seedsmen began applying modern methods to its development. Today, there are many distinct varieties of sweet corn, and it is one of the most satisfying of all the home vegetables.

For all its popularity corn is, in a number of ways, a difficult customer. It will grow almost anywhere in almost any soil, but unless it has plenty of food, water, and sun, the plant looks more like the overgrown grass stalk that it is than a vegetable. The ears will be small and possibly empty.

Therefore, if your soil is not yet fertile and you want corn this coming season, it is advisable to mix a lot of composted manure or chemical fertilizer into the earth. If you use fertilizer, dig a trench 8 inches deep and 12 inches wide the length of your projected row of corn. Place about three-fourths of the removed soil on one side of the trench, and the remainder on the other side. Mix 5-10-5 fertilizer in with the larger quantity of soil at the rate of about 7 pounds per 100 feet of trench. Return the fertilized soil to the bottom of the trench. Tamp firm. Return the remainder of the soil to the trench. Now you can seed without danger of the seeds themselves making contact with fertilizer particles.

Some farmers mix the chemical fertilizer into the soil about 2 weeks before sowing, but the trenching method, while more troublesome, is safer.

Among the many varieties of sweet corn now to be had, Royal Crest is often selected for first and last plantings of the season because it matures in just 60 days. It is a medium-size plant producing 7-inch-long ears with 12 rows of bright yellow kernels. Honey & Cream ripens in 78 days. Its ears run about 6½ inches in length and have 16 to 18 rows of yellow and white kernels on the same ear. Iochief stalks reach 8 feet in height. Its ears may be as long as 8½ inches with 16 to 18 rows of golden kernels. Iochief needs 85 days to do its thing. Golden Cross Bantam, probably the most popular of all sweet corn varieties, also produces 8½-inch-long ears, most of which are doubles, and does it all in 84 days. There are many other excellent varieties, some whose flavor, growth characteristics, and disease resistance may be better suited to your farm than those listed here.

Planting and cultivation. Corn seeds cannot be sown before the earth is warm. If they are, they will rot. Should you wish to push the growing season up, there are two approaches. You can start the seeds indoors, or you can risk it: Plant early, and if nothing shows in 10 days or so, dig a few seeds up to see whether they have germinated or died. In the latter case, plant some more.

Corn seeds are sown to a depth of between ½ and 1 inch, 4 inches apart, in flats and outdoors. Later, the plants are set or thinned to about 8 inches apart. Corn is naturally open-pollinated. Pollen discharged from the male tassels at the top of the plant sift down through the air until they reach the receptive silks. Therefore it is best to plant corn close together in groups or rows instead of in one long row. Row spacing of corn is today closer than it used to be. Whereas corn furrows used to be spaced as much as 42 inches apart, experience has found the better distance to be closer to 12 inches. Since you can't walk between rows 12 inches apart, set out four rows and then a walking space. So long as you can reach into the rows for picking, you're in good shape. As for hills or groups, go to four or five plants instead of the usual three.

Plants spaced this closely will prosper if there is sufficient water and food, but they will draw a lot of nutrients from the soil; so you may have to use fertilizer for a few years. Keep tabs by measuring your soil's nutrient content.

Corn requires a little weed picking when it is young. Later you can mulch or not mulch for weeds. It makes little difference. Once corn takes off, very little excepting certain companionate plants can grow near it. Corn throws too much shade.

Some farmers gather the nearby soil up against the lower end of the stalk and cover the secondary or prop roots that appear. The purpose is to firm the plant against the wind, but 2 or 3 inches of loose soil against the bottom of a 7-foot stalk isn't going to hold it up in a high wind; so don't bother forming hills around each plant. Secondary side shoots, sometimes called suckers or tillers, are sometimes cut off by farmers. That too is a waste of time. Let them be.

Harvest. Don't get anxious. Wait until the silk has shriveled and turned brown. Then cautiously pull a bit of husk back. If the ear has filled out (be advised that some never fill completely), if the kernels are plump, start the kettle boiling. The less time lost between picking and eating, the better. Even a few hours can make a tremendous difference in taste. If the ear is not filled out, replace the husk. No harm done.

Cucumbers

Cold-sensitive.
pH 6.0 to 7.2.
Loam.
Plant 1 week or more after last frost, ½ inch deep, 3 inches apart, and thin to 6 inches apart or in hills (groups) of three plants.
Yields anywhere from 5 to 10 pounds per individual plant.
Harvest in 55 to 65 days.

Cucumbers are easy to grow. Half a dozen vines will supply the needs of an average family over the summer. Cucumbers ramble, but they are easily trained to a trellis, and they don't mind sharing a pole with tomatoes, as cucumbers do not need full sun to thrive. They prefer fertile loam, but will make do in average soil.

There are any number of excellent varieties. Spartan Salad is resistant to most cucumber diseases and is excellent for the small farmer because it bears fruit over a long period. Early Surecrop is ready in 58 days and forms long slender fruit up to 9 inches long. Wisconsin SMR is chosen for pickling; cucumbers are 6 inches long and about 2½ inches in diameter. Ready in 60 days, they can also be eaten fresh. Burpless Hybrid is long and thin. It doesn't need to be peeled and is easily digested without burping by those who have difficulty with cucumbers. It is ready in 65 days.

Planting and cultivation. Although the cucumber is reputedly difficult to transplant, this farmer has never found it so. I have even moved small plants from one part of my field to another without loss. So, you can start your cucumbers indoors if you like, or sow the seeds directly outdoors. As stated, the seeds are sown about ½ inch deep, 3 inches apart, and are thinned to where they are about 6 inches apart. Indoors, they should be started about 2 weeks before the last frost so that they are ready for transplanting 2 weeks or so after the last frost. You won't lose time by waiting 2 weeks. Cucumbers like warmth, and they will just hang in there doing nothing if it is cool.

You can't let them trail about on the ground, because they will take up lots of space, and each cucumber that rests on the earth will rot and attract slugs. The best arrangement is a trellis or a convenient fence. Space them out along its bottom about 6 inches apart, with the thought that you can lose a few and still get a good crop.

Once they are a foot or more long, you can mulch fairly close. After that there is nothing to do but guide the vines every once in a while. If you don't watch them, they will take off across the grass. The only precaution to remember during this period is that you must move them gently and never when wet, as whatever microbial disease may be present will be spread about.

Harvest. You can pick the cucumbers at any point during their growth, but you must not let them even begin to show signs of yellowing. For if they yellow, they quickly change texture and flavor and become inedible. When you pick, take care not to pull the cucumber loose, but either cut its stem or push it off the fruit with your thumbnail. And look sharp. Cucumbers have an unholy knack of hiding right under your nose. They also grow rapidly after a good summer rain.

Eggplant

Warm weather crop.
pH 5.5 to 6.5.
Fertile sandy loam.
Plant ½ inch deep, 3 inches apart, in flats, 8 weeks before setting out; then space 2 feet apart, 3 feet between rows.
Yields about 2 pounds per plant.
Harvest in 100 to 140 days.

Eggplants used to be called mad apples, perhaps because they are distant cousins of the Deadly Nightshade family. Around the Mediterranean, this handsome fruit is a staple. Here, it isn't too well known. (Did you know there is a white variety?) It deserves a better fate. It makes many tasty dishes though it doesn't contain much nourishment.

One reason they aren't popular here is that they are difficult to grow. They like to drowse in the summer sun, taking as much as 140 days to mature. A touch of cold, even a cool summer night that goes below 50°F, can damage them, and such temperature dips are common when you get away from the ocean or Great Lakes shores. If your summer nights are chilly, if you do not have sufficient warm weather, even if the plants spend their first 2 months indoors, chances are your eggplant crop won't make it.

The most popular variety is Black Beauty, which bears four or five large purple-black, globe-shaped fruit. It matures in about 85 days. The New York Improved

Eggplant mulched with leaves.

produces somewhat longer and lighter-colored fruit. It ripens a little earlier, as does the New Hampshire Hybrid, which was developed primarily for northern farmers. Unfortunately the New Hampshire Hybrid tends to droop, and its fruit lays on the ground. This variety of eggplant must be either propped up by staking or underlaid with clean straw or other mulch.

Planting and cultivation. The seeds are sown about ½ inch deep about 3 inches apart in flats, approximately 8 weeks before the day you plan to set them out. This day will be about 2 weeks or more after the last frost. For a more exact figure, see the tables in Chapter 13. In any event you want your plants about 5 or 6 inches high when you harden off and transplant them. In order to transplant plants of this size, you will need either to start the seeds in 4-inch pots or to move them from the flats to pots well before you bring them outdoors.

When you set them out, cup the soil around the plant so that you form a bowl that can be filled with water. Eggplants need plenty of water at transplant time. In addition, if there is a strong sun, shade them for a few days.

Cultivation consists of mulching, little more.

Harvest. The eggs can be cut off—their stems are woody—as soon as they reach half-size or more, or any time afterward up to the point where they lose their surface shine. If you want a few large plants, pinch off some of the blossoms. Some farmers pinch off all the blossoms that form too late in the season for fruit.

Kohlrabi

Very cold-hardy.
pH 6.0 to 7.2.
Fertile loam rich in nitrogen and potassium.
Plant indoors and transplant for spring crop, or outdoors for late fall crop.
Sow seeds ¼ inch deep, 2 inches apart; thin to 6 inches apart and rows 12 inches apart.
Yields about ¼ pound per plant.
Harvest in 54 to 60 days.

Another, not too well known member of the cabbage tribe, kohlrabi has the flavor of cauliflower and beet combined, but with the cold hardiness of the cabbage. It may be sliced and eaten raw like a cucumber; or it may be peeled, sliced, and boiled. In the latter form, it can be buttered and eaten with pepper and salt.

The plant itself is strange in appearance. The stem swells out to form a ball about 2½ inches in diameter. The leaves project from the ball, which is the edible portion of the plant.

Kohlrabi is cultivated exactly like cabbage. It is harvested when the edible heads are full. Don't wait too long, as it grows fibrous past maturity.

Two varieties are popular: White Vienna and Purple. The Purple is believed to reach a slightly larger diameter before becoming tough. Its skin bears a pale purple tint, but its evenly textured flesh is pale green. In taste it differs very slightly from the White variety.

Leeks

Cold-hardy.
pH 6.4 to 7.6.
Loam.

Early White Vienna kohlrabi. *(Courtesy W. Atlee Burpee Co.)*

Plant as soon as the ground can be worked, ½ inch deep, 3 inches apart; thin to six or more
  inches apart, in rows 2 feet apart.
Yields about 2½ pounds per 100 feet of row.
Harvest in about 130 days.

Leeks are an unappreciated member of the onion family. They have a slightly
onion flavor, but are much milder and can be cooked and served as a side
vegetable, much like asparagus. Or leeks may be added to soups and stews and
salads, just like onions.

Leeks are cold-hardy and tough. They can be sown directly in the field, but their
growth is so slow that you can't grow them outside in one season up North. There,
they must be started indoors. In milder climates you can start a second crop in late
August or September and then, by protecting the plants with mulch or the likes
from frost, you can harvest them early the following spring.

Three varieties are generally available: Large Flag is most popular, followed by
Broad London. Giant Musselburg, which was developed in a Scottish town of the
same name, is a bit larger and better suited to cold weather. Incidentally, leeks and
leekers, who are farmers specializing in leek production, are very popular in
Scotland where the cool, moist weather favors the onion and cabbage tribes.

Planting and cultivation. Sow the seeds ½ inch deep and 3 inches apart, either
indoors or out. When the plants reach a height of 8 inches, several courses of action
are available. Conventional practice calls for the plants to be cut in half and
transplanted in the bottom of a furrow 6 inches deep. Just enough soil is returned
to the furrow to cover the plant roots. The remainder of the soil is returned slowly
over a period of weeks. Covering the lower portion of the plant blanches (whitens)
it and makes for a more succulent, milder leek.

Alternatively, you can cut off the top half of the plants, and draw soil up against
the plants without transplanting them. And still another alternative is to let them
be and harvest them in the normal way. You will get leeks a lot earlier, and they
will probably have a little more pep to them.

Harvest. Simply pull the plants whenever you wish. They are edible from the
moment they poke their tops above the soil.

Lettuce

Very cold-hardy.
pH 6.4 to 7.6 for head lettuce.
pH 6.0 to 7.2 for leaf lettuce.
Fertile loam.
Plant outdoors as soon as the ground can be worked, ½ inch deep, 1½ inches apart, in
  rows 6 to 10 inches apart.
Yields about ½ pound per plant (head).
Harvest in 40 to 90 days.

Lettuce is probably the single most important vegetable in our salads when
judged by frequency of appearance. It doesn't deserve it, for lettuce has only a little
more food value than mushrooms, which have none. However, both lettuce and
mushrooms do provide jaw exercise; so they are favorites with dieters.

In any event, lettuce is fairly difficult for many beginners to grow. There are
several reasons for this, and if you keep them in mind, you can easily avoid failure.

Lettuce has a poor root system. Therefore, the soil must not only be friable and
fertile; it must also be fertile near the surface. Deep-down fertility does lettuce
absolutely no good. So when you add fertilizer (or manure, which is best), make

**RAISING
LETTUCE.**

(*A*) Seedlings
emerging from a seed
strip containing Black
Seeded Simpson
lettuce seeds.

(*B*) Second thinning of
the row of lettuce.

(*C*) One of the trans-
planted seedlings.

183

certain you keep it within the top few inches. Lettuce must grow quickly if it is to be crisp. This means, as stated, that the soil must be fertile and friable, but in addition the plant must be well watered, by rain or hose. However, lettuce cannot survive water-logged soil; so do not choose a continuously wet spot on your farm for lettuce culture. Lettuce is a cool-weather crop. If you misjudge your seeding time and let the plant grow through midsummer's heat without a sunshade, the plant quickly goes to seed. Heads will not form, and you will have a sort of little tree. (Still edible and tasty, though.)

There are three kinds of lettuce: head, leaf, and Cos or Romain. They are planted and cultivated alike, though there is a slight difference in their pH preference. (Cos is classed as head.) The leaf varieties can be spaced as little as 6 inches apart in rows 6 to 10 inches apart. Head varieties require more space.

Head lettuce is the kind most frequently encountered on your greengrocer's (fruit store) shelves. The plant forms a head much like cabbage. Most of the leaves are blanched (white). It is crisp and tasty but contains the least nourishment of all. A few of the better-known head lettuce varieties include Butter Crunch, which forms a small "bib" head about 4½ inches across in some 67 days. Iceberg has a compact, medium-sized head with light green fringed leaves edged in light brown. Its center is silvery white, and it is ready for picking and eating in about 85 days.

Leaf lettuce, so called because the plant forms a very large, loose head of light green, frilly leaves, is popular with do-it-yourself gardeners because the outer leaves alone can be removed for use. The plant grows new ones.

Salad Bowl, ready in 45 days, is a leaf variety that forms a large round head with medium green leaves. Another is Oak Leaf which matures in only 40 days and has dark green leaves. Still another is Slobolt which can be harvested (its leaves cut) over a longer period of time than the others before it bolts (goes to seed). This variety needs 45 days.

White Paris is a good strain that is self-folding. Its leaves do not have to be tied together to blanch its interior (if that is what you want). It is ready in about 70 days.

Planting and cultivation. Generally leaf lettuce is sown directly in the field, while the head varieties are started indoors in flats. The reason is simply that the head varieties require a little more time. When you sow directly (you will find seed tape most advantageous), space the seeds closely, about 1½ inches apart. Then remove every other one when they are a few inches high, and use them for salads. Later, thin them out again with the same alternate-plant out scheme, leaving the plants a proper 6 inches or so apart. When you start them in flats, either start them close and later prick them out and replant indoors before setting out, or start them 3 inches apart and transplant directly. In either case be certain to give the young plants at least a week of hardening off before transplanting.

Don't cultivate. Lettuce roots are close to the surface and easily damaged. And don't bring the mulch too close. Lettuce is prized by slugs (snails without shells), and they will use the mulch as a cover while they feast.

Harvest. As stated, a few leaves may be cut at one time from the leaf-type lettuce. The other heads are cut as soon as they fully grown. Some authorities advise that the heads be cut early in the morning, before the summer sun has time to remove the dew. Others state quite plainly that lettuce should not be harvested before 10:00 A.M., after which time they definitely show a vitamin increase. A difficult decision.

Burpee Hybrid cantaloupe. (Courtesy W. Atlee Burpee Co.)

Cantaloupe (Muskmelon)

Cold-sensitive.
pH 6.0 to 7.2.
Fertile, sandy loam.
Plant well after last frost, ¾ inch deep, five seeds to each hill, spaced 5 feet apart.
Yields three to six melons per plant.
Harvest in 80 to 120 days.

There is more than a little confusion attending the cantaloupe or muskmelon. Although it is eaten as a fruit, it is actually a member of the gourd family and is therefore technically a vegetable. Its name differs from place to place and from farmer to farmwife. The original melon was a muskmelon and was brought by church travelers from Western Asia to the town of Cantalupo near Rome and planted in the papal gardens there. The first melon had a faint musklike odor and coarse green skin. The original is still grown in Europe. The variety grown here and usually called both cantaloupe and muskmelon has a heavily netted body. The net portion turns yellow first, and the spaces follow, changing from green to yellow as the plant ripens. This is one way of determining a muskmelon's state of eatability: The web's spaces have turned yellow. Another way, if you have a sensitive nose, is to smell it. It has no odor when it is green. Squeezing melons just angers the fruit man, and doesn't tell you anything. Incidentally, melons ripen slightly when removed from the vine.

Melon vines are sensitive to transplanting and cold. So in any place more or less north of the Mason-Dixon line they must be started indoors early enough to permit the young plants to be set out at least one week after the last frost-free date. It is best not to start them in flats, but in individual pots so that the roots are disturbed as little as possible when transplanting.

When set out, they must be well watered and protected from the wind as well as the cold. You need mulch only in the area around the plants, but not too close.

Once the vines reach out, they shade most of the weed competition out of business. One trick to speeding ripening is to place each melon on a board or square of tar paper.

Harvesting. Simplicity itself. Follow the directions for recognizing ripe melons given previously, and when you put your knife to the vine, just before cutting, say a prayer for the melon experts of ancient Baghdad. Among other tasks they were responsible for harvesting the melons, which were highly prized. When one was cut too early or too late, Baghdad cut a melon expert permanently from its payroll.

Onion

Very cold-hardy.
pH 6.4 to 7.6.
Loam.
Plant seed outdoors 4 weeks before last spring frost, ¾ inch deep, 3 inches apart, in rows
    12 inches apart. Or plant "sets" (small onions) 3 inches apart in similar rows.
Yields about 10 pounds per 10 feet of row.
Harvest in 95 to 130 days.

The onion has been cultivated for at least 7 millennia. It is to be found in almost all diets and all kitchens. It is very popular with most backyard farmers, yet comparatively few noncommercial onion growers meet with much success growing this root crop.

The reason may well be that the onion appears able to survive anywhere. It

Planting Spanish onion seedlings.

Pull the Spanish onions early, and you have scallions.

won't prosper in poor, hard soil, but it will remain alive. As a result, many inexperienced farmers plant onions in their poorest fields, whereas onions require light, fertile soil in order to grow fat and mild. You will get some return if you plant onion sets in poor, rocky soil, but it is doubtful that you will get back 3 pounds for every pound of starter onions set out. Onion sets give you faster results, as they are small onions, up to about ½ inch in diameter when you plant them. Seeds, of course, have a much longer way to go. However, unless you grow your own (by pulling small, immature onions, drying and storing them for the following season), onion sets at today's prices are an expensive, hardly profitable way of growing onions.

Onions may be divided into two kinds; scallions or bunching onions, and bulb onions which form the tear-jerking ball-shaped vegetable we are all familiar with. There are also a few exotic types, one of which bears little onions on top of its stalks, and another which has a bulb that sort of splits to form clusters, each part of which may be separated and planted in the fall.

Sets are not usually classified any further than color. They are available in red, white, and yellow, and produce onions of the same color and flavor.

Onion seeds are another matter. Many varieties are to be had. To list a few: White Lisbon forms a crisp white, flat scallion that is ready in 60 to 100 days. It can be pulled earlier. Yellow Spanish requires 110 days and forms a sweet, golden-yellow bulb that is very mild and up to 6 inches across. Its flesh is white. White Spanish also needs 110 days to mature, and it is pearly white. Ebenezer is popular for pulling early as sets. It matures in about 120 days and forms flattened bulbs about 3 inches across. It is mild, has a yellow-brown skin, and keeps very well through the winter. Evergreen Long White Bunching is a scallion that does not form a bulb and requires 120 days to mature.

Planting and cultivation. Onions can be started from seeds indoors or from seeds planted outdoors. The usual depth is about ¾ inch, with the seeds spaced about 3 inches apart in rows about 12 inches apart. Sets are planted no deeper than their midpoint, which is about where they will remain as they grow and mature.

Onions are partial to light, fertile loam, doing particularly well in well-drained muck soils. They are sensitive to acidic soil; so take care to check that before trying onions.

Onions don't throw much of a shade so they are almost defenseless when it comes to weed invasions. A strong weed attack can wipe out a stand of onions in a few weeks. So be certain to mulch well and hand-pull whatever weeds crawl in between the mulch and the onions.

Harvest. Onions are edible as soon as they leave their seeds. If they show green, you can eat them. So harvest anytime you wish. You can pull bulbing onions early and use them as scallions if you wish. You can pull scallions when they are small and when they are large, in this way you can have fresh onions available over a longer period of time.

If you want bulbs, however, you must plant the bulbing type of onion, and you must wait until it forms a bulb. This can be hastened by knocking the plant's stalks over when they are large. The pulled onions must be cured before they are stored if you want them to last the winter without rotting. This is done by laying the plants out in the sun or on the floor of a dry room and leaving them there, well spaced, until the stalks have shriveled. Then the stalks are cut about an inch above the bulb. Whatever dirt remains on the bottoms of the onions is dusted off, and the vegetable may then be put away in a dry place for later use.

Parsnip

Cold-hardy.
pH 5.6 to 6.8.
Plant seeds ¼ inch deep, 1 inch apart, in rows 18 inches apart, as soon as the frost leaves
   the ground. Thin to 3 inches apart.
Loam.
Yields about 6 pounds per 10-foot row.
Harvest in 90 to 120 days.

Parsnips aren't too popular with the backyard farmer for some unknown reason, but should be. They are one of the most nutritious and easiest vegetables to grow. Parsnips are very hardy and can be left in the ground until needed. Cold weather does not affect them at all, but doesn't improve their flavor either as many people believe.

Guernsey is a popular variety. Each parsnip grows to 12 inches in length and 3 inches across its top. Hollow Crown, Model, and All American are others. The last mentioned is shorter and thicker and perhaps better suited to farms with shallow topsoil.

Planting and cultivation. Parsnip seeds more than a year old should not be used, and sowing should always be somewhat heavy, as these seeds do not germinate well. Although the seed is planted no more than ¼ inch deep, farmers often cover the soil with paper or boards or mulch to speed germination. A few radish seeds may be mixed in with the parsnip seeds to help mark the row. The starting aids must be removed as soon as the parsnips show.

Parsnips are a long-season, cool weather crop and will do much better up North than in the South. Cultivation is very easy. The plants are hardy. Outside of mulching and perhaps a little weeding, there is really nothing to do.

Snow peas emerging from the soil.

Snow peas starting to blossom. They are mulched with an assortment of leaves and grass clippings.

Burpeeana Early peas grown on a wire trellis. (*Courtesy W. Atlee Burpee Co.*)

Harvest. The plants are ready for eating anytime, but they should not be pulled but dug up when desired. If you wish, you can let them remain in the ground through the winter; just protect their tops with mulch of some kind. In the spring they must be harvested, or they will run to seed, and you will be plagued by wild parsnip weeds.

Peas

> Very cold-hardy.
> pH 6.0 to 7.2.
> Loam.
> Plant outdoors 4 weeks before last spring frost, 1 inch deep and 2½ inches apart, in double rows 2 feet apart.
> Yields about 4 pounds per 10-foot single row.
> Harvest in 59 to 68 days.

Peas, like corn, taste best when cooked and eaten as soon as they are picked. Peas are high in proteins, mineral salts, vitamins, and sugar. The weight of a good pea is nearly one fourth sugar, which changes quickly into starch when the pea pod is removed from the vine.

Peas are a cool weather crop and should be sown as early as possible. They do not thrive in midsummer heat. Where the climate permits, a late summer sowing can be made for a fall crop.

There are a large number of varieties to choose from. Sparkle is one of the earliest. It forms 3¼-inch, dark, blunt pods on 18-inch-high, self-supporting vines in only 59 days. The peas are ideal for freezing. Laxton Progress, named after the great English pea breeder, Thomas Laxton, of the nineteenth century, ripens in 60 days. It produces large pods with deep green peas on 18-inch vines. Triple Threat produces triple pods when planted in fertile soil. Its vines are about 32 inches high, and its pods are up to 3½ inches long and may contain up to nine peas. Wando matures in 66 days and has medium-size peas on a 26-inch vine. It is noted for its resistance to heat as well as to cold. Mammoth Melting (Snow Peas) matures in about 75 days and produces an edible pod. (Cook and eat like string beans, if you pick them early enough.) The vine grows to a height of 4½ feet and must be supported.

Planting and cultivation. The seeds are best set out in a single row if the variety is more bush than vine and can support itself. For the taller types, set the seeds out in double rows with each seed alongside the space between two seeds in the adjoining row so that the seeds are about 1½ inches apart. This makes it easier to set up brush, sticks, or even a woven wire fence between the rows and thus support the vines.

Most pea seeds are planted 1 inch deep, but some are best at 1½ or even 2 inches, especially in the fall when there is usually less moisture in the earth. Pea seeds are sensitive to chemical fertilizers. So if your soil is poor and you are going to use chemicals, take any of the precautions suggested in an earlier chapter. Make certain that you press the soil firmly down atop the seeds, and have patience. Some

Sugar peas (edible pod). *(Courtesy W. Atlee Burpee Co.)*

Mulching a young pepper plant with peat moss.

varieties germinate in as few as 7 days, others require two weeks, and some varieties have to be guided onto their supports.

Peas may be mulched like any other vegetable. They are sensitive to drought and should be carefully observed for water shortage, but watered only if necessary.

Harvest. The trick to picking peas is to gather them when their pods are nearly but not entirely filled out. Generally, the pods nearest the ground ripen first. The edible pod varieties are picked earlier. If you let them hang on too long, you won't enjoy eating the pods though the peas remain tasty.

Pepper

Warm weather crop.
pH 5.2 to 5.6.
Loam.
Start indoors 6 weeks before last spring frost. Transplant after all danger of frost is gone.
    Set plants 18 inches apart, in rows 2 feet apart.
Yields about 1 pound per plant.
Harvest in 60 to 80 days.

There are two types of peppers, hot and sweet. As one hot pepper can keep the average American palate burning for a year, there really isn't much need to grow your own. But sweet peppers, like tomatoes, can be eaten as a fruit and it is therefore difficult to grow too many of them.

Peppers are warm-weather creatures. Unless you are in the Deep South and have a long growing season, it is best to start the plants indoors and let them get 8 inches or higher before setting them out.

There are a fair number of varieties to choose from. Early Calwonder Sweet forms thick-walled, dark green fruit that matures in 68 days. Yolor Wonder is ready in 75 days. Its fruit is somewhat blockier and very sweet. Permagreen, developed recently by the University of New Hampshire, remains green to maturity and after. Exceptionally thick-walled, dark green, and very sweet, it is reportedly a heavy bearer. As it was developed up North, it is probably a little more cold-resistant than the others.

Planting and cultivation. Peppers do best in light loam. If your soil is poor, try mixing some composted manure in with the soil at the spot where you are going to place the plant. But don't make it all manure; peppers do not like an over-fertile soil. Peppers like a pH of 5.2 to 5.6, but they will tolerate soil with a pH of up to 7. Peppers usually need stake support. In general, their cultivation is much like that of tomatoes. Use mulch to conserve moisture and hold down the weeds.

Harvest. Peppers can be picked any time they form. The longer you wait, the larger the fruit will grow until it (most varieties) turns red. The flavor changes slightly and becomes ideal for pickling. Many people prefer the flavor of the red pepper over the green.

Potatoes

Very cold-hardy.
Sandy loam.
Plant seed potatoes as soon as the ground can be worked, each piece 4 inches deep and 1 foot from its neighbors, in rows 3 feet apart.
Yields more than 1 pound per plant.
Harvest in about 100 days.

Potatoes are native to South America, having been first cultivated by the Incas in the Andes Mountains and reported by the invading Spaniards. Today, potatoes are probably one of the most widely used vegetables in the world. When conditions are right, they are among the highest yielding per acre of all the vegetables.

They are a cool-weather crop that can be started as soon as the frost leaves the ground and can also be started early in June for a fall crop.

They are easily grown and flourish in sandy, loose loam that is acidic. But potatoes grown in tight, high pH, infertile dirt are plagued by bugs and scab. It is not uncommon for bugs to chew weak plants down to the ground in a couple of days.

If you can purchase seed potatoes from a reliable seedman, you will probably find that he carries Irish Cobbler, Chippewa, Green Mountain, and Katahdin. The Cobbler is a good early variety with a round shape and creamy white skin. The Chippewa looks the same, but is supposed to have a higher resistance to mild mosaic (a fungus disease). Green Mountain is a late variety with a large, flattened, long body that is russet colored. Katahdin is somewhat like the Cobbler, but it is usually sown for late harvest.

Planting and cultivating. If you can't purchase seed potatoes, you can always use what you can buy at the market. Select tubers of the type you prefer. Make certain they are free of scabs and black specks that look like a touch of tar. The black is *Rhizoctunia* bacteria. Discard for seed use those tubers that have one or more long

Potato plants coming up in early spring.

stems growing from the eyes. Pick potatoes that have no stems, or no more than two very short ones per eye. Now, place the potatoes you have selected to use for seed out in the sun for a few days. The air temperature must be below 60°F but above freezing. This encourages the tubers to develop short, tough shoots that speed growth (much better than the spindly ones grown in warm darkness).

When you are ready to plant, cut each potato into several chunky pieces, each piece to have one or two eyes, but no more. Plant the pieces as suggested: 4 inches deep, 1 foot from its neighbor in rows 3 feet apart.

Now there is nothing to do until the shoots emerge from the ground. At this time you mulch exactly as you would for any other plant. Now again there is nothing to do until the potatoes are ready.

Harvest. The tubers are ready when the plant tops wither. You can now dig them up or wait as long as a month if you prefer. Use a garden fork and dig carefully to avoid mashing your potatoes before they are cooked. Once unearthed, let them lie in the sun until the adhering soil is dry. Then brush the soil off, and store your crop in a dark, cool place with a temperature preferably around 37°F. If potatoes are exposed to light, they turn green. The small, sometimes green potatoes you find near the surface of the soil are called new potatoes and are especially good when boiled. These should not be stored but should be eaten more or less directly.

Pumpkin

Cold-sensitive.
pH 5.6 to 6.8.
Loam.
Plant seeds well after first frost, 1 inch deep, six seeds per hill, with hills 6 feet apart. Thin to two or three plants per hill.
Yields over 100 pounds per pumpkin (depending on variety).
Matures in 95 to 120 days.

Most pumpkins are vine crops closely allied to squash. Pumpkins ramble along the ground, taking up lots of space and demanding cool, steady temperatures and fertile loam. If you are short on space and still want these jolly fellows, you can plant them near an established lawn, and let them ramble across for the summer. Or you can plant them between rows of corn—some farmers even put a few pumpkin seeds near the corn seeds. If you haven't the required soil, you can fool them by digging a hole, discarding half of the soil, and replacing it with rotted manure. Make the hole about 1 foot across and equally deep.

There is little you can do about their temperature requirements, except make do with what you have. Up North you can extend the growing season and keep the pumpkins out of the cold spring night air by starting them indoors and holding transplanting off until well into spring. Down South you can cater to their heat sensitivity by planting them in semishade, which brings us back to the cornfield. Lacking a cornfield, you can try planting the pumpkins a distance from pole and trellis crops, but positioned so they are shaded part of the day.

There are a number of pumpkin varieties: some are grown for their seeds (which are eaten, not planted), some are bush types, and some are grown for their size.

Lady Godiva matures in 100 days, has green and yellow stripes, and was developed by the U.S. Department of Agriculture for its highly edible, high-protein seeds. Fruits are only 8 inches in diameter. Big Tom ripens in 120 days and has thick, dry sweet flesh. Its fruit is excellent for pies and weighs up to 18 pounds. Big Max isn't ready for show for 120 days. By then it may be 70 inches in circumference and weigh more than 100 pounds. It makes a whopper of a pie. Small Sugar is best for all-around use. Ready in 100 days, it is about 7 inches in diameter with bright orange, sweet flesh. Cinderella is a bush-type pumpkin that needs only 6 square feet of growing space. Its 10-inch fruit is ready in 95 days.

Planting and cultivation. Wait until the frost is gone, then plant as suggested above. Mulch as soon as the plants show any size. Pumpkins need no attention; they are easy to grow in this respect.

Harvest. Cut the vine about 5 inches from the fruit. Let it remain in the fields a few days to permit its skin to harden. Pumpkins can take a little frost, but a hard frost will damage them; so don't wait too long.

Radish

Cold-hardy.
pH 6.0 to 7.2.
Sandy loam or loam.
Plant seeds as soon as ground can be worked, ½ inch deep, 1 inch apart, in rows 12 inches apart. Thin to two or more inches apart, depending on variety.
Yields vary with variety.
Harvest in 22 to 60 days.

Radishes are the easiest of all vegetables to grow and certainly are the first to show a return. They will grow anywhere if watered, but to be crisp and palatable, they must have loose, friable soil.

There are three general classes of radishes: spring, summer, and winter. The division is made on the basis of temperature preference and growing time. The spring radishes grow most rapidly and are most appreciative of cool weather. The summer group grows a little more slowly and prefers warmer weather. The winter radishes grow most slowly and taste best when they complete their growth in cool and cold weather.

The list of available varieties is very large. Here are just a few.

Spring types: Burpee White, ready in 25 days, tastes best when under 1 inch in diameter. Cherry Belle, round, red, and smooth, is ready when it is ¾ inch across, and that takes only 22 days.

Summer types: Champion, similar to Cherry Belle but larger and more heat-resistant. Ready in 28 days. White Icicle reaches a length of 6 inches, sweet and mild. Also resists heat well.

Winter types: Round Black Spanish, ready in 55 days, has a large globe-shaped root up to 4 inches in diameter with rough black skin. This one is pungent if not picked on time. White Chinese, sometimes called Celestial, is the mildest of all the winter radishes and has a pure white root up to 6 inches long and as much as 3 inches in diameter. Takes 60 days to reach full size but can be removed and eaten anytime.

Another that is called All Seasons White Radish requires 45 days to reach maturity, but can be left in the earth another 6 weeks without its texture or flavor changing. In fact, it is tasty and edible even when it has reached an unbelievable radish size of 12 inches in length and 2½ inches in diameter. This variety can be grown anytime.

Planting and cultivation. The seed is sown no more than ½ inch deep, even less for the quick-grow varieties. As the seeds are very small, you probably will do much better with the seed rolls. In any event, start pulling alternate radishes as soon as you see that one is interfering with another. Except for the All Seasons variety, your radishes will taste better if pulled a little before maturity instead of afterward.

To keep a crop coming all summer long, plant your second batch as soon as your first batch sends up its first pair of leaves.

Harvest. Just remove when ready and eat.

Rhubarb

Cold-hardy perennial.
pH 6.0 to 7.2.
Highly fertile loam.
Plant root cuttings 5 inches deep, 4 feet apart.
Yield depends on plant age and soil.
Harvest in 2 years.

Rhubarb is a perennial that produces a fair return once every spring in view of the little attention it requires. It can be started from seed, but the most practical method is to purchase roots and plant them. As the roots last for many years, their cost is not excessive, though not cheap either.

Rhubarb was first cultivated by the Chinese 40 centuries ago. Whether they ate its stalk is unknown, but they did ascribe valuable medicinal properties to the plant's roots. Our present plants came to us via Russia, reaching England some-time in the early 1600s, when it was still grown as a medicine. Just when Englishmen stopped treating themselves with rhubarb root extract and began treating themselves to its stalks is unknown. Present-day varieties were developed only recently. The first and still the best-known and most expensive variety is called the MacDonald, after the college of the same name in Quebec where it was developed. The MacDonald stalks have a brilliant red color. Their skins are tender and need not be peeled off. Sauces and pies have a pink color. The Valentine has deep red stalks, and the Victoria has green stalks shaded in red.

Planting and cultivation. As the crop you harvest will depend on the fertility of the soil, you are advised to work in as much well-composted manure as you can before planting the root cuttings, which incidentally must be planted with the shoots pointing upward. Simply dig a hole of sufficient depth and size, insert the root, and cover it with soil and press firmly down. Weed until the stalks show, at which time they will fend for themselves.

Harvest. The plant is ignored the first year. No stalks should be pulled. When the frost gets the stalks, cover them with mulch. The following spring you can "pull" a few stalks, and the word is used advisedly. The stalks are not cut but pulled off by grasping each one near the ground and pulling it back and away. Do not pull more than a few, and stop when they grow back weak and spindly. When a stalk bearing a flower head appears, pull it off.

The following year you can pull more stalks, again stopping when the new stalks become thin, indicating that the root has given up much of its reserve energy.

Sometime after the seventh year the crop will fall off. There will be fewer stalks, and each stalk will be thinner than before. This is the time to dig up the root and examine it. Cut the old portions away, taking care to leave at least two "eyes" in each of the portions that you are going to keep. Replant the "new" roots, and you are back in the rhubarb business again.

Note that the leaves are never eaten but always cut off along with at least an inch of attached stem. The leaves contain some form of poison.

Rutabaga (see also Turnip)

Very cold-hardy.
pH 5.5 to 7.0.
Loam, high in phosphorus.
Plant seed as soon as ground can be worked, ½ inch deep, 2 inches apart; space to 5 inches apart, in rows 12 inches apart.
Yields up to ¾ pound per plant.
Harvest in 85 to 90 days.

Sometimes called the Swedish turnip, the rutabaga is larger, more cold-resistant, and firmer-fleshed than the turnip. It keeps better through the winter. Some rutabagas are elongated much like a carrot, and others are globe-shaped. Some varieties have white flesh while others are yellow.

The Macomber is possibly the best of the white types, while Purple-Top Yellow, which is ready in 90 days is possibly the best choice among the yellow-fleshed varieties. The Purple-Top does show purple aboveground, but is light yellow below. It cooks to an orange color, however, having sweet, fine-grained flesh.

Planting, cultivating, and harvest. Except for allowing more space between the plants, the rutabaga is treated exactly like the turnip.

Spinach

Very cold-hardy.
pH 6.4 to 7.6.
Well-drained loam.
Plant seeds as soon as ground can be worked, ½ inch deep, 2 inches apart, in rows 18 inches apart. Thin to 5 inches apart.
Yields something less than ½ pound per plant.
Harvest in 48 to 70 days.

If we stretch the facts a little, we can say that there are two types of spinach. One is cold-hardy and heat-sensitive, bolting to seed when the weather turns hot. The other is both heat- and cold-hardy. The first is the good old spinach some of us hate (and some love). The second is not really spinach, but is *Tetragonia expansa*, whereas the real stuff is *Spinacia oleracea*. The second doesn't look like spinach when it is growing, but when prepared, it looks, tastes, and has all the nutritional value of spinach.

It is called New Zealand, after the land of its origin. It can be harvested in 70 days, produces an abundance of fleshy, crisp green leaves which can be picked through the summer. There is no need to pull the entire plant. There is only one variety of *Tetragonia expansa* available, and it has just been described. That is it.

There are possibly a dozen or more varieties of "real" spinach to pick from. Here are some of the better known. Bloomsdale Long-Standing, ready in just 48 days. It grows erect, is slow to bolt, and produces a heavy yield of thick, crinkled, dark, glossy green leaves, which can be eaten raw or cooked. America requires 50 days, produces thick, tender green leaves in masses of up to 10 inches across. Also reputed to be slow-bolting and especially popular with backyard farmers, Hybrid No. 7 does it in just 42 days. It grows upright and is resistant to downy mildew. Fordhook also is ready in about 42 days. The young leaves can be used in a salad.

Planting and cultivation. The seeds are sown in the open just as soon as the earth can be worked, which can be as early as 4 to 6 weeks before the last frost-free day of spring. The seeds are buried ½ inch deep and 2 inches apart for regular spinach, and a little more for New Zealand. The rows can be 18 or so inches apart. Thin by pulling alternate plants as soon as you have little more than a half-dozen leaves on each plant. Repeat a second time when the plants are approximately half grown. Pull the regular spinach when it is full grown; just trim the outside leaves from the New Zealand.

For a continuous crop of standard spinach, make successive plantings every two weeks up until 2 months before the start of summer's heat. Resume planting at the tail end of summer, and stop 2 months before the first hard frost.

If your winters are mild, cover your last unpicked crop with mulch, and you should have a real early harvest the following year.

Spinach is sensitive to soil conditions; so check soil pH before planting. Spinach is also subject to damping off; so don't overwater, and don't crowd the young plants with mulch. You'll just have to hand-weed a little at first.

Harvest. The standard spinach is simply pulled when ready or even earlier. The outer leaves on the New Zealand are carefully cut and removed.

Squash

Cold-sensitive.
pH 5.6 to 6.8.
Well-drained loam.
Plant well after frost is out of earth, ½ inch deep, 6 seeds to a hill; thin to 3 plants; space
  hills 6 feet apart. Or start indoors and transplant.
Yield depends on variety and harvest time.
Matures in 50 to 110 days.

There are bush-type squash, vine-type, and summer, fall, and winter types. Some are eaten before maturity. Some are used only after they have matured. Some are cooked, some are baked, and some are merely ornamental.

The entire squash family is sensitive to the cold. Neither the seeds nor the

Summer squash (zucchini) being mulched with grass cuttings.

seedlings should be planted outdoors until the ground is fairly warm. Plantings must be timed to permit your variety to go to maturity or ripen to your taste before the onset of frost, because it doesn't take very much cold to destroy the leaves of the plant, though the hard-skinned fruit can remain outdoors for quite a while.

There are many fine varieties of summer squash to choose from. These can be picked anytime before maturity. Here are a few.

Early White Bush, ready in 54 days, fruit starts out pale green and changes to creamy white, forming a flat pan 7 inches across, 3 inches deep, with scalloped edges. St. Pat Scallop, ready in just 50 days, has bell-shaped fruit that tastes best when a little less than 2 inches across. Early Summer Crookneck needs 54 days, is bright yellow, and has the crooked neck common to this variety. It is best when picked under 4 inches in length. Burpee Golden Zucchini, ready in 54 days, forms a golden cylinder and has a true Italian flavor.

And here are a few of the fall and winter varieties. These are picked only after their skins harden, and they are usually baked. Notice there is a much longer wait for harvest.

Burpee Butternut Squash, needs 85 days, has a sweet-nutty flavor when baked. Its flesh is orange, and its fruits reach a length of up to 10 inches. Pick them all when winter comes; you can eat the young ones. Royal Acorn needs 82 days; shaped like a giant, ribbed acorn, it is dark green outside but turns to orange upon

Winter squash two weeks after transplanting.

storage. Depending on soil and moisture, this variety can reach 7 inches in height. True Hubbard, ready in 115 days, is a most popular winter squash because if properly stored it will keep until spring. Excellent for pies, boiling, baking, etc. Has a dark, bronze-green skin and will reach 10 pounds in weight. Burpee's Bush Table Queen is a semibush type, requiring less space than the vine type and producing a large number of acorn-shaped fruit 5 inches long. Cooks dry and sweet; tastes much like a sweet potato when baked.

Winter squash planted next to pole beans.

Planting and cultivation. Squash prefer soils that are high in organic matter; so if you have some humus or composted manure, work that in. They also prefer well-drained soil, so if your farm is a bit on the wet side, build a low hill, say a few inches high, for the seeds.

The vine types are planted in hills, no more than two to three plants per hill. The bush type can be planted in rows, in which case the seeds are thinned to plants 18 inches apart, or the seedlings are set out this far apart in rows 3 feet apart.

Mulch as soon as you have a fair-sized plant. If you wish, you can try an old farm trick; place a few shovels full of earth here and there on the sprawling vines to encourage them to put out side roots; it is supposed to increase yield. Also, with care you can guide the galloping vines away from trellises and poles, which they will climb if handy.

Harvest. You can't harvest summer-type, soft-skinned squash too early. Most of them taste best when small; all taste poorly or are inedible when oversize. And frequent harvest encourages the plant to produce more. The hard-skinned fall and winter squash can be permitted to grow to size, but lift them up now and again to prevent slugs from attacking, which they may do if the fruit lies on wet earth. Incidentally, squash have an uncanny ability to hide, so when frost comes, use a rake to turn all the vines over. You'll be surprised at the number you have overlooked.

Strawberries

Cold-sensitive.
pH 5.9 to 6.5.
Sandy loam, well drained and high in organic matter.
Start seed indoors midwinter, and transplant, or purchase plants and set out after first
   frost, 18 inches apart.
Yields up to 2 pints per plant.
Harvest some varieties 8 weeks after setting out plants.

Strawberries are the most appealing of all the fruits and vegetables, and the most demanding in terms of time and labor. However, with good soil, a little experience, and a system, work can be held to a minimum, and if you have a well-trained pussycat or use a muslin cover, you won't share your harvest with the birds.

There are many new varieties to choose from, including two new bush types, which are available only in seed form. The others can be purchased as full-size plants ready to be set out.

Earlidawn and Midland are both early types. Earlidawn produces berries up to 4 inches around. Midland is excellent for freezing. Catskill, Midway, and Robinson are midseason varieties. Sparkle, Ozark Beauty, and Ogallala are midseason to late varieties, with Ozark Beauty reputedly the heaviest and most hardy of the fairly recent hybrids. The group just listed can also be considered everbearing. Marlate is a very late, single-crop variety, as are Gardian and Superfection.

All the above are available as plants. Alexandria and Harzland are two bush varieties, available in seed form only at this writing. Neither produces runners, and the Harzland is everbearing. Both produce berries the first season and are, like other strawberries, perennials.

Planting and cultivation. Strawberries do best in sandy loam that is loaded with rotted manure or humus. Although the plants appear to have a short-root system and other writers may advise shallow soil preparation, if you have manure or fertilizer to add, work it into the soil for 6 or 8 inches.

Harvesting strawberries.

To set the plants, thrust your trowel or spade edge into the earth to make a deep, wide slit. Lower the plant's roots into the slit. Try to keep the roots fanned out. Do not try to position the roots as you would those of a bush; the roots are too soft. Position the plant vertically so that its crown (the lump) just rests on the surface of the soil. Press the earth around the roots and water. It is important that the roots not be exposed. If they are, the plant will die. It is also important that the crown not be positioned beneath the surface; if it is, it will rot and the plant will die.

Every strawberry farmer has his own system for setting out the plants in relation to each other. Here are four arrangements. The last is the most common commercial arrangement.

The individual plants are spaced 18 inches apart in two rows 12 inches apart, with footpaths between the double rows. All the runners are pinched off as they appear. This is called the hill or hill row system. It is generally used with everbearers.

The plants are spaced 24 inches apart in rows 30 inches apart. This is called the hedgerow, single. All the runners are pinched except two from each plant, which are guided to open spaces between the plants. A variation of this system is called the double hedgerow and is simply two rows. These two systems provide additional berry plants, which you will need in time, as will be explained. They take a little more work and the individual berries may be a bit smaller.

The matted-row system involves no runner pinching. The plants are set out 20 inches apart in rows 3 feet apart, which includes space allotted to walking. Only those runners that cross the path are pinched off. This system requires the least work but supposedly results in smaller berries and a smaller yield per plant: the runners absorbing some of the food that would otherwise go into the berries.

This writer suggests a modified matted-row system. Simply pinch a few runners off whenever convenient.

In order to clarify the systems of dispersing the plants over the field, one important step has been left out, and that is mulching. To keep the berries from lying on the earth and rotting and to keep moisture in and weeds out, it is advisable to mulch the earth around each plant heavily with clean straw. Without it you will have a heck of a time keeping up with the weeds. Strawberries are too weak to defend themselves.

Mother plants and runners. Excepting for the bush types which we will discuss shortly, all strawberry plants send out runners—wire-thin arms—which they use for self-propagation. Every half dozen inches or so the runner puts down a shoot and before the season is over you have a new, baby strawberry plant right there. You need some of these new plants because the old plants, which are called mother plants when they give birth, lose their ability to bear. When the aforementioned crown becomes about 2 inches high, the plant has had it. So, if you don't want to be purchasing new plants every 3 or 4 years, you must let some of the runners take hold.

To secure the new plants some farmers half bury a small, dirt-filled pot in the earth beneath a runner and hold the runner in place with a mound of soil. The runner sends its roots into the pot and the new plant is formed there. In the fall the runner is cut and the new plant set into the earth where desired. A simpler method is to pinch and move the runners selectively so they form plants where you want them, in time replacing the overage plants.

Bush types. Start the seeds indoors during the winter, and set the plants out as soon as they crowd their pots. They can set as close as 12 inches apart because they do not form runners. To replace these plants you have to start with seeds again.

Harvest. The everbearing and the bush types can be harvested the first season. The others should not. Instead, pinch off their blossoms as soon as they appear. Pick the fruits as soon as they are red. Most types cannot remain on the plant for more than a few days without spoiling.

When the last berry has been picked, cover all the plants with several inches of straw or hay to protect them from the frost. Do not use leaves, as they will mat down and damage the plants.

Tomato

Cold-sensitive.
pH 5.2 to 5.6.
Loam.
Plant seeds $\frac{1}{4}$ inch deep, 3 inches apart. Transplant, and space 3 feet apart after all danger of frost is past.
Yields 10 pounds per plant and more, depending on climate.
Harvest in 75 to 90 days.

The tomato is still another plant brought to Europe from South America by the Spaniards. No doubt they brought the plant home in the form of seeds, which not surprisingly are still worth more than their weight in gold, even at today's gold prices. A packet containing 20 hybrid seed selling for 65 cents contains approximately 50 milligrams of growing power. This works out to be roughly 5 times more expensive than gold. In the long run, the plants brought away from South America proved to be more valuable than all the tons of stolen gold.

If you protect them from frost, tomatoes are an almost nonfail crop. That and the high cost of tomatoes in the shops is probably the reason tomatoes are to be found in almost every backyard farm. In the South you can sow the seeds directly

Cherry tomatoes grown with string beans.

outdoors. Up North, you can either purchase young plants or grow your own. Though they like rich, acidic, humus-filled soil and lots of sunshine, they will struggle along almost anywhere.

There must be hundreds of tomato varieties sold through seed catalogs and the garden supply shops. My favorite is Burpee's Big Boy, but no doubt you will find your own after a few tries. Here are just a few to start with. (Incidentally, since the sales people have taken over many seed outfits, you have to read the packets more carefully. Harvest in 52 days, or less, usually means harvest from the time the plants are set out.)

Burpee's Pixie Hybrid is an early-crop, high-yield, small-size plant developed for window box gardeners. It does not exceed 18 inches in height. Scarlet Dawn is another early tomato. Livingston's Globe, named for a pioneer in tomato development, produces pink fruit. Jubilee has yellow fruit as much as 3½ inches across. Yellow Pear bears in clusters. The tomatoes are yellow and pear-shaped, and excellent for pickling as they are very firm. Beefsteak is an old-time favorite with a distinct, strong flavor of its own. Burpee's Delicious reaches 2 pounds in weight and has very solid, scarlet fruit. Big Boy also can reach 2 pounds. Its fruit is a deep red, smooth and solid.

Planting and cultivation. Since almost everyone grows tomatoes, a considerable amount of lore has been accumulated in this field. Some is the result of scientific testing, and some the accumulation of informal experimentation. Let us start with the "hard" data and then drift off.

Tomato seeds do not germinate readily and are subject to damping off. They are best started in a sterile growing medium at a temperature of between 70 and 80°F. The hybrid seeds need plenty of warmth. Seedlings do best at a temperature of 60

You can make a hotkap or a tiny cold frame by using three sticks and an ordinary plastic bag. Bag raises plant's temperature and protects it somewhat from frost.

to 70°F; so when the plants show, move them to a cooler spot. Don't skip hardening off the plants, and be careful; a touch of frost can do them in.

Don't set them out until all danger of frost is past. If you set them out early, protect them with hotkaps or a temporary cold frame made of a sheet of plastic stretched over a wire frame.

Plants to be individually staked should be spaced 3 feet apart or more. Plants to be trained to a fence or trellis can be closer, but there is no point in loading the space up. Three standard plants on 8 feet of trellis will produce as much as eight standard plants on the same trellis. Dwarf types can be set closer.

Some of the methods of supposedly securing more root from each plant have been discussed before, but we will repeat for convenience. One trick, setting the plant very deep, doesn't do any good. Dig the deep-set plant up after the season, and you will not find that it has more roots than others. Setting the plant in the soil at an angle may help; this writer never tried it. The standard method, setting each plant in a bowl-shaped depression, always works out fine as it helps you water the plant generously when you set it and helps you water at other times; the bowl holds the water in place and keeps it from running off.

The use of a sheet of black plastic as mulch for setting tomatoes has a number of advantages. (Clear plastic produces higher temperatures but encourages some weed growth.) It kills off the weeds, raises soil temperature, and appears (at least in my neighbor's yard and in the literature) to speed harvest. The sheet must be laid down before the plants are set out and must be held in place with a few stones or what have you. The sheet doesn't enrich the soil by any means, and it is questionable whether the plastic will speed tomato harvest more than a heavy layer of organic mulch.

Mulched with black plastic covered with wood chips to hold it down, these highly pruned tomato plants produced earlier than usual, but didn't produce as much.

Some farmers prune their tomato plants. The thought is that mere branches do not produce tomatoes; therefore they reduce the crop. In this system the suckers or side branches that grow out from the axils where the leaves join the main stem are cut off, preferably with a razor. Some gardeners just leave the main stem with a few main leaves. (Incidentally, when cropping, make certain you are not removing a stem that is going to open out into tomato buds. Let the stem form before you cut.) The result of this system is a skinny plant with a number of large tomatoes.

My thoughts and observation lead me to conclude that pruning tomato plants reduces the total crop because it reduces the plant's ability to convert the mineral waters that its roots provide into sugars and starches. The leaf is where it all happens. Remove the leaves, and you remove the sugar factory. This is dramatically demonstrated by the grapevine. Cut off side canes while its grapes are unripe, and many of the grapes will shrivel up.

I cut off the bottom leaves and branches on my tomato plants because they drag in the mud and the fruit resting on the ground tends to rot.

Staking, that is tying a single plant to a stake, is the simplest method used for keeping tomatoes off the ground, but it is a poor one because the plant's arms droop and fold over the supporting tie. When they do, circulation is cut off and the arm dies. A trellis of some sort is much better because you can let the arms spread without folding. Incidentally, you can bend vines in any direction so long as you do so over a period of days. Stakes and trellises are discussed in Chapter 14.

Harvest. Pick the fruit as soon as it shows the proper color. You can delay a few days, but if you delay too long the fruit will burst, especially if there has been a rain. In the fall let the plants be, even though you expect a mild frost. Tomatoes are fairly hardy at this time, and by putting off cleanup you can sometimes get two or

Pruning a tomato plant. The branch growing out of the axil—the joint between a true branch and the trunk of the plant—is twisted off. Some farmers believe this improves harvest; this farmer doesn't.

three more weeks of Indian summer. During this time you can harvest more tomatoes. Just keep picking the red ones; they are more easily damaged than the green. And don't discard the green. Collect them all, and store them in a cool place. When you want some, remove them and place them in a warm dark room. In this way you can have ripe tomatoes, albeit a little dry, up until December.

Turnip

Very cold-hardy.
pH 5.6 to 6.8.
Loam, high in phosphorus.
Plant seed as soon as ground can be worked, ½ inch deep, 2 inches apart; space to 4 inches apart, in rows 12 inches apart.
Yields up to ½ pound per plant.
Harvest in 35 to 60 days.

Turnips are grown for both their leaves (greens) and roots. They are tough, winter-hardy plants that will make a showing anywhere but do their best in loam that is high in phosphorus. Start your sowing early in spring, and make successive plantings about two weeks apart to secure a constant crop. Quit two months before you expect the full heat of summer, and resume planting in late summer, continuing up until two months before the frost hits the pumpkins.

Purple-White Globe is perhaps the best all-around variety. It is good cooked or raw and is ready in 55 days. Its roots are smooth, nearly round with bright purple tops. It grows to 5 inches across, but tastes best when only 3 inches across. Tokyo Cross and Early Milan are ready in 35 and 45 days, respectively. The Cross has high resistance to virus and other diseases and is best when only 2 inches across.

New Hampshire Midget watermelon. *(Courtesy W. Atlee Burpee Co.)*

The Milan is best when no more than 3 inches in diameter. The leaves of the Shogoin are ready for cooking in only 30 days. Its root needs 70 days. The foliage of the Just Right Hybrid is ready 30 days after seeding. Its root measures 5 inches long and 3 inches thick when ready in 60 days.

Planting and cultivation. The seeds are sown early, and alternate plants are pulled as soon as they crowd one another. Then the soil should be mulched close but not up to the roots.

Harvest. Keep tabs on the variety you plant so that you won't let them grow too large, as they will then become tough and bitter. The only exception is Tokyo Cross, which can be left in the ground until it is 6 inches across without turning pithy and bitter.

Watermelon

Cold-sensitive.
pH 5.0 to 5.6.
Sandy loam high in organic fertilizer.
Plant seeds well after all chance of frost is gone, ½ inch deep, eight seeds in a 1-foot circle, in hills 7 feet apart. Cull to three plants to a hill.
Yield depends on variety.
Harvest in 70 to 100 days.

Watermelons are the luxury fruit of the backyard farm. They require lots of space and long, lazy summers, free of little boys who can't resist sleeping watermelons lying unprotected in the fields.

Today, there are many excellent varieties to choose from. There are baby melons only 7 inches long with yellow interiors and big green daddies that can go to 50 pounds of pure, unmitigated joy. Here are a few.

Burpee Hybrid Seedless is ready in 80 days, goes to 14 pounds, and has red flesh with few seeds. Yellow Baby Hybrid is an oval melon under 7 inches in length with bright yellow, sweet, juicy flesh. It is ready in 70 days. Charleston Grey goes to 35 pounds, is ready in 85 days, and resists *Fusarium* wilt, anthracnose, and sunburn. Hybrid Dixie Queen can reach 50 pounds, ready in 85 days; it has few seeds and crisp, sweet red innards. New Hampshire Midget, well suited to northern climate, ripens in 70 days and reaches the size of a large cantaloupe, weighing about 6 pounds when ready to eat.

Planting and cultivation. Watermelons like well-drained, sandy loam rich in rotted manure. Old-time farmers recommend that at least half a wheelbarrow of manure be mixed into each hill before planting. The seedless varieties are started indoors. The others are usually started directly in the field. Wait until all danger of frost is past. Sow the seeds ½ inch deep in circles 1 foot across, eight or more seeds to each circle, and space the circles 7 feet apart for the midget varieties and 9 feet for the big boys. Cull the weaker plants when they show, leaving no more than three vines to each hill; two if you haven't enriched the soil. Mulch, and wait for harvest.

Harvest. When the melons have reached their advertised size, when their underside shows yellow, when they thud and do not resonate when you tap them, when they feel heavy for their size, when an experienced melon expert says they are ready, they are ready. The only exact guidance this writer can offer is that it is better to pick watermelons a little after maturity than earlier. When they are immature, they are not sweet. On the other hand, wait too long, and they go bad. It is a problem.

CHAPTER SEVENTEEN

Bush Fruit

RASPBERRIES

ALTHOUGH THE TERM bush fruit is by no means an exact description, it is apt for raspberries, blackberries, blueberries, and their ilk. These are bushes of varying sizes and temperaments, and they do belong together because they all have two things in common. They provide delicious fruit and require very little work.

Probably the most popular of the bush fruits, raspberries are perennials that produce fruit on 1-year-old canes which then die with the onset of winter. Usually a plant will thrive for 5 or 6 years and then simply dry up, at which time it is removed.

Raspberries are not started from seed but from small plants available from nurseries. Once in the soil and growing, the plants propagate themselves in one or both of two ways, depending on variety (excluding their seeds which lie in the fruit). The plants may form suckers, which are canes (shoots) that grow directly from a root a distance from the plant itself.

And, or, the plant may bury its head: literally push the tip of one cane or more into the soil and form roots that very summer. The sucker and a portion of the attached root may be cut from the old plant and replanted to form a new, independent plant. The buried tip of the cane may be cut from the remainder of the old cane, at which time the tip with its own roots becomes an individual plant that may be left where it is or moved. Thus, once you purchase a number of

Planting a raspberry bush alongside a house. Roots are given plenty of room. Canes are cut back to 6 inches after planting.

raspberry plants, you have all you need and more for the rest of your farming days.

Soil, climate, location. Raspberries like many other plants relish rich, humus-filled loam. But unlike many other plants they will make do very well with almost anything they can get, so long as it is not water-logged. Their pH preference ranges from about 5 to 7, but isn't at all critical.

Raspberries are a cool-weather crop and will not do well in the Deep South. At the same time, the plants cannot withstand extreme cold either. If you live up in Minnesota and parts of North Dakota where the temperature can drop to 40 below, you had best check with your local nurseryman before investing in raspberries. Even the most generous mulching will not protect the plants from arctic temperatures.

Varieties. There are red, golden-yellow, and black; there are early, midseason, late, and everbearing raspberries. Here are just a few.

Ranere favors a sandy soil, is an everbearing red with small to medium berries. It is hardy and propagates rapidly.

Pruned raspberry canes in early spring.

June produces large, bright red berries. Its canes are almost thorn-free. It prefers clayey soil and does not send out as many suckers as Ranere.

Bristol produces glossy *black* berries in midseason.

Cumberland is another black with large berries in midseason.

Indian Summer is another red everbearer that produces in June, July, and again in the fall. It is more cold-resistant than the others.

September is equal in cold resistance to the Indian Summer, but its red fruit is larger, and it produces in midsummer and fall.

Southland is an everbearing red that is better suited to the mid-South than the others.

PLANTING AND CULTIVATION

You will not harvest any berries the first year, and not too many the second. Not until the third year will you be inundated with fruit. So select your berry patch area with care. You don't want to move the bushes about, but want them to remain in place forever.

They like the sun and the open air, but they will take some shade and confinement, as in an alley between houses. They don't mind trees, but they must be well clear of the drip line. As for the number of bushes to set out, the way this farmer cultivates them, there isn't much work; so don't worry about having too many. You can always find friends who will be pleased to pick themselves a bowlful.

Control. Raspberry bushes and their ilk will overrun your farm in a year or two if you let them. They must be confined, even the upright varieties. The easy way is a single fence, to which they are roped, or a double fence, between which the canes are guided. The latter arrangement is the simplest and easiest. You only need to tie the bushes once in a while.

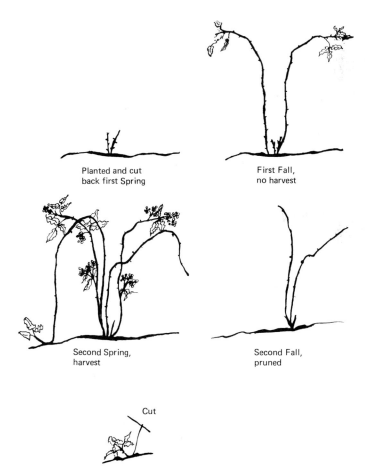

Planted and cut
back first Spring

First Fall,
no harvest

Second Spring,
harvest

Second Fall,
pruned

Cut

Second Fall, rooted tip separated from cane
and permitted to grow

Planting, growth, and harvest sequence in life of a raspberry or blackberry bush. Note that berries appear only on year-old canes, after which they are pruned back.

Blackberry sucker rising toward the sun from a mulch of leaves.

The fencing itself need be no more than two parallel bars about 3 and 4½ feet from the ground, supported by suitable stakes. Almost any material will do for the fencing. You can use pipe driven into the earth with heavy, galvanized wires as the bars; or fir, which is the cheapest kind of lumber; or tree branches, limbs cut off and wired together into lengths. The fencing needs only to be strong enough to support itself; the pressure of the canes is negligible.

Make the fences about 1½ feet apart, and as long as your row of bushes. Install them before or after you set out the young plants, but before they grow, or you will have a mess of wild cane. I have a single fence of wired branches that backs up to a neighbor's wire fence. Works fine.

Generally, directions call for the plants to be set out 3 feet apart, which is fine if you don't want to invest too heavily in a row of plants. But you will get more per foot of row if you set out twice the number of plants, say 1½ feet apart.

Dig a hole for each plant about 1 foot across and 8 inches deep. Remove the soil, discard half, and replace half with composted manure (or skip the manure if you wish). Now make a cone-shaped hill on the bottom of the hole; the apex of the cone to be just a fraction of an inch below the level of the soil. Examine the plant's roots. Cut broken ends cleanly off. Then position the center of the plant atop the cone, and spread the roots. Cover with soil, and tamp firm. You now have a plant, the crown of which is level with the soil and whose roots head downward. Water well, and mulch with whatever organic material you have. Spring and fall are the best times to set out bushes, but no matter, raspberries are tough, and if you see that they are watered, they will take hold anytime within the growing season. Next, cut the cane or canes back to 6 inches from the ground. Now there is nothing to do until the following spring.

Blackberry canes tied to a trellis.

Pruning. In the spring the plants will send up a number of canes. Cut the skinny ones back, leaving no more than two thick canes the first year, and no more than three in years following. Guide the canes up between your fencing. Tie the more rambunctious canes in place. There will be no berries on these canes this year. In the early fall, cut all canes off at a height of about 5 feet. Leave only those earth-seeking canes that you desire to root themselves. Cut these canes off close to the new root just before winter.

Cutting the canes short encourages them to send out laterals. Some farmers merely pinch (squeeze) their canes at the 5-feet point. I have found that cutting is simpler, neater, and much more convenient. I don't have the canes intruding into the rest of my plantings.

Harvest. The following year, blossoms and then fruit will appear on the canes which are now in their second year. At the same time the plants will send out new canes. Pick the berries as soon as they are ready. And they are ready if they fall into your hand at your touch. Pick earlier, and the fruit is a bit sour; pick too late, and the fruit is on its way to becoming wine; it's loaded with yeast. Picking or not picking doesn't appear to affect the health of the plants one way or another.

However, in the fall, those canes that produced fruit must be removed. This is done by cutting them off about 2 inches from the ground. If you don't, they will interfere with next year's harvest, and the wind blowing on them can break the plant at the root.

At the same time, thin out the new canes. Remove the suckers, unless you want to cut them free and form new plants. And remove all the skinny canes even if there is nothing left but one thick cane. Take the new plants you have permitted to form, and plant them between the old plants. All of them will not take, and all of them will not grow as sturdy as you might wish; so don't worry about having too many replacement plants. Incidentally, use a small stone to encourage plants tips to root.

This all done, mulch away, and wait for the next harvest.

I don't know about other bush-fruit farmers, but this is all I have done with my plants over a dozen years or so and have always had a good crop except for the year my bushes were run down by an automobile. No cultivating, no fertilizer, no insecticide. If this appears improbable, think of the berry patches of your youth (or at least my youth). Interminable rows of bushes alongside rough stone walls marking the edges of fields. Nothing was ever done to the plants except to harvest the fruit. (The old cane, however, was a nuisance.)

BLACKBERRIES

All that was said about raspberry culture can be repeated for blackberries. There aren't as many varieties to be had; but those that are, are good.

Darrow, an improved old favorite, produces mid-July and continues for much of the season. Berries are about 1 inch long.

Thornfree has no thorns. Its one crop of berries are medium large, firm, and glossy.

Smoothstem, another new variety without thorns, is reported to be exceptionally vigorous and hardy. It will bear up to 40 large, sweet berries on a single cane. Harvesting begins in August and continues until frost.

BOYSENBERRY

This member of the bramble family is a cross between a blackberry, loganberry, and dewberry. It forms the largest berries of all. They are usually jet black, filled with juice, are sweet, and have few seeds. None of the bramble berries keep well, but the boysenberry keeps most poorly of all. It has to be used a day or two after picking.

Thornless is the most recent development. As its name implies it has no thorns. This variety does well in our Southern states and on the Pacific Coast where the winters are mild. North of Washington, D.C., the Thornless requires considerable winter protection.

Planting and cultivation. Boysenberries differ from raspberries and blackberries in that their canes ramble much more. They are far longer and have to be sort of hung on their supports. The young canes are sometimes guided along the ground or the lower horizontal support, out of the way of the producing canes. When the older canes have done their bit and are cut back, the new canes are moved up and into their place.

BLUEBERRY

When I was a boy and spent a portion of my summers on a farm, we used to walk a mile or so to a neighbor who had a giant blueberry patch. There, for five cents a quart we could pick berries to our heart's content. No charge for the berries we ate. I don't remember how tall I was at the time, but the bushes stretched over my head and the narrow paths between them formed a maze. The earth was always mucky underfoot.

I learn now that this was a "natural" or wild patch of blueberries, and that not

Mulching the base of a blueberry bush.

until half a century or so ago were blueberries cultivated successfully. The berries grew where they would and nowhere else. It wasn't until the late Dr. F. V. Coville of the U.S. Department of Agriculture put the finger on the causes that blueberry cultivation became a science and not a game of chance. He found that neutral and alkaline soils are fatal to blueberry plants and that they thrive only in highly acidic soils where certain fungi are present.

Now that we know, it is no trick at all to find or convert existing soil to suit blueberry growth. And it is a good thing too. Blueberries are even easier to grow than the bramble fruit, and the berries can be kept much longer.

Blueberries like an acidic soil with a pH of 4 to 5.2 that is constantly moist, but not water-soaked. So, if you have a low spot on your land, this is the place for blueberries.

They like their soil loose with plenty of organic matter. One of the old-time formulas for preparing soil for blueberries consisted of one part sand to two parts rotten wood, oak leaves, or rotted sawdust. A good-size hole would be dug in the ground, and the existing earth removed and replaced with the aforementioned mix.

It is a good mix if the organic material is well rotted; it is not if the organic matter is not rotted. Humus from a compost heap has a pH of 4 to 5, but fresh wood chips or leaves do not. So if you are going to prepare the soil for the blueberries, take care that you use the proper ingredients.

As an alternative, you can simply mix a quantity of sand in with the soil, and if the soil isn't neutral (pH 7) or more, the plant will squeeze by. If you mulch heavily as you should, the mulch will lower the pH, and the following season, preferably in the spring, you can mix about one teaspoon of sulfur in with the soil around each plant. I don't know why most books on the subject recommend that you wait

Blueberry blossoms. Each blossom will form a berry.

a year before adding the sulfur (usually mentioned as aluminum sulfate, which is not as desirable), but that is what they say.

If the soil is up near pH 7, I wouldn't advise planting the bush; I'd either heel the plants in, if I already had them, or I would put off purchasing plants until I could bring the pH down, either by adding sulfur, as explained in Chapter 7, or by adding humus. Incidentally, watch out for the pH of most composted and bagged ruminant manures. The ones I have tested read out pH 7—neutral.

To heel a plant in, you dig a shallow trench and lay the plant across the trench so that the roots are in the trench and the plant itself is lying on its side. Then the bare roots are covered with soil. Lying on its side this way confuses the plant, and it remains safe but dormant as long as its roots are moist.

Planting and cultivation. Assuming that your soil's pH is right, or close to what it should be, or at least down to pH 5.5, dig a hole large enough to easily accommodate the roots. Try not to disturb the ball of earth around the roots, or if there is merely moss, remove the moss, cut the ragged edges from the broken roots, stand the plant up, and spread its roots out so that the upper group is about 3 inches below the surface of the soil. Replace the soil, making a sort of saucer around the plant. Water thoroughly, and cut the plant back about one third. Space plants about 5 feet apart.

It is always necessary to cut plants back, because when they are removed from the earth, their roots are partially destroyed, and if the plant tries to supply more leaves with water than its roots can draw from the earth, the plant will dry up and die.

The root-leaf systems of all thriving plants are in balance. Remove some branches, and their leaves and the plant will put forth new branches and leaves. But remove some roots, and the plant will suffer because it has no way of putting out new roots quickly enough. If the major portion of the root system has been destroyed, as it is when plants are simply pulled up by the roots—a practice common to many bargain nurseries—a major portion of the leaf system must be cut off; otherwise the leaves drain the roots, and the plant dies.

In any event, it is better to cut back more than necessary, rather than less, but always leave at least two buds for growth.

While on the subject, here are a couple of tips: You can judge the condition of a plant by scraping a little bark from the ends of a branch. If the branch end is dry, the plant has run out of water. If you scrape a little bark near the plant's trunk and it is dry, the plant is most likely finished.

If you encounter a plant that appears dry or almost dead, cut its branches well back, and then set the plant in a bucket of water. Sometimes this treatment will revive a half-dead plant.

Getting back to our blueberry bushes. Water once a day until the bushes have obviously taken hold. Mulch generously with sawdust and similar granular material that rots quickly, or with whatever you have.

You won't get much of a crop the first season, but the crop will increase each year if the plants are watered sufficiently by either rain or hose (if the leaves droop, hit them with the hose), and if you mulch sufficiently to bring the pH down to where it belongs.

Do not cultivate the soil. Blueberry roots are close to the top, and you will damage them. Do not prune any more than is necessary to remove deadwood and clean up the bottom of the bush; you don't want berries near the ground. After a number of years your plants may develop thick, coarse branches that do not produce much fruit except at their extremities; they should be cut off during the plant's dormant season.

Harvest. The deep black fruit produced by the blueberry is deceptive. The berries may look ripe, but they really aren't until they drop into your hand when you merely touch them. If you force them off, you will find them sour. All the berries do not ripen at the same time; so you have a more or less extended harvest period.

Not really harvest time. Berries are still not quite ripe. They need to be a mite darker.

CHAPTER EIGHTEEN

Grapes

G RAPES HAVE BEEN cultivated over much of the world since prehistoric times. Very possibly, man has cultivated grapes even before he began with wheat and rye. It is therefore not surprising that we know a great deal about grapes and viniculture, the science of growing and harvesting grapes, a science to which many men devote their entire professional lives. What is surprising is that the much-cared-for and studied grape is so compliant, so willing to produce so generously for so long with so little assistance. No other fruit rewards the grower so well or is so adaptable. A single vine can produce upward of 25 pounds of grapes, depending on soil, sun, and water. An ordinary grapevine can be harvested profitably for 50 years. Grapes will grow where any other food crop will grow. They are to be found almost everywhere. In America alone there were almost 30 wild species of grapes growing before the advent of the white man.

If these aren't reasons sufficient to start you planting grapes, there are several additional reasons, products of our times you can say, for growing grapes. Store prices have never been higher; quality never lower. The big red (Tokay) variety of grapes sold in our supermarkets (super to what?) is all water and absolutely no flavor. Its juice is exactly like that of a mixture of sugar and water. The green grapes (they are never called anything but that in my market) are so green that they can curl your teeth, and the big black grapes (Reiber) are usually soft and semirotten.

By comparison, the grapes on my vines, and I do nothing but prune and harvest, have a flavor that you can recall half the winter through. I grow Himrod Seedless, Interlaken Seedless, and Catawba; and I think the flavor of my grapes is better than

Author staking a grape-
vine the first year after it
was planted and cut back.

Install the poles that hold
the wire trellis that will
support the vines at an
angle. This enables the
pole to better resist the
pull of the wires.

Grapes form very early on the vine—sometime in April or May, but will not be edible until September or October.

average because I let the grapes remain on the vines several weeks after they are ripe enough to eat. Obviously, it is easy enough for you to do the same.

Another reason why this is a good time to start your own vineyard, be it one vine or hundreds, is that a number of excellent new table and wine grape varieties have been developed.

Stark Blue Boy is an improved Concord (blue) that ripens a week earlier than usual, has a more mellow flavor, grows well in poor soils, and has tight clusters of grapes that can be left on the vine for 3 weeks or more. Good for eating, jam, juice, and jelly.

Golden Muscat is a new, midseason, golden table grape. Bearing its fruit in large clusters, it is vigorous and hardy, and an extremely heavy producer.

Steuben, a new, late midseason dark blue grape can withstand temperatures to 20°F below zero. It makes a fair wine but is best for eating: jams and jellies. Its berries are of medium size and have a sweet yet spicy tang.

Himrod Seedless, a very early, golden-yellow grape, is suited to table use. It keeps well and has a flavor like those of its parents combined, which are Thompson and Ontario.

Interlaken Seedless is a very early, golden-yellow table grape.

Niagara is one of the best known white grapes. Rates with Concord in vigor and crop size. Great for wine making as well as eating.

Buffalo is a new, extra-early, blue-black grape that makes excellent eating, is fair for wine making, and makes very tasty jams, jellies, and marmalade.

Vinered is a new, late-ripening grape that is good all around: table, wine making, jams, and jellies. In color it is light red; it has a tender skin and forms very large clusters.

Catawba bears dark copper-colored grapes late in the season. Each grape is very sweet and large and keeps very well. It is an old favorite and is prized as a source of wine.

Aurora, a new variety, is the result of crossing classic European varieties with hardy, disease-resistant wild American species. Its fruit is white-pinkish, excellent for eating, and producing a fine, delicate white table wine.

Foch is an extra-early, cold-hardy variety, also the result of crossbreeding, that can be used for a burgundy wine without blending.

Baco Noir bears an abundant quantity of blue grapes early in the season which form large tight clusters. Vines are disease-resistant and highly productive, and are grown commercially for making red table wines.

SITING

Vines require a number of years before they do their best, and, as stated, they last a long, long time. So take care in selecting your vineyard site, be it one vine or a hundred.

Grapevines like hillsides, where they are somewhat protected from the wind, but yet are exposed to air movement and a full sun. Grapevines do best in soil that is a mixture of gravel, loam, and a little clay, and has a pH ranging from about 6.5 to 7. But grapes are practical, hardy creatures. They will do well in almost any soil, under any conditions, so long as they have some sunlight and the ground beneath them is not waterlogged.

Grapes need 170 frost-free days to ripen. They can stand cold but not much more than 20°F below zero. Some varieties withstand cold better than others.

You can train your vines to grow on a supporting trellis made of stretched wires, up the side of your home, over a patio or garden trellis, or over an arbor in the garden. Remember, the root of the plant need not see the sun; only its leaves must. In the field, vines are usually positioned 8 to 10 feet apart in rows 8 to 10 feet apart. Wire trellises used in the field can be installed a year after the plants are set out.

PLANTING

Purchase 1 or 2-year-old vines. There is no point in buying more mature plants. The roots of older plants are usually damaged in transit; and no matter how mature your plant is, it will not produce grapes the summer you plant it, and very possibly it will not produce grapes the following summer.

Prepare the ground by digging a hole large enough to accommodate all the roots without crowding, and more than deep enough by several inches. Snip off the broken root ends. Mix a little humus, if you have it, in with the soil. Spread the

Examining the vines in midseason. This is a Himrod variety vine.

roots naturally, and cover with soil. Tamp firm, but do not fill up the hole. Leave a few inches unfilled. This arrangement will help you water the vine, which you should do as soon as you have the plant in its home. Fill the hole with water at least three times the first day, and at least once a day every day thereafter when it doesn't rain. Then at least twice a week until there is a good show of leaves, indicating that the vine has taken hold.

When the vine is first planted, it may extend several feet in length from its root. This is the way it should be for transit. However, as soon as you have planted and watered it, cut the vine back to the bottom two or three buds. If there are several vines, leave the thickest—with several buds. Never cut a cane off close to the main cane or stem. Always leave at least one joint (lump) on the cut cane to prevent loss of sap (bleeding).

Drive a 7-foot stake into the earth close to the vine, but not so close that you injure the roots. This done, you will have 6 vertical feet of stake, onto which you will guide, with light string, the most likely shoot that comes out of your new grapevine. You want this shoot to grow straight up. The shoot may not want to do so; it may curl a little here and there. No matter, so long as its general direction is upward. Tie the cane lightly so as not to damage it. Outside of this and keeping weeds out of the vine's hole by mulching or pulling, there is nothing to do but wait.

PRUNING

This is the tricky part. If you aren't certain of the following instructions, don't prune at all, which is a far, far better course of action than the one I took. For five years straight I pruned too heavily and saw nary a grape. Finally I got some old-timer to explain it to me. Anyway, I ended up with a very strong, well-developed root and stem.

This is the way a grapevine works. Let us start with the one or two-year-old vine we just planted and cut back. It has a root system and several buds. No body or canes, as they are called. By the end of the summer, each bud will have produced canes and leaves. Let us consider just one cane, and ignore all the rest. They work exactly the same.

Our cane will be several feet long and will carry a dozen leaves and a number of buds. There will be no grapes on this cane or on any of the other canes.

Comes the following spring, and our cane will be almost one year old. For convenience we will call it a year-old cane. During this summer, the summer of its first year, the cane will do three things. It will grow longer by anything up to more than a dozen feet. It will put forth a few side canes and leaves, and it will put forth grapes. In the summer that follows, the section of cane that put out fruit the year previously will do nothing but put out leaves and hang in there. The 1-year-old section will grow longer and put out fruit. No fruit will appear elsewhere. Clutch this fact of viniculture to your bosom, and you will never go wrong pruning grapevines. Grapes never grow on old cane, only on year-old cane—cane that grew the year immediately preceding.

Now, at the end of the third year our cane has grown through three summers; a few feet the first year, perhaps a dozen more the second and third year. It is now more than 30 feet or so long. If we let it continue to grow, it will reach a hundred or more feet in length. Should we let it do so, we will find our grapes appearing farther and farther away from the root of the plant, with a reduction in grape size and quantity. In addition to which, we will have trouble finding the tiny grapes among all those leaves and vines. For maximum productivity, we must prune our vine so that the grapes are never formed more than 20 or so feet from the plant's roots.

However, since we must have 1-year-old canes to secure a crop, how can we cut our cane back and still get grapes? Easy. Cut alternate canes back.

To explain, let us go back to our original plant. It is just a root and a couple of buds. The first season the plant will extend several canes, none of which will bear fruit. Let us cut back all but two, and call one the upper cane and the other the lower cane. In the second summer both will bear fruit. At the end of the second summer we cut one back to the main stem. The other cane, let us say the upper one, remains along with the new section it has formed.

The following summer the lower cane forms a new shoot. We harvest the upper cane and cut it back. Thus, at the end of this summer, we have a very short upper cane and a one-year-old lower cane. The next summer the lower cane, being one year old, produces grapes. The upper cane forms a new shoot. Thus, after the first or second year we always have a year-old cane and a new cane a-forming. In practice, we do this with however many canes we wish to permit on our vine.

Actual practice. The vine is planted and cut back to two or three buds. Next, one cane is encouraged to grow more or less vertically up our stake. The others are ignored. In the fall the vertical cane is cut at a height of 6 or so feet, or ignored if it hasn't reached this height. The other canes are cut back to the root. In doing so, always leave a few inches of cane. Never cut the cane back flush with the root or main stem the way you would with a tree. And always do your pruning well after the plant has stopped growing. To be certain, best wait for the first frost.

Around this time install a two- or three-wire trellis consisting of a pair of vertical poles with two or three wires stretched between them. The top wire is usually about 6 feet above the ground. The other two are spaced equidistant between.

The following summer, canes, leaves, and possibly fruit will spring from the buds on the single vertical cane. Guide the side canes onto the horizontal wires to make two or three crossarms; one cane in each direction. Be advised that the plant may not cooperate. It may not thrust forth canes nice and neatly at the correct cross-points. If so, *don't argue.* Bend the canes, wherever they may be headed onto the nearest wire, even if you have to turn one in a soft arc back on itself. Should you cut off a cane growing in an undesirable position, aesthetically, you will find that the plant will not put forth a new cane from a bud that lies exactly in the desired position. So just work with what canes appear. The arrangement doesn't have to be precise. Cut back all the extra cane; just be certain to leave a little stub.

At this point you now have a vertical stem and several crossarms. At the end of summer, cut each crossarm back, if necessary, so that none are more than 6 feet in length as measured from the vertical stem. From this moment on, your vertical stem and its crossarms are your permanent plant. You never prune this portion of the vine, but let it grow thick and strong.

The following summer the crossarms will be one year old, and they will produce grapes. At the same time they will extend themselves and produce laterals. Well after harvest, cut the crossarms back to their 6-foot length, and then cut *every other* cane that projects from the crossarms back to the next to last bud or joint.

The following summer, again after harvest, prune the canes that project from the crossarms. This time you cut the long canes almost back to the crossarms, leaving the new, one-year-old canes in place. This is the way we set up our alternate new and old cane system, working from the crossarms.

A few tips. Never cut the vines during the growing season. Supposedly useless leaves do reduce the crop: Cut off any canes and the plant will cut back on the grapes; they will actually shrivel up. Cut some canes and they will bleed: sap will drip out in clear, transparent drops.

At the start of summer, the new cane is pale green. By the end of summer, when you are ready to prune, the new cane will be as brown as the old. To prevent confusion, mark either the new or old cane with string or tape.

HARVEST

Keep tasting the grapes until you are satisfied. Then use a sharp knife or scissors to cut each bunch free. Do not pull them off. They all do not have to be removed at once, but usually can be left on the vine several weeks or more. It all depends on the season and variety.

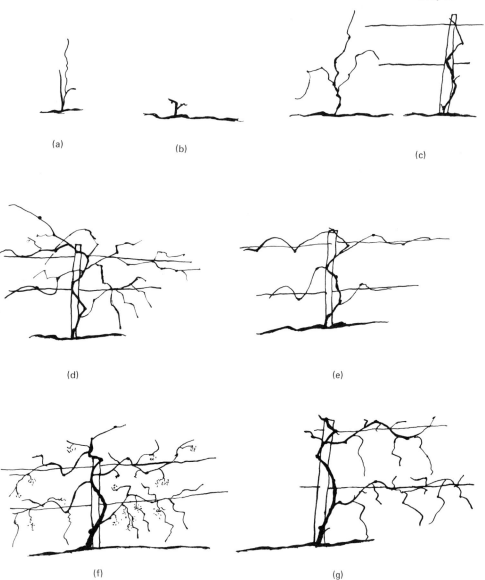

(a)

(b)

(c)

(d)

(e)

(f)

(g)

Grape cultivation. *(A)* The vine is planted as received. *(B)* It is cut back, leaving just three or four buds on the vine. *(C)* After the growing season, sometime in the fall, when the leaves have fallen from the vine, it is staked as shown and pruned back to a single erect cane. *(D)* At the end of the second fall, a multitude of new canes will have grown out of the single vertical cane. There may or may not be a few grapes. *(E)* The canes are pruned as indicated, after the second fall. *(F)* By the third fall, there will be a harvest of grapes on the year-old canes. *(G)* After the third fall, the canes are pruned back as indicated. These canes, growing from the horizontal arms, will bear grapes the following season. Leaves and the left side of the last drawing have been omitted for clarity.

LAYERING

To provide yourself with additional grapevines, a technique called layering is used. Take a long, low-growing cane. Lay it on the ground. Place a mound of fresh soil over a short portion of the cane. Direct the end of the cane upward again. Let it be for several years. Cut the cane between the soil and the main vine when roots have formed in the mound of soil. Move the new plant wherever you wish. Cut it back after planting.

The foregoing by no means exhausts the science of viniculture, but it will start you on your way and assure you of a bountiful harvest.

CHAPTER NINETEEN

Tree Fruit

MOST OF THE difficulties attending the growing and harvesting of tree fruit—apples, pears, and so on—can be easily eliminated by growing dwarf trees. The hard part with big trees is reaching up there. No such problem exists with small trees. You can reach the highest fruit standing on a box. Dwarf trees do not go over 15 feet in height. In addition, dwarf trees require very little pruning. Whereas full-size fruit trees are pruned heavily to hold down their vertical growth, which produces rashes of suckers and other undesired branches, which necessitates still more pruning, no such problem exists with small fruit trees. There is no need to limit their height. Pruning on a small tree is minimal.

At the same time, dwarf fruit trees produce as much fruit per square foot of earth surface as their larger relatives. The fruit on a dwarf tree tastes the same, looks the same, and cooks the same as fruit grown on a full-size tree.

Dwarf trees produce fruit the second year they are transplanted and will continue to produce for perhaps 30 years, depending on type. Full-size trees require a minimum of 3 years before they produce fruit, and some don't bear for as many as 10 years after planting. On the full-size, plus side, the trees last longer. Apple trees can be productive for 50 years.

A full-size apple tree (continuing our example) will grow to 50 feet if not heavily pruned. It will also shade a circle of earth 50 feet across. Therefore, to grow a full-

PLANTING DISTANCE, MATURE HEIGHT, AND YEARS TO BEARING FOR VARIOUS DWARF, SEMIDWARF AND STANDARD FRUIT TREES

Fruit trees	Planting distance, feet	Mature height, feet	Bears after planting, years
Apples, semidwarf (Understock: Malling Merton 106)	12 × 15	12–15	2
Apples, standard size	35 × 35	20–25	3–10
Apricots, dwarf (On *Prunus tomentosum* or *P. Besseyi*)	10 × 10	8–10	2
Apricots, standard	20 × 20	15	3
Cherry, sour—dwarf (North Star—natural dwarf)	10 × 10	8	2
Cherry, sour—standard	20 × 20	20	3
Cherry, sweet (Available in standard size only)	25 × 25	30	3–4
Peach and nectarines, dwarf (Understock: *Prunus tomentosum* or *P. Besseyi*)	10 × 10	8–10	2
Peach and nectarines, standard	20 × 20	20	3
Pears, dwarf (Understock: Angers quince; also on special northern understock)	12 × 15	12–15	2
Pears, standard	20 × 20	30	3–4
Plums, dwarf (Understock: *Prunus tomentosum* or *P. Besseyi*)	10 × 10	8–10	2
Plums, standard	20 × 20	20	3

Courtesy W. Atlee Burpee Co.

size apple tree you have to give up sufficient space for a produce garden large enough to feed a family of four. You need far less space with a dwarf tree. The exact space depends on the height of the tree. The Golden Glory peach, for example, grows no more than 6 feet tall and 5 feet across. You can space these trees 7 feet apart, leaving 2 feet of clearance between them. On the 15-foot trees you need no more than 17 feet between trunks.

And when you practically eliminate pruning, when there is no need for ladders or power spraying equipment, tree fruit becomes as easy to grow as bush fruit, and far more profitable, as you can certainly harvest more fruit from a tree than a bush that would occupy the same space. In addition, all the fruit trees are beautiful when in flower. The aroma of the apple blossom is particularly entrancing.

There is one drawback. Good dwarf fruit trees from reputable nurseries are not inexpensive. They cost about a third more than standard trees; and if you are planting a large number, the cost does mount.

Starkspur Golden Delicious dwarf apple tree. *(Courtesy Stark Bros.)*

Incidentally, if you have the space, consider a small orchard as an adjunct to your income. As mentioned previously, the pick-it-yourself system of farming has proved very practical. You plant, and the customer picks his own. With short fruit trees, the system is imminently practical. Many of the nurseries offer generous discounts on large orders.

Dwarf-tree crop yield is high—higher in some respects than that of the large trees. With some varieties you have to prop up the limbs to keep the weight of the fruit from breaking them off. With dwarf apple trees, for example, an acre planted

Dwarf peach tree. *(Courtesy Stark Bros.)*

with 450 trees will produce upward of 1,000 bushels; so you can readily see how this could be profitable, especially if the purchaser does the hardest part, which is to gather the fruit.

THE MAKING OF A DWARF

With the exception of few natural or genetic dwarf fruit trees, all the dwarfs are the result of grafting a scion onto a root taken or developed from another variety of tree. The choice of root-top relation limits the growth of the scion or the added-on

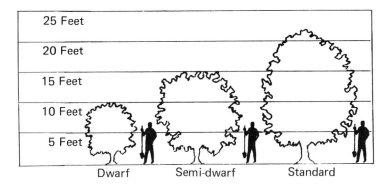

| 25 Feet |
| 20 Feet |
| 15 Feet |
| 10 Feet |
| 5 Feet |

Dwarf   Semi-dwarf   Standard

Relative sizes of dwarf, semidwarf, and standard fruit trees. *(Courtesy W. Atlee Burpee Co.)*

section. If you examine a full-size cultivated fruit tree, you will see where the top section has been grafted onto the lower section. There is a change in bark texture and color, and possibly a noticeable lump when the tree is merely a whip—a single thin, vertical stem. Dwarfs are "produced" the same way. The difference in growth is a result of the choice of root.

PLANTING

Fruit trees will grow well in almost anything except heavy clay and pure sand. They do best in full sun, but will make do in partial shade, but not under another tree. They will not grow in muck or water-logged soil.

All the fruit trees are planted in a like manner. Where differences exist, they will be mentioned under the specific fruit tree. If you wish, add humus or moss to the starting soil. It will speed growth.

When you are ready to dig, remove the burlap or plastic covering the roots. Clip off the ends of whatever ragged or broken roots may exist. Make a mental picture, or use a rule and measure the natural root configuration. Dig a hole more than large enough to accommodate the entire root system without folding or compressing any of the roots and deep enough by more than several inches to hold the tree in its original relation to the surface of the soil. Next, take some of the topsoil you removed, and cover the bottom of the hole. Set the tree in place. Its graft—that lump we talked about—must be higher than the level of the surrounding earth. Take the remainder of the topsoil. Toss it on top of the roots. Follow with the rest of the soil, after removing all the stones. Stop when there is a hole about 1 inch deep. Take the remainder of the soil, and make a little wall around the hole. Fill the hole with water. Hold the tree in a vertical position. Pour more water in the hole. Except for filling the hole with water twice a day for the next week or so, that is it for the planting. Do not add any chemical fertilizer. Do not mulch up to the tree's trunk. Leave a bare area.

INITIAL PRUNING

If you recall, we discussed the importance of holding the top of the plant in balance with its root system. The roots of your new plant have been all but removed. To prevent the leaves that will form from drying out the roots, the top of the plant is cut back about a third.

Cut those branches that appear to have dried out, if there are any. Cut those branches that are opposite one another on the trunk (just cut one). Cut whatever branch may be pointing upward at a sharp angle. This is where the tree will be weak.

Use sharp pruning shears or a fine-toothed saw such as a hacksaw to do your cutting. Make your cuts close to a bud on the side of the branch away from the trunk. The cut should be about ½ inch from the bud. Doing so speeds recovery. Cut too far from a bud, and the branch will not heal quickly if it heals at all.

Seal all of the major cuts—trunk or heavy branches—with roof cement or any of the preparations sold for the purpose. Sealing helps keep the fungus out.

If you have purchased a whip, which is a single-stem young tree and is, incidentally, the best buy, cut the stem about one-third of its height from the ground. Again, take care to cut at a point where there is a bud, and on the upper side of the bud by a small distance. This is called heading, and forces the tree to put out side branches or laterals. Otherwise the tree will grow mostly straight up.

MIDGROWTH PRUNING

There are many views and opinions on pruning and a few facts. And, as in many other fields of human endeavor, only the facts really count.

First, pruning does not help the tree grow. Pruning is a shock to the plant's system. The balance between the roots and leaves is disrupted. Wounds are opened which admit fungi.

Orchardists prune for their advantage, not the tree's. They prune standard trees heavily to reduce their height, to make their branches spread out so that the fruit is more easily harvested and so that more fruit is exposed to the sun, which improves their color.

Secondly, pruning does not increase the harvest; on the contrary, you lose fruit every time you prune. Prune heavily enough and consistently enough, and you will have a tree with a magnificent shape and no fruit. Fruit is formed on branch tips at least one year old. Thus, if you consistently cut back the year's growth, there will be no old tips and no new buds which will flower and produce fruit. (Incidentally, if you are puzzled by the presence of the tiny leaves at the bottom of the pear and apple, as I was for many years, be advised that it is the remains of the blossom. The fruit forms immediately behind the blossom's leaves.)

Therefore, when you prune, and you need to do very, very little pruning with a dwarf, bear in mind that you are balancing a better branch configuration and perhaps better-spaced fruit next year or the year following against fruit this year.

Thirdly, when you prune you remove a group of leaves and a branch. The tree's root system now has more food and energy than can be accommodated by its leaf system; ergo the tree will form another branch where it desires. Such branches may appear anywhere, and they usually head straight for sunlight. They are called suckers and will not produce fruit for several years (if you let them remain). Therefore, once you prune heavily you are condemned to continue to prune heavily each succeeding year. You have but to inspect the trees in an abandoned orchard to see the results of heavy pruning. The old trees are covered with suckers, which are branches the tree favors, not the farmer. A fruit tree planted and grown for ornamental purposes alone has a tall beautiful shape and no suckers. Such a tree produces a tremendous quantity of fruit; but in the case of an apple tree, for example, there is no practical way of getting to the fruit. It is too high.

Returning to our fruit tree. You have planted the dwarf and cut it back to aid its growth and starting as recommended. The tree has fruited and grown. Should you prune it? Yes, but only if one branch is interfering with another; one branch has taken toward reaching for heaven, another is touching the ground, and/or a branch is damaged.

In other words, clean up and correct, but don't cut away to shape the tree or make its branches even out or fill an empty space. The less you prune, the better the tree will fare.

When you do prune (excepting for when you first plant the tree and that is best done early spring or late fall), do it when the tree is dormant. This will reduce the shock of amputation.

APPLE TREES

Far and away the most popular of all the fruit species for backyard planting, apple trees are highly productive (some dwarfs can produce up to 6 bushels per season), vigorous, and disease-resistant. There are any number of varieties to choose from in the dwarf and semidwarf sizes, plus trees that bear five varieties and trees that bear 2-pound apples.

Although a single apple tree will pollinate itself, it is best to plant two or more varieties for cross-pollination; you will harvest a much larger crop from each.

The first dwarf apple trees were made by grafting a selected branch of apple tree onto a Malling IX root. The results were satisfactory except for the weakness at the joint, which was brittle. A strong wind could snap the tree at the joint.

Today, dwarf trees are assembled from as many as four different trees; one furnishing the roots, another the top, another one section of the trunk, and so on. Whether or not the problem of the brittle graft has been eliminated by new techniques is something this writer has so far been unable to determine. It is therefore suggested that unless otherwise assured, dwarfs be fully supported by stake or trellis for at least their early years.

Here are just a few of the dwarfs and semidwarfs offered for sale by reliable nurserymen:

- Golden Grimes, a yellow-skinned apple with excellent flavor. Ripens early in the fall.
- Jonathan, red, medium-size fruit suited to eating and cooking. Ready in the fall, stores well.
- Red McIntosh, a red apple with snow-white flesh, sweet and juicy, good for eating, cooking, and cider. Ready early in the fall.
- Red Delicious, a big, firm juicy apple, very sweet. Has five knobs on the bottom, which is a characteristic of this variety. A late fall producer.
- Yellow Delicious, the best of all the eating apples to this writer's taste. Bright, golden-yellow fruit, very lovely blossoms. Bears late.
- Starkspur Red Rome Beauty, the world's best baking apple, excellent for applesauce too and many people who enjoy chewing enjoy eating Romes. Ripens around mid-October.
- Starkspur Arkansas Black, a dark red apple with a tart flavor, good for cooking or eating. Ripens late in October.

Apple blossoms.

PEAR TREES

Pears are the second most popular fruit planted and enjoyed by home orchard-ists. Their planting and pruning are fairly similar to that of apples, with one exception. Pears should not be planted in soil high in nitrogen. For some reason, soil high in nitrogen makes pears more susceptible to fire blight, which attacks pear trees more than other species. (This disease and its cure are discussed in the next chapter.)

You are not likely to find soil rank with nitrogen except if you plant, as this writer did, a pear tree atop an old drain field. A drain field consists of partially open pipes covered with gravel and sod. The field receives and thus drains a septic tank of its effluent. Said effluent is, of course, partially decomposed human waste and is naturally rank with nitrogen. There is no pathological danger in the effluent beneath the soil, but two of my pear trees suffered fire blight in succession. The first had to be removed. The second struggles on with medical assistance. Two apricot trees atop the same field are unharmed.

SEQUENCE IN WHICH APPLES RIPEN (LISTED IN ORDER OF RIPENING)

®Stark Earliest	Priscilla	®Starkspur Golden Delicious
Lodi, Early Golden	®Stark Jon-A-Red	®Stark Rome Beauty
®Starkspur Lodi	Cortland	®Starkspur Red Rome Beauty
EarlyMcIntosh	Grimes Golden, Double-Life	®Stark Splendor
Summer Champion	Spartan	®Stark Blushing Golden
®Starkspur EarliBlaze	Super ®Starking Delicious	Turley Winesap
Wealthy, Double-Red	®Stark Red Bouquet Delicious	®Stark Red Winesap
®Stark Gala	®Starkrimson Delicious	®Starkspur Winesap
Prima	®Starkspur Red Delicious	®Stark Scarlet Staymared
Ozark Gold	®Stark Jumbo	®Stark Red York
®Stark McIntosh, Double-Red	IdaRed	Northern Spy, Double Red
®Starkspur McIntosh	®Stark Jonalicious	®Starkspur Arkansas Black
®Stark RedGold	®Stark Golden Delicious	®Stark Tropical Beauty

Courtesy Stark Bros.

Pear blossoms.

**SELF-POLLINATING AND NON-SELF-POLLINATING FRUIT TREES, AND
SUGGESTED POLLINATORS**

Type of fruit requiring pollinator	Suggested pollinator
All apples, *except:* Golden Delicious—Jonathan Red Rome Beauty Stark Tropical Beauty	Any other variety of apple tree except the Winesaps and Stark Scarlet Staymared. Most potent pollinators: Starkrimson, Starkspur EarliBlaze, and Starkspur Golden Delicious.
Peaches: Stark Hal-Berta Giant Stark Honeydew Hale J. H. Hale	Any other variety of peach tree. Most potent pollinators: Burbank July Elberta, Starking Delicious, and Stark Early Elberta.
All pears, *except:* Duchess & Kieffer	Any other variety of pear tree, except Magness. (Bartlett and Seckel are not compatible). Most potent pollinators: Starking Delicious and Moonglow.
All sweet cherries	Venus, Stark Gold or Van.
All plums, *except:* Giant Damson and Green Gage	Any other variety of plum tree. Most potent pollinator: Redheart.
Prunes: Burbank Grand Prize	BluFre or Stanley.

Courtesy Stark Bros.

Since pear trees may be attacked by fire blight, it is customary to prune them even less than dwarf apples. So that when the damaged limbs are removed or cut back, there are some left. Initial cutback, however, should not be stinted.

Another difference between pear tree and apple tree cultivation is in the matter of harvest. You pick apples when they are ripe. You pick pears when they are at the point of changing from dark green to light green. A difficult moment to ascertain with certainty, and it will take patience to learn. However, the pears cannot be permitted to ripen on the tree. If they do, they taste badly. Instead, they are picked pale green, wrapped in a paper napkin, and put away in a dark, cool place to ripen. The ripe, red pears you see in nurserymen's ads have been faked somehow.

Here are some of the pear varieties offered in dwarf and semidwarf size. Note, plant two varieties for cross-pollination. If you plant Bartlett and Seckel, you must plant a third because these two do not pollinate each other.

Bartlett is a long-time favorite, good for eating and canning. The fruit is golden yellow, soft, fine-grained, and sweet.

Beurre d'Anjou grows vigorously; its fruits are large and tasty. They ripen early in the season.

Clapp's Favorite resembles the Bartlett somewhat. Its fruit is large, pale yellow. Excellent for cooking and often thrives where other varieties do not. Harvest in August.

Seckel, sometimes called sugar pear because of its sweetness, has brown skin with a touch of red. Good for eating and pickling.

Moonglow is a blight-resistant variety. It bears large, dark-yellow fruit touched with red that is ripe in mid-August.

Duchess produces one of the largest pears grown, but despite its size its flavor is excellent. This variety is self-pollinating, bears late in September.

Tyson, another blight-resistant variety, produces medium-size yellow pears that are very soft and juicy. Harvest around the beginning of August.

**RIPENING SEQUENCE OF PEACHES,
PEARS, AND CHERRIES, LISTED IN THE
ORDER OF THEIR VARIETY AND
RIPENING**

Peaches

®Stark Early White Giant	Sunapee
Desertgold	Loring
®Stark EarliGlo	Madison
Candor	Cresthaven
®Starking Delicious	®Stark Early Elberta
®Starking Delicious	®Stark FrostKing
®Stark Sure-Crop	Belle of Georgia
Com-Pact Redhaven	®Stark Elberta Queen
Redhaven	J. H. Hale
Reliance	®Stark Honeydew Hale
®Stark SunBright	Redskin
®Burbank July Elberta	®Stark Hal-Berta Giant
®Stark Starlet	®Stark Autumn Gold
Babygold 5	Monroe
Glowhaven	
Glohaven	

Pears

Tyson	®Stark Grand Champion
®Starkrimson	Seckel
Fame	Duchess
Moonglow	Buerre Bosc
Bartlett	Anjou
®Starking Delicious	Kieffer
Magness	Comice

Cherries

Early Richmond	Hedelfingen
Vista	®Stark Lambert
Emperor Francis	Schmidt's Biggareau
Meteor	®Stark Montmorency
North Star	®Starkspur Montmorency
Van	®Stark Gold
Napoleon (Royal Ann)	Suda Hardy
Venus	
Bing	

Courtesy Stark Bros.

PEACHES

Peaches are another fruit that is very popular with backyard orchardists. The trees produce generously, and, as stated earlier, it is almost impossible to purchase properly ripened peaches in the supermarkets.

Peach trees like well-drained sandy and gravelly soils. They can withstand a shortage of water for a while, but they are easily drowned by flooding. They also need lots of air; so don't select the peach if your orchard is shut off from the wind by buildings and walls.

The full-size trees cannot stand cold weather that drops lower than 20°F below zero, but dwarf-size peach trees have reportedly withstood temperatures to 25 below zero with the aid of a little mulch around their base. The mulch should not

Ripening Bartlett pears.

be positioned until after the first frost. Placed there sooner, it will make a home for field mice.

The mulch must be removed well before spring thaw, and the earth around the base of the tree should be lightly cultivated with an eye to keeping it bare. Peach trees are often attacked at root level by a bug called the peach borer. Keeping the base of the tree free of grass and weeds makes it more difficult for the bug to sneak up on the tree and makes his presence more readily observed (a gummy red mass).

Peach trees bear heavily, and one of your problems will be to reduce the crop somewhat. This can be done by judicious pruning. Just cut a few small branches here and there; don't hack away, or the tree will respond by sending up more branches.

For best taste let the fruit cool for a day indoors after picking.

A few of the many dwarf varieties available:

• Reliance, a very cold-hardy strain. Ripens early in August. Has yellow, sweet flesh. Fruit is medium to large in size. Good for canning, freezing, and eating.

• Elberta, a freestone peach with a bright yellow color and thick, juicy flesh. Ripens in midseason. Fruit is fairly large. Self-pollinating.

• Hale Haven is also self-pollinating; fruit is also large, yellow, with free pits. Good for canning as well as eating. Harvest midseason.

• Red Haven. Ripens early, has large fruit, almost solid red and especially delicious.

APRICOTS

I chose apricots for my limited space because fresh apricots are the most rare and expensive fruit for sale locally. The harvests have been excellent, although we don't care much for the fruit from one of our trees. Makes wonderful jam however.

Apricots are related to peaches and will grow almost anywhere the peach will grow—almost. The apricot blossoms early and is sensitive to a late spring frost. The blossoms are lovely, and it is an attractive tree at this time. However, the varieties I have aren't particularly attractive during the remainder of the year. Although textbooks state that the apricot is self-pollinating, most nurserymen advise planting two or more varieties for better results. Apricots ripen before early peaches. In my neck of the woods, New York State, apricots are ready for picking and eating as early as the 4th of July.

Here are a few dwarf varieties:

• Chinese Golden produces large, smooth-skinned fruit with an orange-yellow color touched with red. Its stones are free.

• Moorpak, an extra-large freestone, has orange-yellow fruit flecked and splashed with red.

• Wilson Delicious is a semidwarf that grows to a maximum of 15 feet. It is very hardy and will bear crops where others fail. The fruit is thick, luscious orange yellow with a distinctive flavor. Good for eating, canning, cooking, and freezing.

CHERRIES

Don't grow cherries unless you love birds, for unless you protect your tree with a metal screen or a birdproof cloth netting, you will lose more cherries to the birds than you will be able to pick.

If you do decide to favor our feathered friends, bear in mind that there are two general types of cherries, sour and sweet. The sour are not as sour as they used to be, but are still favored for pies and jams. The sweet are for eating, but may also be used for pies and jams and such.

The sour varieties are a bit hardier, bear a little sooner, and will accept a wider range of soils. Preferentially the sour varieties prefer clay loam. The sweet-cherry trees do best in sandy loam. Both cannot stand wet soil, but at the same time cannot stand drought either.

Apricots just forming. Their blossoms still attached.

Apricots midseason. Another month to go.

North Star is a sour variety of cherry, with large fruit having a delicious tangy flavor that is dark red when fully ripe. It is a hardy and productive strain that can be harvested early in the season.

Stark Montmorency is another sour, but isn't really sour. It is sweet when fully ripe. The skin is bright red, but inside the flesh is yellow. Will often bloom the first year, and bear the second after planting. Can be used as fresh fruit and for pies and the likes. Unlike the North Star, Montmorency is a semidwarf.

Meteor, another semidwarf, grows to about 12 feet and produces large, tart cherries that are excellent for pies and preserves.

CHAPTER TWENTY

Pests

S OMETIME BETWEEN THE start of your farming and the beginning of a truly
fertile soil, your vegetables may be attacked by a horde of ravenous insects.
You can, if you wish, stand idly by, secure in the knowledge that no single insect
genre will devour all specie of plants. Therefore, even if you do lose all your
cucumbers, for example, your turnips will remain unscathed. You can also rest
easy on the assurance that no matter how heavy the infestation may be this year,
the year following will see far fewer of these particular pests, and the year after you
will have to search to find even one. For this is the nature of insects. When they
multiply out of all normal proportions, their enemies quickly multiply in equal or
even greater numbers.

On the other hand, you needn't stand by. There are several methods and means
you can use to protect your vegetables, none of which are harmful to man or beast.

In the case of fruit trees you cannot stand by. Hordes of insects may be permitted
to destroy the leaves and fruit on your trees. The leaves will grow back, new fruit
will form, and the insects will disappear in a season or two without counteraction.
But you cannot do the same with the trunks and roots of the same trees. They must
be protected prior to attack.

This may be contrary to a purist's approach to farming. It is certainly not
completely organic farming, but it is imminently practical. For the damage that can
be done by even a few insects and grubs to fruit tree roots and trunk can be
permanent and even fatal. Self-healing after an attack takes years at best, and most
often the tree never bears as well ever again.

This then is the reason for a chapter on pest control in a book that earlier stated:
Little pesticide is necessary, sometimes none.

GUARDIAN PLANTS AND FLOWERS

Probably the most generally effective are chives, onions, and garlic, which planted here and there are reported strong repellents of many insects and especially aphids. Most often chives and garlic are planted next to lettuce and peas for aphid protection.

Beans are planted near or among potatoes to discourage Colorado potato beetles. In turn, potato plants act to repel the Mexican bean beetle, which loves bean plants.

Asparagus can be protected from beetles by planting tomato plants nearby.

Cucumbers can be protected from cucumber beetles by planting radishes in the center of the hills. The striped and spotted cucumber beetles find radishes abhorrent for some reason.

Cabbage worms and cutworms can be kept from cabbage plants by planting tansy between the cabbages.

Geraniums near grapevines ward off Japanese beetles, which love to chew on grapevine leaves.

Marigolds between potato plants also discourage the Colorado potato beetle.

Marigolds will also protect corn against Japanese beetles.

Nasturtiums planted near beans thwart the Mexican bean beetle; near broccoli they guard against aphids; between cabbages nasturtiums ward off white cabbage butterflies.

Onion is good everywhere as a pest and fungi deterrent, but do not plant near beans or peas.

INSECTS THAT FIGHT INSECTS

There are insects that feed on other insects. Most notable are the ladybug and the praying mantis. A ladybug can devour 50 aphids in a single day without really trying. A praying mantis, the largest insect found in these parts, reaches a length of 4 inches and is protected by law. He or she (how can you tell?) will eat anything it can get its lobster-like claws on, and it is hungry most of the time.

Suppliers. Write to any of the following companies, if you will, for prices and data on ladybugs, praying mantis, wasps, and other helpful insects that you can introduce to your farm to protect your plants from other insects.

Bio-Central Co.
Rt. 2 Box 2397
Auburn, California 95603

Eastern Biological Con. Co.
Rt. 5 Box 379
Jackson, New Jersey 08527

Ecological Insect Services
15075 W. California Avenue
Kerman, California 93630

Gothard Inc.
P.O. Box 370
Canutillo, Texas 79835

Lakeland Nurseries
Hanover, Pennsylvania 17331

Mincemoyers Nursery
R.D. 5 Box 379
New Prospect Road
Jackson, New Jersey 08527

Schoor's Sierra Bug Co.
P.O. Box 114
Rough and Ready, California 95975

Vitova Co.
Biological Control Division
P.O. Box 745
Rialto, California 92376

World Garden Products
2 First Street East
Norwalk, Connecticut 06855

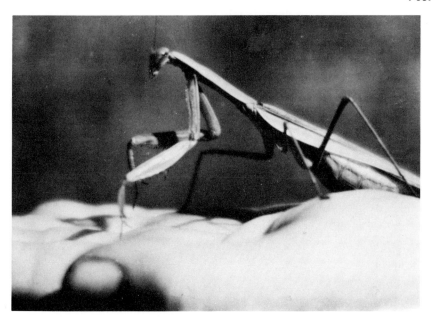

Praying mantis. He, she, or it can grow to a 4-inch length. *(Photo courtesy Bio-Control Co.)*

FEATHERED ASSISTANCE

Birds consume a tremendous quantity of insects. They have a tremendously high metabolism and must eat several times their own weight each day to remain alive. Birds are never overweight and never on a diet. The trick is to get them to come to your farm. One method, already mentioned, is tossing kitchen scraps into the fields. Another is planting trees and bushes that birds like.

Here are some of their favorites:

Blueberry
Dogwood
Cranberry
Elderberry
Honeysuckle
Inkberry
Flowering crab
Mulberry
Wild cherry
Sour cherry

HAND-TO-HAND COMBAT

When they are not too numerous, the larger insects can be picked off and destroyed. The simple way is to drop them in a can filled with water topped by a few drops of kerosene or light oil.

Grubs that dig a hole in the side of a plant's stem and then eat their way upward can be recognized by the discolored section of the plant, by the "sawdust" ejected by the dining grub, and sometimes by a swelling in the stem. Use a razor blade, and slit the plant's stem lengthwise along the suspected area; that will do him in.

Aphids and other small insects can be washed away with a strong stream of water from a hose.

Slugs, i.e., gastropod mollusks that have no shell or merely a rudimentary one, can be destroyed by stepping on them, which is far less cruel than covering them with salt, which causes them to dissolve. (The salt removes the water.) They can be trapped by filling a shallow pan with beer and setting it out in the field. Slugs love beer; they crawl in, drink, become intoxicated, and drown. (Suggested by the U.S. Department of Agriculture, honest.)

A more effective method is to lay a flat board on the earth. Slugs crawl beneath the board for protection. Turn the board over in the morning, and the birds will take care of them. Since slugs make their home under boards and such, it is good practice to keep the garden clean of such trash and to turn the mulch over every now and again to expose slugs and other unwanted characters.

CHEMICAL REPELLENTS

Most if not all unwanted insects and fungi can be controlled by one or more of the following insecticides, which are perfectly safe in that they do not persist in the earth or on vegetation and are perfectly harmless to man.

Pyrethrum is derived from a species of chrysanthemum. It is effective against the leafhopper, webworm, cabbage caterpillar, tomato worm, fruitworm, millipede, sow bug, and pill bug.

Shell-less snail or slug

Rotenone is made from the root of the derris plant, a climbing vine with purple and white flowers. It is effective against the asparagus beetle, spotted cucumber beetle, striped cucumber beetle, potato beetle, flea beetle, Japanese beetle, cabbage caterpillar, carrot caterpillar, looper, squash bug, and pea weevil.

Thuricide is not a chemical but a strain of bacteria, *Bacillus thuringiensis,* that is a slow but effective destroyer of tomato hookworms, canker worms, and cabbage worms.

Ryania is derived from the roots and stems of a shrub of the same name, native to Latin America. It does not kill but slows bugs to the point where they die from other causes. It is effective against the Japanese beetle, squash bug, and cabbage looper.

Quassia is a very strong insect repellent made from the roots and bark of the Quassia tree, another inhabitant of the southern continent.

Hellebore, another insect repellent, is made from a flower that was common in Roman times. It is a member of the lily family. The chemical is drawn from its roots and rhizomes.

Nicotine is a yellow oil that is extracted from tobacco. You can make a weak solution yourself by soaking tobacco leftovers in water a few days. In concentrated form, nicotine is a strong poison, but when drawn by an infusion of water, as suggested, or diluted with sufficient water, nicotine is harmless to man, bird, and animal. Generally a teaspoon of 40 percent nicotine sulfate is mixed with a gallon of water and used as a spray.

Nicotine is effective against red, green, or black aphids and thrips.

Sulfur, which is a mineral element important as a plant food, can be used as a dust that is effective in combating the red spider.

While none of the above are harmful in the ordinary sense, that is to say, they are not poisons (excepting nicotine), you must be wary of insecticides that are

Potato flea beetle

Cabbage looper

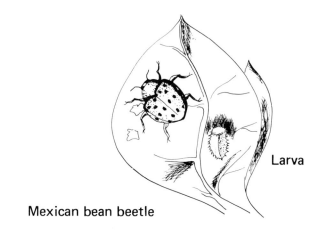

Larva

Mexican bean beetle

touted as organic or nonharmful. The insecticides may very well contain one or more of the "safe" ingredients, but may also contain other substances that are poisonous and that do remain in the fields and on the plants for a long time.

PROTECTION SPECIFICS

BROCCOLI, BRUSSELS SPROUTS, CABBAGE, CAULIFLOWER AND CHINESE CABBAGE

Attacked primarily by the cabbage worm or looper, a pale green caterpillar, up to 1½ inches long that moves along by looping or doubling up. It feeds on the undersides of leaves, making large ragged holes. *Hand-pick and destroy;* apply pyrethrum, rotenone, or thuricide before heads have begun to form. Cover undersides.

ASPARAGUS

Attacked primarily by the common asparagus beetle and its associate, the twelve-spotted asparagus beetle. Shake beetles off, and destroy or dust with rotenone.

BEANS (ALL SPECIES)

Look for clusters of tiny yellow eggs on undersides of the leaves. They are the deposits of the Mexican bean beetle, the greatest troublemaker in the bean patch, and will soon develop into sluggish yellow larvae with destructive eating habits.

Although these string bean vines were badly eaten by beetles, they still produced a considerable crop of beans. Most pods, however, bore small marks indicative of the insects.

Dust or spray with rotenone or pyrethrum if you don't want to squish them by hand. Do this in the early morning when the leaves are moist with dew for best results. Cover both sides of the leaves. But don't touch the leaves when wet.

BEETS AND CHARD

Beets and chard are members of one family and are rarely attacked by insects, but they sometimes are troubled by leaf spot which is a fungus and shows itself as gray dead spots ringed in purple. Remove the infected leaves, and burn. Do not toss in the compost heap.

CARROTS, PARSNIPS, AND TURNIPS

Occasionally one of these vegetables will be attacked by a voracious carrot caterpillar. Pick him off, and send him scurrying. More serious are the results of visits by the carrot rust fly which deposits its eggs in the soil near carrots, parsnips, and turnips. The larvae eat their way into the roots of these plants and

Ladybug larva eating aphid

work down to the tip, leaving "rusty" tunnels in their wake. The fly itself is small and dark green. Its visits can be discouraged by spreading a line of naphthalene flakes over the soil alongside the row. A pound spread over a distance of 100 feet will give almost complete protection.

CORN

The corn earworm is the worst troublemaker. It grows to about 2 inches in length and effects a green to purple-brown suit with lengthwise strips. It reaches the innards of the ear of corn by virtue of having been deposited on the silk as an egg by its moth parent. Once the larva hatches, it eats its way through the ear. What isn't eaten by the worm remains edible; so just cut it away and use the corn. Many corn lovers swear the worms are found in the sweetest ears.

Corn earworm protection can be secured by placing a few drops of pyrethrum mixed with oil on the silk emerging from the corn ears shortly after they form. It is a protection but not a cure. To prevent a repeat performance, carefully collect all corn plants at the end of the season, and toss into the compost heap.

The European corn borer is another son of a night-flying moth. He is about 1 inch long with a white or pink body and a dark head. He digs right in horizontally into the plant's stalk. You may see a tassel fall over and find a small hole underneath or see a small hole near the base of an ear of corn. Look for a white, scalelike mass of eggs on the underside of leaves. Remove the leaf.

There no sure cure for this pest either. Discard the egg-covered leaves in the garbage can, or burn them. In the fall, carefully toss all the corn plant remains into the compost heap, and cover with other organic material.

Just as serious, when it strikes is bacterial wilt. The corn plants shrivel and die. This is most frequent in hot weather when the plants are nearly full size. Cut the stalk of an infected plant, and squeeze it. If a yellow liquid comes out, you have wilt. Burn the infected plants, and switch to a variety with greater resistance to this infection.

CUCUMBERS, MUSKMELONS, PUMPKINS, SQUASH, AND WATERMELONS

The striped cucumber beetle, having a color scheme ranging from yellow to black and three black stripes down its back, is the worst offender. Only about $\frac{1}{5}$ inch long, its larvae are a whitish brown, nearly $\frac{1}{2}$ inch long with brown heads. The parents feed on the leaves and stems. The children tunnel into the stems and roots below. All members of the group spread damaging bacterial wilt.

You can handpick the beetles and give them the kerosene-on-water treatment, or you can dust or spray with rotenone as soon as the plants emerge. Spray after a rain or early in the morning. But be careful not to actually touch the plants. Avoid getting spray or dusting powder on the blossoms.

The squash vine borer eats a hole into the side of the vine close to the ground, makes a right-angle turn, and continues eating. You will recognize his presence by a little mound of vine dust, a color change in the stem, and sometimes a slight enlargement. Use a razor and slit the vine lengthwise in his area. That will do him in without destroying the plant.

EGGPLANTS, PEPPERS, TOMATOES

Flea beetles are one group of insects that love these plants. They are minute in size, only about $\frac{1}{16}$ of an inch overall. They are sometimes black, sometimes brown, and just as often striped; but no matter their color, they jump about and chew numerous small round holes in the plant leaves as they jump, or so it seems. Dust, or spray with rotenone.

Another troublesome group of insects attacking eggplants, peppers, and tomatoes are the cutworms. They reach a length of 1¼ inches, run from dull gray through brown, sometimes adorning themselves with strips or spots. Touch them, and they curl up. (It isn't necessary to touch them.) They don't eat much, but what

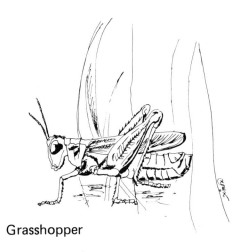

Grasshopper

they do eat is catastrophic; a narrow, horizontal cut right across the plant's stem, and down it goes. To prevent, place a 3-inch collar of aluminum foil, cardboard, or plastic around the stem of each plant, letting the bottom edge of the collar rest in the soil. That stops them.

Still another pest is the tomato hornworm, a wicked customer replete with a horn on his rear and a green suit striped down the side. He doesn't bite; so you can pick him off and destroy him. However, if he is carrying small white lumps on his back, he is infested with a parasite that infects only the hornworm. Pull him off the tomato plant, but let him be. The parasite will destroy more bugs than we can.

ONIONS AND LEEKS

The onion thrip, which is a very tiny, yellow fly, likes to lay its eggs in the leaves of the onion and leek near the base of the plant. The emerging nymphs suck on the plant's juices, giving the leaves the appearance of having been bleached. Spraying with rotenone or nicotine sulfate is very effective. Get the insecticide down between the leaf sheaths.

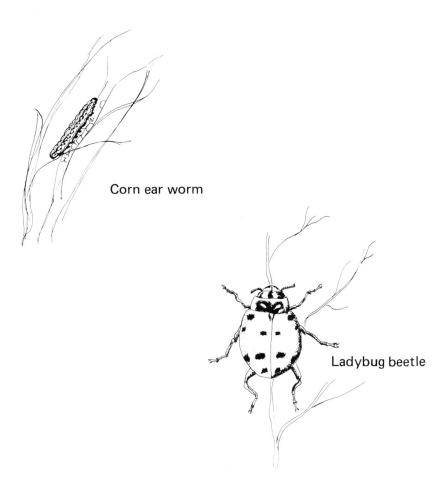

Corn ear worm

Ladybug beetle

Tomato   hornworm

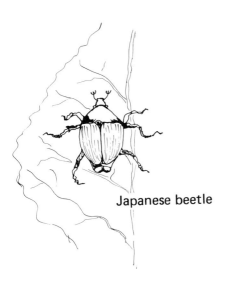

Japanese beetle

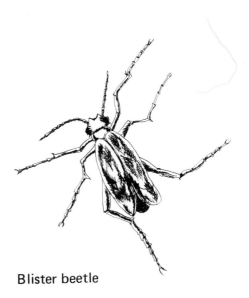

Blister beetle

Another troublemaker, especially up North, is the onion maggot. It is the larva of a small gray fly that looks much like a small housefly. It lays its eggs near the base of the plant, and the grubs eat their way inside. Spray the soil with an oil emulsion, which can be purchased ready mixed for the purpose. Do this as soon as the flies appear, and twice a week thereafter.

LETTUCE

The cabbage looper sometimes wanders into the lettuce patch and chews around. Pick him off, or spray with rotenone or pyrethrum. And keep an eye open for slugs. They love lettuce.

Lettuce drop is a fungus infection. The plant's outer leaves wilt, and a watery rot forms. This is caused by lack of circulating air; perhaps you have the plants too close to one another, and near too much water.

PEAS

The aphid is the insect most likely to be troublesome with peas. There is nothing to be gained by anticipating his attack. Wait till he arrives, if he ever does, and counterattack with rotenone. These pests destroy the pea plant by sucking it dry of juice, at which point the plant shrivels up and dies.

POTATOES

The Colorado potato beetle is the malefactor here. He is a yellow bug, about ⅜ inch long, with black lines on his wing segments. His larvae are pale red and a little longer in size. They chew the plant leaves and stems without stopping until there is nothing left. Handpick the bugs. Search for egg masses beneath the leaves. Cut the leaves off, and destroy the eggs. Spray the plants with rotenone to protect them.

The potato aphid can be destroyed with either a rotenone or a nicotine sulfate spray.

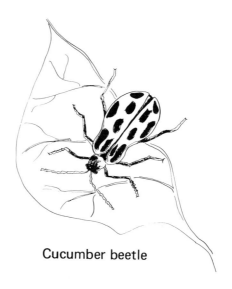

Cucumber beetle

Pear tree carrying on despite fire blight. Fruit bore little signs of the infection.

SPINACH

Aphids are most troublesome to spinach. Apply rotenone or pyrethrum dust or spray to control them.

On occasion, a cabbage looper may show up hungry. Handpick him or let the rotenone or pyrethrum do the job.

STRAWBERRIES

These plants are also troubled with aphids from time to time. Treat as above.

FRUIT TREES (FIRE BLIGHT)

The best way to control and limit fire blight is to keep careful watch on your apple, pear, and quince trees immediately before, during, and after they bloom. If any of the new tip growth wilts or turns black, use a sharp pair of shears, and cut that section off, making your cut at least 6 inches back of the infected area. Remember this is a fungus disease; so don't touch the infected section and then touch the uninfected areas with your hands, or any other tree for that matter, without washing your hands first in strong soap. Dip your shears in gasoline or kerosene before using elsewhere, and burn the infected sections; don't toss them on the compost heap.

If the infection persists, try a combination of malathion, kelthane, and methoxychlor in an oil base. Many of the garden-supply houses carry it. It is a poison and should not be used 10 days before harvest. Mix at the rate of two tablespoons to a gallon of water, to which you add a pinch of any household detergent, to "wet" the water. Spray heavily on the branches and trunk of the tree.

This combination also kills a host of other fruit tree pests. But it is a poison and must be used with care. Do not spray on blossoms; they will either die or fail to fruit.

FRUIT TREES (BORERS)

These insects drill small round holes in the bark of fruit trees. You know they are there by the holes and by the trails of sawdust they leave. Once beneath the bark, they settle down and fool around. In a very short time the bark of the tree in that area is separated from the tree proper, and no sap flows upward. That side of the tree dies shortly thereafter. There is a poisonous paste that is sold, which you squirt into the holes—it is almost worthless.

The best I can recommend is a new antibug compound developed by Union Carbide and marketed under the trade name of Sevin. Its toxicity is extremely low, and therefore it can be used fairly close to harvest time with little danger. It is sold as a wettable powder and in combination with sulfur, and sulfur and zineb.

To treat tree borers, carefully spray the main limbs and trunk of the tree right down to the ground; give it a good soaking once a month, beginning with the first warm days of spring. The usual mixture is one tablespoon of the Sevin to a gallon of water.

If your tree is already infected, cut away the infection, and treat with asphalt or a commercial tree-sealing compound.

FRUIT TREES (LEAF INSECTS)

The same insecticide, Sevin, mentioned above, is also effective on a host of fruit tree pests. Here is a partial list: codling moth, tent caterpillar, bagworm, apple maggot, peach twig borer, fruit leaf roller, pear psylla, green apple aphid, European red mite, leafhopper, stinkbug.

The same substance can be used on many vegetables and will control, kill, or dissuade all the insects we discussed previously. It even controls fleas and ticks on cats and dogs.

PEACH TREE BORER

Peach trees are cursed with a particular moth that lays its eggs near the base of the tree's trunk. The grubs dig into the soil an inch or so down, and attack the soft bark. In a short time they can girdle the tree and destroy it. You can usually detect their presence by the gummy red mass that the tree exudes to protect itself, and some times by the wood dust. And, of course, the infallible sign of their presence is the demise of the tree.

Protect your trees against these insects by keeping the soil near the bottom of the trunk free of grass, mulch, and debris. Dig up the soil a short distance every once in a while to see whether all is clear there.

One method used by old-time farmers to protect their trees from this moth is to place a circle of mothballs in the earth around the base, but not touching the tree. The mothballs are then covered with soil banked up against the trunk.

Vegetables, bushes, and vines not mentioned in this chapter are seldom troubled by pests.

Index

Index